D1452593

Mexicans

in the Midwest

1900–1932

Mexicans
in the Midwest
1900–1932

Juan R. García

The University of Arizona Press, Tucson

The University of Arizona Press

∞ This book is printed on acid-free, archival-quality paper.
Manufactured in the United States of America

01   00   99   98   97   96   6   5   4   3   2   1

Library of Congress Cataloging-in-Publication Data
Garcia, Juan R.
Mexicans in the Midwest, 1900–1932 / Juan R. Garcia.
   p.   cm.
Includes bibliographical references (p.   ) and index.
ISBN 0-8165-1560-3 (cloth : acid-free paper)
1. Mexican Americans—Middle West—History—20th century.
2. Mexican Americans—Middle West—Social conditions.   3. Mexico—
Emigration and immigration.   4. Middle West—Emigration and
immigration.   I. Title.
F358.2.M5G37   1996
977'.046872073—dc20   96-10098
CIP

British Library Cataloguing-in-Publication Data
A catalogue record for this book is available from the British Library.

Publication of this book is made possible in part by the proceeds of a
permanent endowment created with the assistance of a Challenge
Grant from the National Endowment for the Humanities, a federal
agency.

Contents

Preface

*M*exicans in the Midwest, 1900–1932 is a broad survey about Mexican nationals in the region before the Great Depression. This work synthesizes much of the published and unpublished research about midwestern Mexicans since the late 1920s. In this study, the demarcation of the Midwest is based upon geographic locations and prevailing definitions of the region. It includes Illinois, Indiana, Iowa, Kansas, Michigan, Minnesota, Missouri, Nebraska, Ohio, and Wisconsin. The amount of research about Mexicans in each of these states is uneven. I therefore do not attempt to provide a comprehensive discussion about the history of Mexicans in each of these states. Instead, I discuss representative states and communities that had larger Mexican populations.

The study focuses on the experiences of the "Mexican Generation" because the majority of immigrants to the region were Mexican nationals. Although the experiences of these nationals varied, some overarching characteristics distinguished them from their counterparts in the Southwest. Mexican immigrants to the Midwest were largely young, unattached males. Most of them saw their stay in the Midwest as temporary; thus, very few sought naturalization or citizenship. Midwestern economics and employment practices made them a highly mobile population. This mobility and the predominance of males profoundly affected the development and dynamics of Mexican communities in the Midwest.

Because the region was not historically or culturally a part of Mexico, the experiences of midwestern Mexicans paralleled those of other immigrant groups. Unlike Mexicans in the Southwest, who encountered mostly native-born European Americans, Mexicans in the Midwest found a more polyglot population of African Americans and recent immigrants from eastern and southern Europe.

Mexican immigration to the Midwest began in earnest in 1914, when the outbreak of war in Europe created a booming economy for the United States that required more workers. How, when, and why Mexicans began arriving in the Midwest are among the subjects discussed in chapters 1 and 2. The reasons for the severe recession that struck the United States in 1919 and its impact on Mexicans in the Midwest are also covered in chapter 2. Inadequate housing, high rents, unemployment, and discrimination were among the many problems that Mexican immigrants faced. The sources, nature, and effects of these problems are discussed in chapter 3.

Very few women of Mexican descent went to the Midwest. Nonetheless, they exercised a profound influence on the economic and social life of the communities in which they settled. Their presence also created sharp divisions within Mexican communities over the questions of acculturation and changing gender roles. Discussion of these issues, how men and women viewed them, and the economic role of women in midwestern communities form the basis for chapter 4.

Mexican immigration to the United States between 1911 and 1929 influenced and was influenced by political and economic forces in Mexico and the vicissitudes of U.S.-Mexican relations. During this time, government attitudes about emigration from Mexico and the treatment of Mexicans in the United States changed. As a result, Mexican consuls in the United States were increasingly asked by their superiors and immigrant nationals to play a larger role in protecting the rights of Mexicans and promoting loyalty to Mexico. How they did this and the results of their efforts are the focus of chapter 5.

One of the purposes of this study is to show that Mexicans were not passive victims. On the contrary, Mexicans actively resisted political, economic, and legal exploitation and discrimination. This involvement is evidenced by the numerous and varied organizations they established. Although diverse in nature, all of these organizations sought to protect Mexicans and promote loyalty to Mexico. The nature, scope, and effect of these organizations in midwestern Mexican communities are discussed in chapters 6 and 7.

Outside of formally organized activities, Mexicans also experienced a highly diverse social life. Living in the Midwest exposed them to a burgeoning consumer and popular culture that offered them a wide array of activities and products. The influence of this new consumer culture on Mexicans is discussed in chapter 8.

Chapter 9 focuses on the onset of the Great Depression and the mass repatriation of Mexicans. How the crash affected Mexicans, their reactions to the repatriation drives, and the effect of these drives on Mexican communities in the Midwest are among the major points covered in this final section.

Whenever possible, I distinguish the experiences and characteristics that are central or unique to Mexicans in the Midwest between 1900 and 1932. I also strive to place this history within the broader context of events in the United States and Mexico and within the scope of U.S.-Mexican relations. In addition to providing a synthesis, I try to challenge and dispel some of the prevailing historical misconceptions about Mexicans. Toward this end, I have sought to present Mexicans as a diverse and heterogeneous population that perceived and responded to challenges and opportunities in a variety of ways. Although this work covers only thirty-two years, during that brief span of time Mexicans had a profound influence on the growth and development of the Midwest.

Many people, too numerous to mention by name, made this book possible. First of all, I owe appreciation to the knowledgeable and helpful archivists and staff members of the Archivo General de la Nación and the Archivo Histórico de la Secretaría de Relaciónes Exteriores in Mexico City. Staff members of the National Archives, U.S. Department of Labor, Chicago Historical Society, Edison Industrial Archives, Chicano-Boriqua Program at Wayne State University, Calumet Regional Archives at Indiana University Northwest, University of Illinois Archives in Chicago, Chicago Public Library, and Bancroft Library were courteous, patient professionals who provided me with the sources and information needed to complete this study.

I owe special thanks to Heather and Oliver Sigworth, who carefully read and edited the manuscript. Their judicious editing and helpful suggestions greatly improved its quality. I also thank Dennis Nodín Valdés, Francisco Arturo Rosales, Michael Smith, Lawrence Cardoso, Ciro Sepulveda, Gilbert Cardenas, Richard Santillan, and Julian Samora for their insights, ideas, and inspiration during the formative stages of this work. I owe a great deal to Joanne O'Hare, Senior Editor at the

University of Arizona Press, for her interest in my work, her patience, and her editorial expertise.

I give special thanks to Cherie McCollum for the great deal of time she devoted to the final preparation of the manuscript. I am indebted to my lovely wife, Rosalind, and our three daughters, Mariel, Michelle, and Alison, for their love, support, and understanding during my long absences. I offer my heartfelt appreciation to my parents, Juan and Maria García, and to the people who inspired this work—the Mexicans of the Midwest. I hope this study does justice to their lives, histories, and struggles.

This work is dedicated to the memory of Julian and Betty Samora. Their lives, love, friendship, and example touched and guided many of us. They will be greatly missed but not forgotten.

Abbreviations

AFL   American Federation of Labor

AGN   Archivo General de la Nación (Mexico City)

ARE   Archivo Histórico de la Secretaría de Relaciónes Exteriores (Mexico City)

CRA   Calumet Regional Archives (Gary)

DIFC   Department of Immigration and Foreign Communities, YWCA

FLPS   Foreign Language Press Survey (Chicago)

INS   Immigration and Naturalization Service

IPL   Immigrants' Protective League

SFRR   Santa Fe Railroad

UCS   University of Chicago Settlement

YMCA   Young Men's Christian Association

YWCA   Young Women's Christian Association

Mexicans
in the Midwest
1900–1932

CHAPTER 1

Mexican Immigration to the United States, 1900–1917

The industrial growth of the Midwest in the decades following the Civil War was phenomenal.[1] Blessed with vast natural resources, extensive waterways, a centralized railroad system, and a growing supply of labor from Europe and America's farm lands, the region quickly became the center of new industries. Contributing to the growth was an impressive outpouring of technological innovations, including the electric light, camera, telephone, typewriter, refrigerated car, and Westinghouse brake. Between 1860 and 1890, wizards walked the land, as American inventors were granted 440,000 patents, in contrast to the 36,000 patents issued in the decades before the Civil War. Just as innovative advances in technology created the necessary machinery for industrial growth, the so-called "captains of industry" developed new financial and administrative structures that brought bankers, machines, and raw materials together to produce and distribute their products more efficiently and profitably.[2] Finally, a growing market, a good transportation network, marked increases in the labor pool, and the help of the federal government all contributed substantially to promoting economic and industrial development.

Paralleling the growth of industry, the expansion of commerce, and the discovery of new technologies was the nation's urban development. In the years after the Civil War, the United States moved from an agrarian to an urban-industrial society dominated by giant national corporations. By 1890 the ten largest urban centers produced almost 40 percent of the country's manufactured goods. Increasingly Americans were drawn to the cities in search of jobs, entertainment, culture, and adventure. In the latter part of the nineteenth century, an estimated eight or nine million Americans left the isolation and sterility of rural life for the cities. Whereas the rural population almost doubled between 1860 and 1890, the urban population, bolstered by internal migration and immigration from abroad, increased seven times. By 1900 six out of every ten Americans made their living outside of agriculture.

As a result of this growth, midwestern cities began to rival major eastern cities in size, wealth, and power. For example, Minneapolis and St. Paul, Minnesota, and Kansas City, Missouri, each grew in population from about 13,000 in 1870 to well over 160,000 by 1890.[3] Among the fastest growing cities in the nation and the world was Chicago, Illinois, which moved from the eighth largest city in the country in 1860 to the second largest in 1900. By 1900 the Midwest contained seven out of the seventeen cities with metropolitan centers of over a quarter million people. These cities were Chicago, Cincinnati, Cleveland, Detroit, Milwaukee, Minneapolis, and St. Louis. Yet their unprecedented growth, which brought productive activity, vitality, and wealth to the country and its people, also created a myriad of problems. Among them were severe housing shortages and inadequate facilities and transportation systems. Congestion, poor planning, and corruption exacerbated and magnified the problems plaguing cities. Critics described them as monuments to waste, poverty, vice, and social disorganization.[4]

Although the urban-industrial complexes drew rural White and Black Americans from the East and Midwest into the cities, the number attracted proved insufficient to meet expanding labor needs. Increasingly employers turned to immigrant laborers from eastern and southern Europe. By the late 1890s and early 1900s, populations in midwestern cities were a conglomerate of many nationalities and ethnic backgrounds. Employers took little notice of the tensions and uncertainties their recruiting practices engendered. Their goal was to maintain an adequate supply of labor, and for a while they succeeded.

Initially most midwestern industrial employers did not recruit Mexicans to work for them because there was little need to do so. Better wages, greater job security, and the lure of the city attracted enough workers from other sources. Most early Mexican immigrants to the Midwest came as agricultural workers to toil in the beet fields or as members of railway construction and maintenance crews. Later, when a labor shortage caused by the outbreak of World War I and restrictive immigration laws reduced European immigration, employers were forced to seek a new source of foreign labor. This time they looked to Mexico.

Most Mexicans who sought new opportunities in the Midwest between 1900 and 1932 were young bachelors, or *solteros*. *Solos*, or married men who traveled to the United States by themselves, also went to the Midwest. Most came from the Central Plateau of Mexico, where a large population and a severe depression in 1907, which affected mining and ranching and caused currency debasement and starvation, forced Mexicans from their homes in search of relief. Many of these unemployed laborers were among the early Mexican immigrants to the Midwest. The outbreak of the Mexican revolution in 1910 added to the economic and political instability and resulted in even greater numbers leaving Mexico.[5]

During the early phases of settlement (1900–1917), few Mexicans came directly from Mexico to the Midwest. Most job-hopped northward, acquiring skills and learning English as they moved deeper into the interior. In this respect the railroad and sugar beet industries played an important role in bringing Mexicans to the Midwest.

Railroads and Mexican Immigration

During the latter part of the nineteenth century, the United States and Mexico initiated extensive railroad-building programs. In the United States, railway trackage increased from 30,000 miles in 1860 to more than 193,000 miles in 1900. "By 1890 the physical integration of the railroad network had been substantially completed. . . . Standard freight classifications had been adopted and the nation divided into four time zones to facilitate train scheduling."[6]

For Mexico the accomplishment was no less significant. In 1877 Porfirio Díaz initiated the construction of a rail network that would facilitate the shipment of goods and, when necessary, troops. This network was designed to bring Mexico into the modern age, attract foreign investors, and assert stronger control over the northern regions of

Mexico. An unexpected outcome of this construction was that it drew thousands of Mexican workers steadily northward as the lines advanced toward the border. Between 1880 and 1900, railway trackage in Mexico increased from 700 miles to over 12,000 miles, more than three-fourths of which was standard gauge.

For many the railroad represented employment and an avenue of escape. By 1900 Mexico's principal railroads were completed and connected to the major American railway lines along the border. As Mexicans approached the border, many took advantage of the opportunity to cross it. The Mexican government was repeatedly asked to recruit more laborers from the interior to replace those who were lured across the border by the promise of higher wages. In the United States, Mexican rail workers were paid $1.00 to $1.25 per day, whereas in Mexico they received only half as much.[7]

American railroad companies welcomed Mexicans because the curtailment of immigration from Asia and the Europeans' preference for year-round employment and higher wages had led to a severe labor shortage. Mexican laborers also had experience in railroad work and were perceived by employers as docile, hard-working people who did not complain about low wages and poor working conditions. Their desirability as laborers was augmented by the employers' belief that most returned to Mexico once the job had ended. Before long Mexicans were laying tracks and constructing roadbeds for most of the major rail lines. Once this work had been completed, many remained in the United States as track maintenance crews. By the 1920s most workers on some railway maintenance crews were of Mexican descent. For example, in 1910, 55 percent of all track laborers in Kansas City, Kansas, were Mexicans. That figure increased to 85 percent in 1915 and to more than 91 percent in 1927.[8]

The railroads were not only instrumental in bringing Mexicans to the Midwest, but they were also important in determining the location of Mexican enclaves in some states.[9] This was the case in St. Louis, Missouri, and in Kansas City, Kansas, where completion of the Brownsville–Kansas City line in 1904 led to the first substantial settlements of Mexicans there. A year earlier the Santa Fe Railroad had begun hiring Mexicans, although it was not until 1907 that the company actively recruited Mexicans from Texas. In Kansas, many cities recorded the first influx of Mexicans between 1905 and 1910. Initially Mexicans were hired as section crews, who worked from May to October and then returned to Mexico. Yet as early as 1907, railroad officials estimated that at least 30 percent of the section workers remained in the United States and worked in the fields for the remaining six months.[10] It was around these individuals that the early Mexican *colonias* (colonies or districts) in Kansas City, Augustine, Wichita, and Emporia, Kansas developed.

Even when the railroads were not directly responsible for influencing settlement patterns, as they did in Illinois, Indiana, and Kansas, they were important in attracting Mexican immigrants to other parts of the Midwest. For example, hundreds of immigrants who arrived in Michigan as workers on railroad section crews had been contracted in the Southwest. The experience of one Mexican who arrived in Detroit, Michigan, in 1916 is illustrative of this northeasterly flow:

> The first time I was contracted, it was in San Antonio. I didn't come to Michigan. I went to Pennsylvania. There were about two hundred of us on contract on a train to Pennsylvania. And from San Antonio to Pittsburgh, you know how many of us arrived? Only sixty-five. They would reach the stations and go their own way. They already knew where they were going; [they] only wanted the ride. In Cincinnati about thirty-five left. Only the green ones arrived in Pittsburgh.[11]

The practice of leaving the trains before reaching a contracted destination was commonplace and grew as Mexicans left Mexico and the Southwest for specific destinations. Many Mexican contract workers had no intention of laboring on the railroads. This was especially true for those who sought work in industry, where wages were higher and employment was steadier. Learning of these opportunities from friends, relatives, word of mouth, and other sources, an undetermined number of Mexicans signed on with the railroads simply to reach their desired destination. Once there, many "skipped out" on their contracts. Railroad companies complained bitterly of this practice and attempted to find ways to discourage it. At times they were aided by unscrupulous contractors, who chained their men together until they arrived at their destination.[12]

Some railroad companies, however, were loath to do anything that placed them in a bad light with their workers and the Mexican government simply because they needed the labor. This was the case for companies whose rail lines stretched into the Midwest and East, where competition for Mexican workers was often intense. Railway companies realized they faced an uphill battle in recruiting and retaining workers because of the drawbacks associated with seasonal employment, lower wages, and the high mobility required by the job. Confronted by labor shortages and a growing number of "skips," the railroad companies found themselves in difficult straits. The prohibitive cost of finding skips, however, limited the employers' options. According to one contractor, the cost to track down, capture, and deport a Mexican who had deserted his job was about $143.40. The expense and large number of desertions forced railroad companies to continue recruiting more laborers from the Southwest and Mexico.[13]

The widespread skipping of contracts by Mexicans represented a valuable lesson for many employers—a lesson few heeded. Contrary to popular misconceptions, Mexicans were not docile. Those new to the United States might have been confused, innocent, or even naive when it came to believing the promises of employers or recruiters, but they were not fools. Yet employers often mistook Mexican inexperience and silence (which was due to their inability to speak English) for docility. They soon learned that when Mexicans did not find things to their liking, they either left the job, complained to employers, or sought assistance from their government. In turn, Mexicans quickly learned that their labor and unity were valuable commodities that provided them some leverage in bargaining for improved wages and living conditions. This newfound knowledge was apparent in the problems experienced by railway companies that failed to live up to their promises.

The Pennsylvania Railroad was one such company. In 1916 it recruited about 1,800 Mexican laborers to work in the Midwest. Within a few months after their arrival, these employees filed a series of complaints with their government over the death of one workman and the mistreatment of several others by the foreman. By the time the Mexican consul investigated the matter, some 300 workers had skipped out on their contracts. Railroad officials bitterly complained to the consul and accused the Mexicans of being "ungrateful."

Consul T. G. Pellicer chided the officials for their anger. He told them that the so-called ingratitude of their workers derived from "the innumerable lies told them at the time they were contracted."[14] He also noted that the Mexicans, like so many other immigrants, had been recruited at the border before they had had an opportunity to orient themselves. There they had been bombarded with promises of incredible salaries, good housing, and no hidden expenses if they joined the railroad. Both the consul and the workers complained that they or their compatriots were often the victims of unscrupulous contractors who took advantage of their trust and naiveté. Contract guarantees promising proper food, adequate medical care, and good housing often went unfulfilled. Adding to the workers' misery were the abuses suffered at the hands of pernicious foremen.[15]

These complaints constituted most of the charges the Mexican workers leveled against the Pennsylvania Railroad. They complained about abusive foremen and nonpayment of the $1.80-per-day wage they had been promised. According to the workers, the company had made several deductions from their pay, including $.50 per day for food even when they did not work, $.75 per month for hospitalization, and accident insurance and commissary expenses. They told the consul that no mention of these deductions had been made to them when they were hired, nor were they informed that $8 would be deducted from their first paycheck to pay for the food they had eaten on the train.[16]

At first the company representative was not willing to listen to demands for concessions. Instead, he threatened that his company would no longer hire Mexicans if they continued to break their contracts. Similar threats were expressed to other consuls. Yet the general feeling among Mexicans was that these warnings were merely bluffs. It was common knowledge that these companies needed workers. Most Mexican employees believed that company officials would be willing to make concessions to keep them from deserting their jobs.[17]

Railway executives, however, sometimes dug in their heels and refused to yield to demands. This behavior resulted in further protests from Mexican representatives and more "desertions" by Mexicans to other jobs. Employers were then forced to recruit more Mexicans to work in the Midwest, thus augmenting the population of the region.

The Sugar Beet Industry and Mexican Immigration

The sugar beet industry also played an important role in recruiting Mexicans to the Midwest. This enterprise created a permanent agricultural force in the Midwest and became a major pool of laborers for other businesses in the region. Many beet workers, or *betabeleros,* moved to the cities in search of higher wages, steadier work, and education for their children. As a result, they were the core of many Mexican colonias. In time a continuous movement between city and field developed, as laborers moved back and forth in search of work. By the mid-1920s, "midwestern cities [had become] the major destination of beet workers at the end of the season and an important source of recruitment the following spring." Sugar beet corporations are credited with having the greatest influence on "the initial entry and continued presence of Mexicanos in the Midwest."[18]

Like other enterprises, the sugar beet industry benefited from the industrial and population boom that occurred after the Civil War. Part of the industry's growth was due to the increased production of processed foods such as jams and jellies and the need for sugar to sweeten coffee, tea, soft drinks, and cereals. The latter part of the nineteenth century witnessed an increase in the consumption of sugar from twenty pounds per capita in 1860 to more than one hundred pounds per capita in 1920. This growth provided the incentive for American sugar manufacturers to gain control of sugar production and establish favorable policies to guarantee their success. To accomplish this they promoted research in developing a commercially viable sugar beet suitable to local climatic and soil conditions. They and their supporters were also successful in getting the highly protective Dingley Tariff enacted in 1897, which raised import duties on foreign sugar by as much as 79 percent. To provide greater incentives for sugar beet growing, several states, including Michigan, instituted bounties of one cent for each bushel of state-produced sugar. The sugar interests also strongly supported the Spanish-American War of 1898 because it secured American interests in some of the most fertile sugar-cane–producing regions in the world.

In the Midwest this flurry of activity spurred the building of more than twenty sugar beet refineries between 1898 and 1907.[19] By 1920 Michigan had seventeen factories in operation and a reported beet acreage of 149,559 acres. Most production was centered around Bay City and Saginaw in central Michigan, although beet fields and sugar factories dotted most of the state.[20] The eighty-six new factories built in the Upper Midwest between 1898 and 1913 attested to the dramatic growth of this industry. After 1900 and for the next half century, 50 to 75 percent of the sugar produced in the United States came from Michigan, Colorado, and California.[21]

The tremendous growth in the cultivation of sugar beets required a large labor supply. Initially sugar beet companies persuaded local farmers to do the tedious, back-breaking, and dangerous work of thinning, hoeing, and topping beets. The work, however, was onerous to the farmers, who began recruiting gang labor to work in the fields. As sugar beet production expanded and labor shortages became more severe, growers began deferring to the sugar beet companies for the recruitment and management of labor. The companies in turn found that recruiting entire families was more cost-effective for production and maintaining a more stable labor force. Before World War I, many of these families were European immigrants and included large numbers of Belgians, German-Rumanians, Bohemians, Poles, and Hungarians.[22] This source of labor dried up, however, as beet workers saved their earnings and invested in farmland. Some workers received loans from sugar beet companies for land purchases because the companies wished to encourage greater cultivation of beets. Once settled, these former beet workers often sought out new workers to toil in the fields; however, the high mobility of the European migrant population and the advent of World War I drastically reduced traditional sources of labor. Forced to seek elsewhere for an inexpensive and malleable work force, the sugar beet industry looked southward to Mexico and the Southwest.[23]

Farmers were initially leery about hiring Mexican workers. According to a representative of the Continental Sugar Company in Michigan, farmers believed Mexicans were dangerous because they all carried knives.[24] These suspicions and fears, however, tended to abate after the first season of using Mexican laborers.

Mexicans were not new to sugar beet work. As early as 1905 the Sugar Beet Company had been formed in Garden City, Kansas, and had hired Mexican laborers to work in the fields and processing plant. In Kansas, however, as in other midwestern states, the number of Mexicans employed was minuscule compared to the number hired in the years after World War I.

Before the war, many companies that recruited Mexican beet workers preferred to hire solos and solteros. This practice can largely be attributed to the availability of other sources of labor and the strong misconceptions that employers had about Mexicans. Many employers believed that solos were more likely to return to Mexico or Texas once the season ended. At least at the outset, employers had no wish to stir up the community by bringing in groups who were socially unacceptable. This practice, however, largely ceased after the war when it became apparent that keeping Mexican workers around saved transportation and recruiting costs.

The outbreak of war in Europe in 1914 and unrestricted submarine warfare diminished immigration to the United States. At first American employers expressed little concern because of the large supply of available labor. After American mobilization for war and the enactment of the Immigration Act of 1917, with its head tax and literacy provisions, employers were forced to seek out new labor sources to meet the needs of a booming wartime economy. Increasingly employers looked to Mexico as an important source of cheap labor. As a result, "Mexican workers became the core of the agricultural proletariat in the Upper Midwest following WWI."[25]

Nevertheless, many midwestern employers found themselves at a disadvantage in recruiting Mexican laborers. Employers in the Southwest benefited from the cultural heritage of the region and its proximity to Mexico. Midwestern employers, however, countered by offering Mexicans higher wages and free transportation. They also used the services of contractors and recruiters who operated along the border. Before long, hopeful recruits were flocking to such places as La Plaza de los Zacatecas in San Antonio, Texas, where labor contractors, or *enganchistas*, openly plied their trade.

Among the hardest hit by the labor shortage were the sugar beet companies. Unlike other industries, the sugar beet companies had opted for family units because the isolation, seasonal nature, and quantity of the work made retaining single workers difficult. Employers soon learned that family units were a better bargain because they worked more acres, provided a buffer against loneliness and isolation, and increased the likelihood that workers would remain during the off-season, saving large recruiting costs. An early Mexican resident of Detroit recalled that he had been turned away by a recruiter in San Antonio because he was unattached. Not to be deterred, he convinced a young waitress at a local diner to pose as his wife. According to him, this became a common practice among solos who sought work in the sugar beet fields.[26]

Few of the Mexican laborers were prepared to do the kind of work they were hired to perform. Contrary to the stereotypes held by many midwestern employers, many immigrants had been urban dwellers in Mexico and were unfamiliar with field work. Contractors or employers were seldom interested or concerned enough to ask; they simply assumed that all Mexicans came from rural areas and knew how to work in the fields. Recruits, most of whom came from the temperate regions of Mexico's Central Plateau, were put aboard trains and shipped directly to the beet fields. Few of them spoke or understood English, and most were unaware of their specific destination. One early immigrant recalled,

> The companies would send "enganchadores" down to the south to advertise in the newspapers that they needed a certain amount of people, and the enganchadores offices were in San Antonio—people would gather there. I came in a special train where they had 600 workers. We came to a small town named Alma [Michigan]. There the workers were divided to different areas. I got to go to a small town near Marysville

where I stayed for three months. And from there I came to Detroit.[27]

At times the route to the beet fields and city was circuitous:

I went to Pueblo, Colorado, during the First World War. And when it ended jobs were scarce. My father and brother worked in a steel mill. Their jobs ended and we moved to Mexico City. But we liked the United States so we saved up for four years and moved here. We moved to San Antonio where we met a beet contractor. Then we moved to Iowa. Coming from San Antonio where it was hot, we were wearing summer clothes. We arrived in April and it was snowing. We, the youngest ones in the family, were children. We were really young, but we all did the work.[28]

The first trainload of Mexican beet workers recruited by the Michigan Sugar Company arrived in Michigan in 1915. This began a yearly migration that continued unabated for the next fourteen years. A yearly average of 2,000 Mexicans were contracted by the Michigan beet industries between 1915 and 1929.[29] In 1922 Mexican laborers constituted 33 percent of the beet workers in the state. By 1927 this proportion had grown to 75 percent, or nearly 20,000 Mexican workers.[30]

In Minnesota Mexicans were contracted in 1907 by the American Crystal Sugar Company. The state had 5,000 Mexican workers in the beet fields in 1927 and 7,000 in 1928.[31] In 1917 52 Mexicans were brought to northwestern Ohio by the Continental Sugar Company of Kansas City, Missouri. The company brought 382 more workers from Mexico in 1918 and another 943 in 1920.[32] When the season ended, the company provided them with work in the sugar refinery in Toledo, Ohio. The number of Mexicans recruited by Continental increased to 2,697 in 1926. By that time it was no longer necessary to recruit out-of-state laborers because many Mexican beet workers found temporary employment on the railroads during the off-season. This pattern became commonplace in the Midwest after World War I. As a result, Mexican sugar beet workers came to provide much of the industrial and railroad labor for the region. By the late 1920s, many of the midwestern factory workers had initially labored in the beet fields.[33]

Whenever factory production dropped, causing a reduction in the labor force, this process was reversed, as sugar beet companies recruited workers from Mexican colonias in the Midwest. They were aided in their recruiting by the frequent periods of unemployment and underemployment caused by seasonal layoffs, production changeovers, and reduced hours that characterized the lives of industrial workers. Advertisements in Spanish-language newspapers, pool halls, and employment agencies promising $23 to harvest one acre, free transportation to and from the farms, and discounted tickets to destinations in Texas once the season ended enticed large numbers of unemployed Mexicans to the beet fields.[34] Similar recruiting ventures by other sugar beet companies throughout the Midwest ensured the predominance of Mexican workers in the beet fields.

By the late 1920s, between 75 and 90 percent of beet workers in the Midwest were Mexicans, a yearly total of 15,000 to 20,000 Mexican workers.[35] This figure did not include children under the age of sixteen or adult women. If these groups are included, the total estimated population of Mexicans drawn to the region by sugar beet companies is more than 40,000.

Turnover in the beet fields was high because of the difficulty of the work, its seasonal nature, low wages, and the tendency of some companies to disregard their promises of good pay and working conditions. Loneliness, isolation, and dangerous working conditions added to worker discontent. "Chicken coops, tents, abandoned shacks and barns only recently vacated by animals" often served as housing.[36] Employees also encountered unexpected expenses about which recruiting agents and contractors had conveniently neglected to tell them. Some companies, for example, deducted the cost of transportation to the Midwest from workers' earnings even though they had guaranteed free transportation. Other companies required employees to purchase all of their goods from company stores or commissary agents licensed by the company to operate such stores. The exorbitant prices charged at these establishments further reduced the meager wages. At season's end many Mexicans were destitute, unable to finance their return home.

There were also problems with stipulations in the contracts. Mexican workers, unlike their European predecessors, had detailed, demanding contracts that shifted much of the responsibility and risk onto their shoulders. Employers had learned from previous experience with earlier groups of immigrant laborers that changes were needed to give companies greater control over the labor force, increase worker dependence on the company, ensure a more stable labor force, and decrease options for other employment. Contracts, therefore, stipulated pay rates based upon the distance between rows, rather than by the acre. "For topping they were paid not merely according to acreage, but also yield of beets and purity, matters which were largely beyond their control."[37] The result was that workers received less money for their labor.

Employers kept wages to a minimum to preclude Mexicans from accumulating enough capital to purchase land. From previous experience, employers had learned that a sufficient income led field workers to become proprietors, requiring employers to spend more money to recruit replacements. They would not make that mistake again. Their goal was to maintain a seasonal work force sufficient to meet their needs. This was good business, they reasoned, and it complemented the desire of many communities to dissuade Mexicans from becoming permanent residents.

A familiar story, one that Mexicans quickly learned, was this: Mexicans were welcome only as long as their labor was needed. Understandably, turnover was high and bitterness was great. Dissatisfaction manifested itself in high turnover rates; in numerous letters of complaint written to consuls, company officials, and friends; and even in songs. In "Los Betabeleros," one gains a sense of the anger and despair such practices evoked.

> *In the year 1923,*
> *Of the present era*
> *The beet field workers went*
> *To that Michigan, to their grief*
> *Because all the bosses*
> *Began to scold*
> *And Don Santiago says to them:*

"I want to return
Because they haven't done for us
What they said they would."
Here they come and tell you
That you ought to go up there
Because there you will have everything
Without having to fight for it.
But these are nothing but lies,
And those who come and say those things
Are liars![38]

As turnover rates increased and competition for Mexican labor intensified, sugar beet companies were forced to change their dealings with the workers. Those changes, however, benefited the employer more than the employee. As stated earlier, sugar beet companies began recruiting families instead of solos or solteros for the good of the company. Because workers were continually being siphoned off by the railroad, steel manufacturing, meat packing, and other industries, sugar beet employers reasoned that men would be less likely to leave in pursuit of other jobs if they had their families with them. Another advantage to recruiting families was that more people could be put to work in the fields, thus increasing crop yields.

To ensure that workers did not skip on their contracts, companies withheld a percentage of the wages earned until the requirements of the contract were met. Ostensibly workers were told the money was withheld so they would have something left with which to return home. This was often a lie; many workers never saw one cent of what was set aside. Instead, it was used to pay for charges incurred during the season. Because workers were seldom, if ever, given itemized lists of their expenditures, it was virtually impossible for them to ascertain what had happened to their money.

Although companies were required to provide round-trip transportation for their workers, many circumvented this requirement by paying a "travel bonus" directly to them. Employers knew that few workers would ever use the money for that purpose. They often used their bonuses to supplement their meager earnings or to pay their debts.[39]

Good workers or those too destitute to leave were provided with low-cost or rent-free housing and credit during the off-season. This practice only served to perpetuate their indebtedness and provided some employers with a pool of workers with which to begin the season anew.

Not all Mexicans passively accepted their fate. Some sought the assistance of their government and requested repatriation to Mexico. Others asked their consuls to take their grievances to company representatives. Many voted with their feet, leaving the beet fields for the industrial sector. Workers also staged walkouts, slowdowns, and demonstrations, despite threats and physical abuse. After suffering through the season, some workers returned to their homes or drifted into cities in search of other opportunities.

The first Mexicans in these communities were largely unnoticed because of their small numbers. For example, Detroit had only 10 Mexican residents in 1910. In 1920 Omaha, Nebraska, had 682 Mexican residents, and St. Paul had about 400 Mexican men, women, and children.[40] Cold, hungry, and destitute, many were forced to turn to local relief agencies. Initially they were well treated and given assistance. Their numbers increased, however, and private and public charities were unable to accommodate the newcomers. As Mexicans increasingly taxed the meager resources of local relief agencies, some municipalities began imposing residency requirements, which precluded many Mexicans from receiving assistance.

Stories of countless hardships and contract violations made their way around recruiting centers and contract offices. Soon many Mexicans who had signed on for beet work had little intention of working in the fields; most simply wanted to take advantage of the free train ride to the Midwest. Once there, they set off on their own to find work. One recruit, who had signed up to work in Michigan, recalled that his group was being sent to Mt. Pleasant; however, he had little intention of going there. En route he met a Mexican couple who was also taking advantage of the free ride. By the time they arrived at Mt. Pleasant, "We were friends. [The man I met on the train] already knew Detroit, so I went to Detroit with them, preferring to work there than in the fields."[41] This was to be an oft-repeated story.

World War I and *Braceros*

In 1917 the railroads, sugar beet growers, and agricultural interests were assisted in their recruiting efforts when the federal government instituted the first Mexican-labor importation program. This program resulted from lobbying efforts by American employers, who argued that the war and the Immigration Act of 1917 had drastically reduced the European labor supply.[42] They contended that this shortage of workers would adversely affect agricultural production and, by extension, America's ability to supply the war effort.

Persuaded by these arguments, the Secretary of Labor, W. B. Wilson, began exempting Mexican agricultural workers from the literacy and head tax requirements of the act. He did this under authority of an emergency clause in Section 3 of the Ninth Proviso, which authorized the Commissioner of Immigration to admit temporary contract labor when such a need was approved by the Secretary of Labor. This waiver of the act, which also required temporary suspension of the 1885 Contract Labor Law prohibiting the importation of foreign contract labor, lasted from May 1917 until March 1921. It was the first of many such waivers initiated by the United States to ensure an adequate labor supply.[43]

Wilson's decision to suspend the immigration provisions met with opposition from organized labor and some congressmen who doubted a labor shortage really existed. Congressman John L. Burnett, the sponsor of the Immigration Act of 1917 and chairman of the House Immigration and Naturalization Committee, challenged Secretary Wilson's authority to suspend the act's provisions.[44]

To defuse some of the criticism, Wilson's department established rigid standards governing the temporary admission of Mexican laborers, or *braceros*. Under these guidelines, only braceros would be recruited, and their stay would be limited to six months. Employers had to formally apply to the Department of Labor for workers. The applications had to indicate the number of workers required, the wages they would be paid, and where they would be housed. Braceros had to be paid the prevailing wage rate, and housing and sanitation facilities had to meet state standards. Employers were required to notify immigration officials about workers who left their employ before the contract period expired. Any worker who violated the provisions of his contract was subject to immediate arrest and deportation.[45]

To ensure that Mexicans admitted under the bracero program did not remain after their contract expired, the Labor Department devised a wage-withholding program to be administered by the employer. These deductions had to be turned over to immigration officials, who deposited them in a U.S. Postal Savings bank. Workers were then entitled to withdraw their funds once they had been processed and returned to Mexico.[46]

Although employers were happy with the government's decision to import Mexican laborers, they resented the stringent regulations governing the program. They wanted all restrictions and requirements dropped because they believed it made the program expensive and cumbersome. In their opinion, the government was coddling the workers, raising their expectations, and creating future problems with domestic laborers once the war ended, when they too would begin demanding similar guarantees. The employers' protests yielded few results. They did, however, convince Herbert Hoover, who served as Food Administrator during the war, that the program should be continued until the war ended. With his help the list of industries that could employ braceros was extended to include railroads, coal mines, and construction work on government projects.[47] Employers were also successful in getting the requirement of withholding wages discontinued.[48]

Once the war ended, Wilson decided that a bracero program was no longer necessary. On 15 December 1918, he issued orders terminating the program. He again encountered strong opposition, this time from the sugar beet interests. Pressured by western congressmen and their powerful allies, Wilson rescinded his decision. On 2 January 1919, he issued an order permitting the temporary admission of Mexican workers until 30 June 1919.[49] Continuing pressure forced Wilson to renew the bracero program several times. The importation of Mexican workers finally ended in 1921 when the United States experienced a major economic depression, which caused massive shutdowns and created an oversupply of cheap domestic labor.[50] At least for the moment, employers did not need to import Mexican labor.

Nevertheless, the Mexican labor importation program of 1917 to 1921 stimulated the migration of Mexicans to the Midwest. Although the number of Mexicans who came to the Midwest as braceros may have been relatively small, the program served as a catalyst for further emigration from Mexico. The program educated thousands of Mexicans on American immigration policy. For example, Mexicans learned that the United States did not have an effective means of regulating entry, that employers were willing to hire Mexicans regardless of what immigration laws were in force, and that the United States was willing to waive immigration requirements whenever a labor shortage was believed to exist. In essence, the program helped lower several psychological barriers among Mexican emigrants. It led them to believe that employers and the government were one in desiring their services.[51]

Labor Contractors and Mexican Immigration

Throughout the era, the work of enganchistas also affected Mexican immigration. These individuals, whether they worked as part of large employment agencies or as "lone wolves," entered an open field of enterprise. Because no centralized recruitment system existed, they established an informal recruiting network, which netted large profits with little risk.

By 1910 several agencies specializing in recruiting workers for the railroads were in operation. The largest and most efficient were headquartered in San Antonio, Laredo, and El Paso, Texas. At these and other major border-crossing areas, representatives met penniless immigrants and offered them provisions and free transportation to employment destinations.

Although some agencies charged workers a placement fee, others did not. The latter preferred instead to acquire exchange rights in furnishing workers with food, clothing, and other necessities. The cost for these commodities was deducted by employers from workers' wages and turned over to the labor-contracting agency. These agencies often charged up to 15 percent more than retail prices because they catered to workers assigned to desolate or isolated areas. A common practice among recruiting agencies was to assess an employment fee of $1 to each individual contracted. This fee, along with the inflated charges for provisions, allowed the agencies to "reap an enormous profit, all of which [was] paid by the laborer." It was indeed a lucrative business, so much so "that the Commissioner-General of Immigration believed that labor agents were actively engaged in searching out new areas of employment for Mexicans in the United States."[52]

Agents traveled throughout Mexico recruiting, hiring, and transporting Mexicans to the border in violation of the Contract Labor Law of 1885. Their work was aided by massive advertising in newspapers and the distribution of fliers. The leaflets told prospective workers where to report. Some even contained instructions on how and where to cross into the United States.[53]

Independent labor contractors also abounded. Whether they were of Mexican or Anglo descent, these operators used their familiarity with the language and customs to corral new recruits. They easily mingled among the masses of immigrants huddled in border cities, spoke to them, and learned all they could about their places of origin, conditions, and population makeup. This led them to Mexico, where they appeared in towns and villages promising high wages, free transportation, adequate food and housing, and good working conditions in "el Norte." Some carried photographs of neat little houses surrounded by white picket fences that would serve as housing for Mexicans. Others carried promotional literature acquired from local chambers of commerce or booster groups that showed only the rosy side of life in the United States.

To the potential expatriate, using an enganchista made sense because they "knew the ropes." They also promised fewer hassles from immigration authorities. Emigrants from Mexico were told that the process of entering the United States legally was expensive and time consuming. "The railroad fare to Guadalajara is about forty-five pesos for full fare. They spend fifteen pesos on the way, two-and-a-half pesos for birth certificates, and perhaps fifteen days in Juárez because of red tape. They have to pass the Mexican immigration offices, the American consulate, and wait for the vaccinations that the public health officer gives. That takes about fifteen days at three pesos a day."[54]

The head tax and visa cost $18. If emigrants had children, they could expect to pay another $10 for each child under sixteen years of age.[55] Such fees were prohibitive; the average wage earned by Mexicans working on haciendas was 12 pesos per day.[56] Because recruiters handled many of these matters, both employers and immigrant laborers thought they provided a valuable service.

Many of the promises made by contracting agents, however, were illusory. As one disgruntled Mexican complained, he had gone "north" because he was promised food, shelter, and a job that paid good wages. "But I soon found out what it was like. The food was salty and poor and we were all crowded in a car so that we were like pigs. Then I found out that the foreman robbed all the workers of their money by means of the community store and whoever got mad or complained was locked up and beaten." Deciding he had had enough, he left the train, sold his $14 watch for $2 and headed for places unknown.[57] A Mexican consul corroborated such stories when he wrote the following: "All of them came contracted to work six month contracts to maintain and repair the difficult rail lines. These contracts are not often made in good faith, for the majority do not obtain what was offered to them in principal. This office has had to intervene on different occasions in order to effect the promises which were made . . . and which were not met because of the bad faith of contractors and the heads of railroads."[58]

These invidious practices did not go unnoticed or unreported by Mexicans. Mostly through word of mouth, information about dishonest recruiting agencies, farmers with bad reputations, and companies that broke contract promises quickly circulated among would-be recruits. Reliance on recruiting agencies by sugar beet workers and other laborers steadily diminished as they acquired cars, learned more from others about opportunities and working conditions, and made repeated trips to the region. Sugar beet workers who proved reliable were offered continued employment on the farms the following year or were provided with low rent or free housing during the off-season as an incentive to remain in the area. Furthermore, during the off-season, beet workers increasingly sought and found temporary employment on railroads and in industries in small towns and urban centers.

Despite the abuses, dangers, and prevarications that often accompanied the trip north, Mexicans continued to stream in, and contract agents continued to benefit from the needs of both clients and customers. The curtailment of Asian and European immigration, the economic growth of the Southwest, the extensive construction of railroads, and the industrial boom in the Midwest all placed a premium on imported labor from Mexico. Adding to this need was the common practice by agriculturalists of luring workers away from the railroads by offering them slightly higher wages. Agricultural interests, in turn, found their labor pool being drained by industrialists. Faced with a steady loss of workers to other forms of employment, railway companies and agricultural concerns were continually forced to seek replacements. The persistent recruitment of Mexicans by sugar beet companies and other concerns spurred a seasonal migration to the Midwest from Texas and Mexico that became self-perpetuating. Mexican workers often discovered that the promises made by enganchistas and employers represented only the first of many broken promises they would encounter in a strange and foreign land.

CHAPTER 2

Mexicans in the Midwest, 1914–1922

Historically there have been several prevailing misconceptions about Mexicans in the United States. Of particular importance to this study is an incorrect characterization of people of Mexican descent as being primarily rural dwellers engaged in agricultural work. A second misconception is that the Mexican and Mexican American communities did not become urbanized until World War II. Both ignore that a major theme in Mexican and Mexican American history in the United States has been the process of urbanization.[1]

The population of the Southwest grew slowly in the nineteenth century. By 1900 the population of the entire Southwest was less than 10 percent of the national total. Starting in 1900, however, El Paso, San Antonio, San Diego, Los Angeles, and San Francisco began attracting both Anglos and Mexicans in record numbers. Mexicans were drawn to those cities because of their diversified economic structure, favorable transportation and communication facilities, connecting and integrated railroad lines, and relative proximity to the Mexican border.[2] This growth began slowly but gathered momentum in the 1920s, when the Mexican American population more than tripled. By 1930 more than 700,000 Mexican Americans lived in urbanized areas in the Southwest. This figure represented an impressive increase: only ten years earlier the entire Mexican American population in the Southwest numbered only 500,000.[3]

Urbanization of Mexicans in the Midwest, which began in the

early 1900s, also reached its peak during the 1920s. By 1920, 70 percent of midwestern Mexicans lived in urban centers. In Indiana, for example, 91 percent of the Mexicans lived in Gary or East Chicago. The rough-and-tumble company town of Indiana Harbor—the Mexican colonia within East Chicago—had the densest concentration of Mexicans in the United States. By 1930 about 5,000 Mexicans lived near the Inland Steel plant in an area less than a quarter of a square mile in size.[4] In Illinois 67 percent of the Mexicans lived in Chicago, and more than 61 percent of those who migrated to Wisconsin settled in Milwaukee.[5] These figures do not include those who entered the United States illegally, seasonal workers who temporarily moved to the cities during the off-season, or braceros who entered the United States between 1917 and 1921. The difficulty of estimating numbers is compounded by the high rate of mobility among single unskilled and semiskilled Mexicans and poor census collection methods that were inconsistent and imprecise. Most of these "uncounted" Mexicans, however, probably augmented the number of Mexicans in the larger urban areas as they joined their compatriots in search of employment, better wages, and opportunity.

Initially the Mexican population in the Midwest grew slowly because much of the influx from Mexico was drained off by southwestern agriculture, mining, and transportation industries. Before the outbreak of the Mexican revolution in 1910, legal immigration from Mexico had been minuscule. In 1900, 103,393 Mexicans entered the United States legally. This figure was only 0.6 percent of the total number of legal immigrants. Between 1911 and 1920 the percentage rose to 3.8 percent when 221,915 Mexicans entered the country legally.[6] The number of undocumented entries, however, dramatically increased because of the revolution, contract labor program, lack of enforcement by American immigration officials along the border, and efforts of recruiting agents. Low wages, currency debasement, and widespread starvation in Mexico, as well as higher wages in the Southwest, drew thousands of Mexicans into the southwestern labor market. The violence and chaos of the Mexican revolution also spurred emigration. Manuel Contreras, who eventually settled in Minnesota, recalled, "The war brought an end to everything. . . . Life was very sad." At the age of ten he joined the Villistas. Later he left his native state of Durango and came to the United States.[7]

Contreras was typical of those who fled their homeland. The revolution forced more than one million people to emigrate.[8]

Unlike their southwestern counterparts, turn-of-the-century midwestern employers had little need for Mexican laborers because of the availability of workers from southern and eastern Europe. Before World War I, almost no Mexicans lived in the major cities such as Chicago, Gary, and Detroit. In 1900, for example, Detroit's Mexican population was 8; in 1910 it was 27.[9] In 1900 the entire state of Kansas contained only 71 Mexicans.[10] In Illinois the 1900 census listed 156 persons born in Mexico, most of them transient workers or itinerant performers.[11] Events in the United States, Europe, and Mexico soon altered this. In a few years the number of Mexicans coming to the Midwest increased dramatically.

World War I and Mexican Immigration

In June 1914 the archduke of Austria was assassinated by a young Serbian nationalist. Within a few months a heavily armed and deeply divided Europe plunged into war. The news of the assassination and the outbreak of hostilities in Europe at first went largely unnoticed by most Americans. Many could hardly pronounce the word "Sarajevo," much less locate it on a map. Most were at a loss to explain what had caused the war. Although President Woodrow Wilson advised Americans to remain neutral in deed and thought, it soon became apparent that this would be difficult.

From the outset the Wilson administration favored the Allies, led by France and Great Britain. Even though the United States sold war matériel and supplies to both sides, the trade heavily favored the Allies. The war proved a boon to American industry, causing production and profits to soar, yet it also reduced the available labor supply. Throughout Europe, villages and towns were drained of human resources as the war exacted a heavy toll in lives and property. These losses and the hazards caused by the German submarine drastically curtailed the number of European émigrés to the United States. The labor supply was further reduced when the United States entered the war in 1917. Although direct American involvement in the war lasted less than one year, military mobilization drained an additional four million people from the work force. The passage of the Immigration Act of 1917, which reduced immigration from southern and eastern Europe by almost 50 percent, added to employers' problems. By 1918 the annual number of immigrants was less than 10 percent of what it had been in 1914.[12]

Hard pressed to find new sources of labor, American employers quickly enlisted women, southern Blacks, and Mexicans. To recruit Mexicans, midwestern employers used a variety of methods. The simplest was to lure already established workers away from the railroad and sugar beet industries. Employers also hired contracting and commissary agents and added their voices to the chorus asking the federal government to exempt Mexicans from the Immigration Act and to institute a contract labor program. These measures, plus the incentive of higher wages and more stable jobs, failed to draw Mexicans northward in 1917. Prevailing rumors that Mexican nationals were being drafted into America's armed forces kept many from entering the United States. As news spread, thousands of Mexicans fled the United States to avoid conscription.

Along the southwestern border, American consuls reported a mass exodus of Mexican laborers. The American vice consul stationed in Piedras Negras, Coahuila, Mexico, reported, "Not only are those working on a wage scale leaving, but people who have rented farms and already planted their crops, have picked up dog, furniture and family and made a straight line for the Mexican border, all from fear of conscription of their children or themselves." The vice consul believed that rumors about conscription had been

> circulated by German agents, or by German sympathizers, who are doing their share for the country of their blood in cutting down the food supply of Texas and other border states, by working on the ignorant and impulsive minds of the Mexican laborers. The Mexican people are inclined to accept ridiculous rumors or stories, rather than facts at all times. I have often noticed here in Mexico that a story of heroic deeds, or some other ridiculous rumor, would far more attract their minds than would a reserved and well-founded report.[13]

The vice consul was not alone in his beliefs. Colonel F. A. Chapa of the Texas National Guard and editor of *El Imparcial,* a Mexican paper published in San Antonio, attributed the exodus to rumors circulated by agents paid by German sympathizers. In an article published on 24 May 1917, Chapa wrote that he "first became aware of the well organized propaganda through a number of subscribers to his paper . . . who wrote him asking his opinion as to the truth of rumors to the effect that Mexicans would be drafted into the American Army." In his mind there was little doubt the mischief was the work of German agents.[14]

The Mexican consul general, T. A. Beltran, was also inundated with inquiries from Mexicans. "I receive daily a large number of letters, one hundred and fifty to two hundred, from Mexicans all over the state, inquiring whether they will be drafted into service, and in all cases I invariably advise that they should have no fear because Mexico is in the best of relations with the United States, and they, as foreigners of a friendly country, should pursue their occupations without fear of molestation."[15]

All three of these individuals were mistaken. Mr. Beltran's argument that Mexicans had little to fear "because Mexico is in the best of relations with the United States" was fallacious. Existing tensions had been exacerbated by incidents such as the occupation of Vera Cruz by U.S. marines in 1914, rumors that U.S. health inspectors had been "branding" Mexican immigrants with indelible ink as proof they carried no contagious or communicable diseases,[16] the raid by Pancho Villa against Columbus, New Mexico, and the subsequent Pershing expedition in 1916 against Villa. The kidnapping and murder of American citizens in Mexico in 1916 and 1917 also heightened enmity. Demands by Secretary of State Robert Lansing that Mexico show more persistence in capturing and punishing the parties responsible for these acts provoked heated exchanges between the two countries. The United States threatened direct action if the attacks against American citizens and property did not cease. Mexico countered that the United States had failed to protect Mexican nationals in the Southwest, especially Texas, where the Texas Rangers reportedly killed 500 Mexicans between 1916 and 1917. In the midst of all this, the Mexican chargé d'affaires in Cuba informed his superiors in early 1917 that the Cuban subsecretary had warned him about a proposed invasion of Mexico involving American, Canadian, and Cuban forces.

According to Alberto Franco, the invasion of Mexico was designed to secure the Gulf of Mexico from German submarine incursions. The plan called for the occupation of Vera Cruz, Tampico, and Progreso. Franco stated that President Menocal of Cuba had refused to cooperate with England and the United States because of the "grave consequences it would have on Mexican-Cuban relations." The U.S. Secretary of State, however, had increasingly pressured Menocal to cooperate by emphasizing Canada's willingness to participate. The plan, according to Franco, was to have American and Cuban troops seize Progreso while American and Canadian forces dispatched from Texas City occupied Tampico and Vera Cruz. Franco had been very careful to verify these stories and reported that some 2,000 American troops had already been mobilized in Cuba in anticipation of the planned invasion.[17]

Although the plan was never carried out, the idea that the United States might invade Mexico was not farfetched. For years conservative elements in the United States had expressed grave concerns about the state of affairs in Mexico and had advocated greater, more direct intervention there. In February 1917 the British secret service intercepted and deciphered a telegram from the German foreign minister, Arthur von Zimmermann, to the German ambassador in Mexico. In the telegram, Germany requested Mexico's alliance in exchange for Germany's promise to help Mexico recover Arizona, New Mexico, and Texas. When news of the Zimmermann telegram leaked out, U.S. apprehension increased. Mexico's decision to remain neutral during World War I further convinced interventionists that pro-German sympathies ran strong in Mexico. Even if Mexicans were not pro-German, some Americans believed that Mexico could have fallen into German hands because of its instability. From 1914 to 1917, Mexico was repeatedly unable to stop foreign encroachments during its conflicts with the United States; it could never ward off the Central powers if they decided to overrun Mexico. At least this is what American officials, who were keeping a close and critical eye on Mexican events, believed.

The assumption that rumors about conscription were solely the work of German agents and sympathizers was also questionable, as was the information that Mexicans would not be drafted. Mexicans had, in fact, been drafted into the armed forces of the United States. This action had elicited protests to the State Department from the Mexican ambassador and consul general. The protests increased as the Selective Service began inducting thousands of Mexican braceros who lacked certified proof of nationality. To help those without proper documentation, some Mexican consuls issued temporary papers that attested to the bearer's place of birth. They also gave these documents to some Mexican Americans to make them appear exempt from the draft. Selective Service personnel responded by refusing to accept any consular proofs and initiating draft proceedings.[18] The conscriptions ended once the mass exodus began and employers complained they were losing valuable labor needed to support the war effort. Stopping the exodus, however, required more than simple pronouncements.

The situation forced the American government, under the auspices of the Departments of War, Labor, and State, to launch a massive campaign to assuage the fears of Mexican laborers. With the assistance of the military, the Mexican Foreign Office and its consuls, the Roman Catholic bishops of San Antonio, and the press on both sides of the border, the American government disseminated statements that assured Mexicans they would not be drafted. In San Antonio, Bishop John L. Shaw sent circular letters to all priests in his diocese directing them to inform congregations that only American citizens of the proper age would be drafted.[19] Colonel Chapa, through *El Imparcial,* appealed to Mexicans not to abandon everything of value just because of unfounded rumors. He labeled the stories about forced conscription "entirely false" and stated that Mexicans were more important to the United States as laborers.[20] Spanish-language posters carried a warning designed to discourage Mexicans from leaving the United States. According to the posters, those who returned to Mexico and later wanted to reenter the United States would have difficulty doing so because of provisions in the Immigration Act of 1917. "The new literacy law adopted recently forbids entry to this country to all who do not know how to read and write a language. It is better for those who are not educated to stay in the United States."[21] The campaign worked. By late August the number of Mexicans returning to Mexico had dropped noticeably.

Even though the crisis created problems for many Mexicans, some chose to ignore the situation. One resident of Cottonwood Falls, Kansas, viewed the draft as an inconvenience he wished to overlook. In a letter to the local recruiter who had mailed him a registration questionnaire, Santos Martínez said he could not join the army because of his employment obligations to the Santa Fe Railroad. Furthermore, he wondered why they wanted to draft him because he could not read, write, or speak "American." He thanked them for their interest and concluded by writing, "If I should decide to become a soldier, I promise to contact you."[22]

The campaign to dissuade Mexicans from leaving the United States continued well into 1918. Economic problems, however, loomed on the horizon. Within a few years the United States again experienced a debilitating depression, the seeds of which had been sown during the war years.

Mexican Workers in Postwar America

The government's failure to plan for demobilization and reconversion contributed to postwar economic problems. During his final years in office, Woodrow Wilson increasingly turned his attention to foreign affairs. With the outbreak of war, the Wilson administration implemented a series of measures that created an unprecedented partnership between government and business. One measure was to establish regulatory agencies to prevent strikes, allocate raw materials, improve production, regulate the transportation system, and coordinate production schedules. By war's end, approximately 500 agencies administered these programs.

When the armistice was signed in 1918, Wilson's role became that of international conciliator, advocating "peace without victory" and his Fourteen Points. As Wilson focused his energies on battling the Senate over the Treaty of Versailles and securing American support via an arduous, cross-country speaking tour, the economic reconversion of the United States fell by the wayside. Between 1918 and 1920 the situation worsened as Americans were buffeted by inflation, a higher cost of living, increased income taxes, nationwide strikes, shortages of all kinds, and racial tensions created by wartime emotions, propaganda, and the migration of Blacks to northern urban areas. During this period of intense emotion and frustrated expectations, Mexicans began arriving in the Midwest in greater numbers.

Although the railroad and sugar beet industries had introduced Mexicans into the midwestern labor force beginning in 1915, the more stable employment in industry allowed permanent enclaves to develop in some midwestern cities. By 1916 Mexican sugar beet workers were laboring in the meat-packing plants of Kansas; the steel mills of Illinois, Indiana, and Pennsylvania; and the auto plants of Michigan during the off-season. They were joined by other Mexicans from the Southwest and Mexico who came in search of work.

Also by 1916 Kansas City, Missouri, had a Mexican community large enough to warrant its own consul and support, albeit minimal: a major Spanish-language newspaper, *El Cosmopolita*.[23] Because of their central location on the route northward, the railroad centers of St. Louis and Kansas City became major distribution points for Mexicans traveling to the Chicago and Calumet region. Sugar beet companies later turned to these and other cities in the northern Midwest to recruit their labor force.[24]

Many of the early workers hired in the meat-packing, railroad, and steel industries of the Chicago and Calumet region were recruited from the packing houses and rail centers in Kansas and Missouri. They were also drawn from the sugar beet fields in Iowa, Kansas, Michigan, and Nebraska. An employment manager for a steel plant in Chicago recalled a trip to Kansas City to recruit Mexicans in 1922. At the gates of one company, he spoke to Mexicans about the benefits of working for his company. After being told by the superintendent to leave the laborers alone, he secured the services of an employment agent. "Through him [we] got the Mexicans and some others. The whites weren't much good so I took the Mexicans largely. The turnover was very high at first. Without women and Mexican boarding houses the men wouldn't stay. So I brought up a woman to run a boarding house and helped her to get it started."[25] This man's behavior—luring Mexican workers away from other employers—was commonplace. His reflections show that even as late as 1922 the Mexican population in the Chicago area was still predominantly young, unskilled, and highly mobile.

Mexicans chose a variety of avenues in their northeasterly journey.

Some traveled directly from the interior of Mexico to the industrial centers of the Midwest. These included laborers brought directly from Mexico or the Southwest by rail, sugar beet, and steel companies. Once in the Midwest, many seasonal laborers left agriculture during the off-season to look for jobs in industry. There they earned $6.00 per day for auto work, $3.50 to $4.00 per day in manufacturing, $4.00 per day on railroad work, and $3.50 to $4.00 per day on street work.

Many of these industrial jobs were also seasonal. Their peak employment periods tended to coincide with the off-season or down times in sugar beet work. The beet season, which began in April or early May, lasted 180 to 200 days. Of these, only about 60 to 80 days were actually spent in the fields. The number of work days depended on family size, overhiring, weather, contracted acreage, and whether growers had staggered plants. Earnings were paltry. In the late 1920s, for example, male adults averaged about $160 per season. Despite onerous working conditions and low wages, many beet workers were constrained to finish the season because of holdbacks on their pay. They did not receive their first paycheck until three or four months after they arrived. Final paychecks were issued in early winter, long after the season had ended. This system imposed credit obligations on workers that quickly ate away at their meager earnings. The need to supplement their income, support families, and pay off creditors forced betabeleros to seek other work during down times or at the end of the season. The chance of finding other employment, however, decreased during the 1920s as unemployment rose.[26]

Mexicans also gradually job-hopped northward, usually as track maintenance workers. Many left the railroads in search of better pay and year-round employment. Others came on the advice of friends or relatives already in the Midwest. Although their letters complained about the food, weather, and living and working conditions, most midwestern Mexicans painted a glowing picture about job opportunities and good wages. Correspondents often stretched the truth because of their loneliness and desire to be reunited with friends and loved ones. Their letters also carried a common theme: although such an inhospitable environment contained hardships, they would be temporary. Many correspondents wrote that they had come to the Midwest because the wages were

higher than those paid by employers in the Southwest. They believed
that saving enough money to return to Mexico would take less time in
the Midwest. They would use the money to purchase implements, seeds,
livestock, or land and to create a better life.

Mexican laborers also used their wages to buy automobiles. This
practice was so commonplace among sugar beet workers that used car
dealers flocked to the fields. Buying cars and trucks was a calculated
rather than frivolous decision because of the advantages associated with
their purchase. Automobile prices in the Midwest were lower than in
Mexico. The cost of a car was not much more than return train fare.
For those who frequently traveled north, a car was a more economical
means of travel. Workers could transport to their homes merchandise
purchased in the Midwest, could carry paying passengers, and could sell
the cars for a profit in Mexico. Cars also provided greater freedom and
mobility to their owners, an escape from abusive employers, and a
means to look for better jobs. Owning a car also led to higher wages in
the fields. Workers who provided their own transportation to midwestern beet fields from Texas or other distant points received $23 per
acre, $5 more than those whose transportation was paid by the com-
pany. If workers drove in from a nearby locale, they received $24 per
acre.[27] Automobiles and trucks were also seen as status symbols, serving
as tangible proof of the earning power of their owners. This mislead-
ing notion convinced others that opportunity for higher earnings was
indeed greater in the Midwest than elsewhere in the United States.

Not everyone came to the Midwest as a contracted laborer. An
unknown number struck out on their own with a friend or group. For
many the journey to the Midwest was circuitous. Señor Morales, for
example, left Dallas, Texas, in 1917 for Kansas and a year later became a
mine-shaft locomotive operator in the southern Illinois coal fields.[28]
Another young man, José Robles, left Mexico in 1917 with his mother,
two brothers, three sisters, and four half-brothers. After arriving in Dallas and learning English, he worked as an interpreter for a commercial
business. Despite his "success," he was dissatisfied and returned to Sal-
tillo, Mexico. While there he heard about Henry Ford's training school.
He asked his friend, Governor Espinosa Mireles, for support in gaining
admittance to Ford's program, which was designed to train students of

Latin descent in Ford's basic principles of business management for positions in Mexico and Latin America. While the proper documents were being prepared, Robles left for Detroit. Awaiting their arrival, he visited the Ford offices in Detroit and took a job in an auto plant for two months. When they finally arrived, he enrolled in the program. In 1919 the Ford Motor Company forced him to apply for citizenship as a requisite for his continued employment. His light skin color and chestnut hair allowed him to fit into American society more easily. In 1920 he married a German woman from Detroit in a Baptist Church.[29]

A young Mexican woman experienced a more arduous journey. In 1906 Monita Esiguia crossed into El Paso from Chihuahua. At the age of 13, she married. She and her Mexican husband traveled to Emporia, Kansas, and Davenport, Iowa, where they worked in the sugar beet fields and packing houses. In 1917 they went to Chicago, but disliked it and returned to Iowa. They eventually settled in St. Paul.[30]

For some Mexican laborers, crossing the border proved difficult. Louis Medina recalled his attempt to cross in 1916. Refused admittance because of an eye infection, he was forced to return to Mexico. After three more attempts to cross legally, he entered illegally by hiding behind the skirts of a large woman. Medina found work in Laredo and San Antonio, Texas, and later traveled to Oklahoma and Arkansas. In 1924, at the age of 17, he and his father drove to Kansas City, Missouri, in a Chandler touring car his father received as payment for a debt. His father died in 1926, forcing Medina to beg for money so his father would not be buried in a pauper's grave. To repay the cost of the funeral and burial (about $8) he began working for a street car company, which paid him $18 per week. Later he made his way to the Twin Cities area in Minnesota, where he finally settled.[31]

There are many similar stories, and each reflects the courage, determination, and tribulations of men and women who faced numerous obstacles and tragedies in their flight to the United States. By 1914 Mexicans had established small enclaves throughout the Midwest, especially in Kansas, Missouri, Nebraska, Michigan, and Minnesota. From those enclaves larger communities developed—pools of labor from which local industries recruited.

Mexicans first came to Chicago in 1916. Initially they were largely unnoticed because of their small numbers and because employers kept them hidden. Their first experiences were anything but promising. As one immigrant later recalled, "We came here on November 23, 1916, we were 17 solos in box cars. But the box cars had bedbugs and we were cold." He left his lodgings, rented an apartment, and sent for his mother and sister. In 1917 he opened a boardinghouse for Mexicans. Others followed suit and within a short time a Mexican enclave developed on South Halsted Street near Hull House.[32] Many of those who lived in the Hull House district, which was considered the major port-of-entry for Mexicans in Chicago, were former beet workers.[33]

Although Mexicans arrived in Chicago with little or no fanfare, others were not so fortunate. In one community the arrival of Mexicans to work in the steel mills stirred apprehension among local residents. A newspaper account of this event termed it a "veritable invasion of Mexican and Indian laborers. . . . This invasion of Mexican laborers has given rise to many comments, and the laboring element here is asking itself thoughtfully what will be the significance of this immigration to the industrial future of the city."[34] As in other places, these Mexican workers were met by a police detail, whose duty was to protect them. The employers feared local residents might turn their initial hostility into violent action. Residents believed Mexicans were strikebreakers, economic threats, and, because most Mexicans were single males, social threats to women.[35]

The attitudes of these residents were common in many other midwestern communities. Some of the negative feelings predated the arrival of the Mexicans and were vestiges of the long history of conflict that had characterized relations between the United States and Mexico. In fact, Anglo hostility toward Latins was rooted even deeper, in the struggles between Protestant England and Catholic Spain during the sixteenth century. The conflicts gave rise to the English-inspired *Leyenda Negra,* or Black Legend, which denigrated Spaniards.[36] When the Latin American republics threw off Spanish rule during the revolutions of 1810–1821, American representatives such as Henry Clay believed that the Latins would model themselves after the United States. When no such modeling occurred, Americans attributed the failure to "inherent Latin traits." Many of the negative attributes once associated with Spain were now transferred to and imposed on the Latin American people.

Events such as Santa Anna's rise to power, the Texas revolution of 1836, the Mexican War of 1846–1848, and the continued violence between Anglos and Mexicans in the Southwest during most of the nineteenth century reinforced the belief that Mexicans were lazy, backward, and cruel.[37] Many of these negative stereotypes were resurrected by the popular media and jingoistic politicians during the Spanish-American War in 1898 and the Mexican revolution in 1910.[38] Reports from Mexico described the violence, brutality, and chaos of the revolution. These reports reinforced American apprehension and hostility toward Mexicans, who became the personification of anarchy, revolution, religious fanaticism, and uncivilized cruelty. Old stereotypes mixed with new fears, creating suspicion and resentment.

Mexicans in the 1919 Steel Strike

Although Mexicans had entered the Chicago and Calumet regions in the early 1900s, it was not until 1919 that they arrived in large enough numbers to establish noticeable enclaves. The stimulus to this increase was the steel strike that began on 22 September 1919. During World War I the government strengthened labor's position. The American Federation of Labor (AFL), which had abandoned efforts to organize steel workers in the aftermath of the bloody Homestead strike of 1892, decided it was time to organize the steel mills again.

The grievances of the steel workers were legitimate. They complained about the long, twelve-hour work days, seven-day weeks, paltry wages, and primitive, drab shacks that served as their housing. Autocratic leaders such as Judge Elbert Gary, a fierce defender of the open shop and head of the U.S. Steel Corporation, refused to yield to pressures and demands. In a show of strength and unity, 365,000 steel workers nationwide went on strike. Initial sympathy for the strike vanished as detractors successfully painted it as another radical movement. Black and Mexican strikebreakers imported from the deep South, the Southwest, and Mexico also hindered the strike. Within two months the strike was broken, and workers returned without a single gain. In addition to the twenty deaths and more than $100 million in lost wages, there was another casualty. For years after the strike, Mexicans were barred from the union because many in the rank and file considered them to be strikebreakers and scabs.[39]

Most of the Mexicans brought to South Chicago, East Chicago, Gary, Hammond, Indiana Harbor, and Calumet to work in the steel mills in 1919 did not see much of their new home. Brought in on trains, usually under the cover of night, they quickly disembarked and were taken to quarters set up for them inside the plant walls. About 500 Mexicans from El Paso, San Antonio, Kansas City, St. Louis, Omaha, and Chicago and 1,000 southern Blacks were recruited in 1919 as strike-breakers.[40] Upon arrival they were quickly dispatched to their barracks and bunk beds; it was not what they expected. Anticipation and anxiety gripped many of these young men as they lay in their beds listening to the strange sounds of the mills. Those who traveled to Indiana Harbor represented the beginnings of La Colonia del Harbor, which in a few years became one of the largest Mexican communities in the Midwest. These steel workers were the nucleus around which other Mexicans followed and eventually established sizable Mexican enclaves in the Midwest.

During the steel strike, between forty and fifty workers, including Mexicans, arrived every few days.[41] Although many refused to cross the picket lines once they realized they were being used as scabs,[42] this show of solidarity was not enough to dispel the mistaken belief among strikers that all Mexicans were scabs.

The work situation deteriorated for Mexicans; soon they were competing with thousands of American servicemen who were discharged from the military. In Chicago Consul José Sepulveda reported that groups of unemployed servicemen had caused a great deal of trouble over the shortage of jobs. Employers, anxious to defuse the situation, fired foreign workers and replaced them with American veterans. "This measure," wrote Sepulveda, "caused many problems and hardships for many of our compatriots, most of whom . . . were forced to leave their work without much hope of finding another job." According to him, Mexicans helped each other through the hardships because his office had no resources.[43]

Nonetheless, the precedent for hiring Mexicans in the steel industry had been established. By 1920 Mexicans constituted more than 18 percent of the workers at Inland Steel, and in 1926 2,526 Mexicans (24.6 percent of the work force) were Inland Steel employees. By the end of the decade Inland Steel was the largest single employer of Mexicans in the United States.[44] Mexicans became a major source of labor for the steel, auto-manufacturing, meat-packing, railroad, and sugar beet industries.[45] Chicago, East Chicago, Indiana Harbor, Gary, and other cities enticed more nationals by their higher wages and more stable communities.

Contrary to the beliefs of many Americans at that time, many Mexicans who came to the region had already spent time in the United States. Many Anglos mistakenly believed that Mexican workers in the Midwest could not adjust to industrial life because of their strong rural antecedents. Mexicans were perceived as nothing more than displaced, nineteenth-century rustics who had suddenly been transported into the twentieth century. Although this description may have been true for some Mexicans, it was not true for all.

Recent studies of Mexican steel and auto workers in East Chicago and Detroit have begun to dispel that myth. Many who came to Chicago and the Calumet region to work in the steel mills in 1919 were recruited not from Mexico, but from American cities where they had worked on railroads, in meat-packing plants, and in mines. In his study of Mexican steel workers, Francisco Rosales found that Inland Steel employed 3,600 Mexicans between 1918 and 1930: 33 percent had entered the United States during World War I but practically all were hired by the company after 1923.[46] In his study of Detroit auto workers, Zaragosa Vargas found that 68 percent of the 1,208 Mexicans employed by Ford between 1919 and 1933 had previously worked in the auto industry or in auto parts plants. Another 25.1 percent had worked in foundries and steel mills. Thus, 93.1 percent of the Mexicans employed by Ford had prior work experience in industry.[47] Paul Taylor reported that many of the Mexicans employed in the steel plants in 1928 had previous work experience in the United States; most had worked for the railroads. In Illinois 201 of 554 Mexicans employed in a steel plant had previous work experience in the steel industry.[48] Although more studies are needed for other cities and industries in the Midwest, these preliminary findings indicate that the Mexican work force was more industrially experienced than employers and detractors believed. The rationale used by unscrupulous employers and foremen that Mexicans lacked industrial skills and thus deserved lower pay and the dirtiest and most dangerous jobs may well have been without foundation.

Employers who hired Mexicans to work in skilled and semiskilled jobs were usually pleased with the quality and caliber of work performed. A steel works superintendent stated, "The Mexicans are . . . quick and alert. . . . [T]hey are steadier . . . and are not so servile. . . . [T]hey don't cringe and curry." Another stated that "Mexicans are the best class of labor we get now. . . . If the American people will just treat them right, we'll have a fine class of people and a fine class of labor. . . . They are honest and trustworthy."[49] This praise, however, is tempered by the knowledge that corporations preferred to hire Mexicans instead of Blacks. Employers considered Mexicans a suitable substitute for Europeans. They also believed that Mexicans had several qualities that made them desirable workers: they were responsive, seldom complained, worked for low wages, lacked unity, exhibited little interest in politics, and had a habit of disappearing when the work ran out rather than staying and causing trouble.[50]

Although the United States faced economic problems at the end of the war, the momentum created by wartime demand spurred production well into 1920. As a result of this expansion and the concomitant need for inexpensive labor, the Mexican population continued to grow. By 1920 several midwestern communities had sizable Mexican enclaves: Kansas City, Kansas, included almost 4,000 Mexicans; Indiana's Calumet region, 1,920; Chicago, about 1,200; and Detroit, about 800. These numbers were dramatically reduced during the depression of 1921.

The Depression of 1921–1922

The depression of 1921–1922 was catastrophic. In October 1921 unemployment in the United States among men and women reached the six-million mark.[51] More than 100,000 businesses declared bankruptcy, and more than 450,000 farmers lost their land.[52] For Mexicans the effects were devastating. An estimated 100,000 of the 478,383 legal immigrants registered in the 1920 census lost their jobs as employers undertook massive layoffs and firings.[53] Unemployment, increased discrimination, and forced and voluntary repatriation caused between 200,000 and 400,000 Mexicans to leave the United States.[54]

A major employer of Mexicans in Kansas, the Santa Fe Railroad, reduced its overall work force by one-half. In Kansas City, Kansas, between 1,500 and 1,700 Mexican meat-packing employees were released from their jobs. Newspaper and consular dispatches described the hardship and suffering of those forced to sleep outdoors and live off donations of meat provided by the Swift and Armour companies.[55] Those fortunate enough to keep their jobs did so with wage reductions of from 8 to 22.5 percent.

The Mexican consul in Kansas City, Kansas, reported to his superiors that many Mexicans were in difficult circumstances. He estimated his district had approximately seventy Mexican families who were destitute and about 300 unemployed Mexicans. Their needs were being served by members of the Mexican community who had sponsored festivals to raise money for relief. He added that religious organizations, including the Catholic Church, had set up kitchens to feed the poor and unemployed. The employment situation promised little relief. After a 50-percent cutback in employees, the meat-packing houses in Kansas City announced that they would again reduce their work force by another 12.5 to 15 percent. This reduction would be nationwide and would affect more than 200,000 employees. The wages of hourly workers would be reduced by $.08, or about 15 percent. The consul also received news that pay for about 8,000 employees of the Missouri, Kansas, and Texas Railroad would be cut. He noted that 97 percent of these workers were of Mexican descent.[56] The consul found himself with few, if any, resources to help the nationals in his district.

In desperation Mexicans left Kansas City to seek work in Chicago and the Calumet region, believing that conditions there would be better. They were not. The Mexican consul, Francisco Paredes, wrote to Mayor William Thompson requesting assistance for his countrymen, whom he described as being in a "most desperate poverty stricken condition." The steel mills and cement factories laid off about one-third of their Mexican workers. Across the country wages for steel mill workers were reduced by 20 percent.[57]

Detroit was hit the hardest. By the end of 1920, 80 percent of Detroit's auto workers were jobless. "The one-industry nature of Detroit's economy made its unemployment the worst of all American cities. More than four-fifths of the industrial labor force was out of work by January, 1921, and an estimated 75,000 individuals left the Motor City." Among the unemployed were almost all of the Mexican auto workers at Ford. Before being fired, however, "they suffered the most relentless speed-up in the history of Ford Motors."[58] As a result of the depression and ensuing unemployment, the number of Mexicans in Detroit dropped from 4,000 to 2,500 between November 1920 and February 1921.

The depression also left many of Michigan's beet workers stranded. The companies that recruited them completely abdicated their responsibility for them and turned a deaf ear to their plaintive cries for help. They foisted desperate workers and their families onto the hapless cities and towns; like others, beet workers streamed into Michigan's cities in search of jobs, relief, and repatriation. The hard-pressed communities and overtaxed agencies denied these unfortunates services and relief.

The administration of President Alvaro Obregón was inundated with letters and telegrams from consuls, local Mexican organizations, and individuals asking for help. Most of them simply desired enough funds to return to their homeland.[59] In March 1921, a local leader in Chicago wrote the Mexican government asking that something be done to assist Mexican nationals. Jesus Rodríguez stated that the depression had clearly demonstrated the precarious position of Mexicans in the United States. He criticized the consuls for failing to help. He suggested that a department be established as soon as possible with the sole responsibility of repatriating all Mexicans. He also urged that lands be distributed to those returning so they could begin cultivating them upon arrival.[60] The government's response to his letter was an assurance that the secretary was "intensely preoccupied with the situation of his compatriots living in the United States."[61]

Ramon Denegri, the Mexican consul general in New York, reported that large numbers of Mexicans came to his office daily asking to be repatriated. His office also received letters from different cities in the Midwest detailing the anguish and suffering caused by the depression. He asked the Mexican government to warn its people about the critical situation and urge them to remain home. It was not uncommon, he wrote, for Mexicans to fall ill because of lack of food, inadequate shelter, and harsh winters. "[M]any Mexicans seek treatment at the hospitals suffering from pneumonia. . . . [They] have no food or coats to protect them from the elements thus they fall victim to the inclement weather."[62] The only solution to the problem, he said, was to keep Mexicans from emigrating. "For years I have fought to end the exodus of Mexicans, describing in detail all of the problems which await them here where life is so hard. . . . Thus far, however, I have been unable to convince our Government to implement measures to end this emigration." He again urged his government to take all possible steps to prohibit the emigration of Mexican workers, including a broad-based campaign to inform them that only hardship and discrimination awaited them in this "inhospitable" country.[63] Obregón responded that he would comply with the consul's wishes and ask Mexico's press to cooperate in this important matter of national concern.[64]

As the depression deepened, more requests for help deluged consular and government officials in Mexico. The Mexican government, still suffering from the economic problems created by the revolution and its aftermath, was hard-pressed to provide funds to so many needy people. One Mexican official estimated that it would cost the government 1.5 million pesos to repatriate 1,500 Mexicans. This was about 100 pesos per person. In 1921, 2 pesos were equivalent to $1 in U.S. currency. The government was flooded with so many requests that in many cases, it simply said no assistance was available. At times the most the government could do was to provide transportation from the border into Mexico. Those who wished to repatriate were left to fend for themselves or forced to seek help elsewhere.

In many cities local self-help organizations known as *sociedades mutualistas,* or mutual aid societies, raised funds to pay for repatriation. In East Chicago the first organization of Mexican workers, La Sociedad Pro-Patria, was formed in 1921 to deal with unemployment and assist Mexicans who wanted to leave.[65] In Detroit the Mexican consul and his civilian board of helpers succeeded in repatriating 5,500 Mexican nationals within two months.[66] In his report about the departure of 497 Mexicans from Detroit, the local consul attached articles of related interest from a local paper. Across one of the articles he typed, "What irony! This picture shows part of the riches in Detroit." It showed $80 million being transferred to a new bank. He noted this was taking place at the very time that Detroit was repatriating 497 Mexicans, "because there is no money for them—Nor work either."[67]

Mexicans were also a source of concern to local municipalities and social welfare groups. Although elected representatives and spokespersons for private charity groups in the United States pressed the federal government to fund the repatriation of Mexicans, the Department of Labor ignored their requests. The government did not wish to set a precedent for helping indigent foreigners who found themselves stranded. Instead, the government ended its waiver of immigration restrictions for Mexicans, throwing even more Mexicans out of work.[68]

The lack of federal aid forced municipal governments, chambers of commerce, and local charities to assume the cost of repatriating indigent Mexicans. In some cities, such as Kansas City and Topeka, Kansas, the cost was shared by local organizations and the Mexican consul. Through these efforts about 1,500 Mexicans left Topeka in May 1921, and 800 more left Kansas City in June. The repatriations in Kansas continued until October 1921. In Detroit similar repatriation measures were initiated. Reports described Mexicans living in shacks and boxcars in "a state of semi-pauperism" and being kept alive by donations of food and clothing from the charitable people of Detroit. Because of the gravity of the situation, the St. Vincent de Paul Society and Mexican Catholic Society collected funds to return these unfortunates to their own country.[69] Henry Ford also helped in the repatriation drive by providing free transportation back to Mexico for 3,000 unemployed workers.[70]

Effects of the 1921–1922 Depression on Mexicans

The repatriation movement ended as quickly as it had begun. By 1922 the American economy was on an upswing. The effects and lessons of the depression, however, lingered and were not easily forgotten. The depression delayed the development of stable Mexican communities in the Midwest, as thousands of Mexicans left the region. In Michigan, for example, the Mexican population dropped from 18,000 to about 2,500.[71] In Chicago 65 percent of the Mexicans lost their jobs as a result of the depression.[72] Most of the 1,200 Mexicans who lived in Chicago in 1920 returned to Mexico, the Southwest, or the beet fields. In East Chicago fewer than 200 Mexicans remained in 1922.[73] Approximately 200,000 Mexicans left the United States as a result of the depression and repatriation efforts. Although their numbers began to increase again in 1922, the disruptive effects of the depression took several years to overcome. In the Midwest, smaller enclaves disappeared completely, never to be revived.

Another effect of the depression was the hardening of attitudes toward Mexicans. The economic problems endured by Mexicans and the attendant publicity occurred while the United States was in the midst of an immigration debate. Critics of the Immigration Act of 1921 argued that quotas should have been applied to the western hemisphere as well. They pointed to the burdens Mexicans placed on the resources of local governments and charities. They argued that Mexicans were likely to become public charges and should thus be excluded. Even though proponents of this view failed in their attempts to formally restrict immigration from Mexico and Latin America, they continued to use economic as well as racial arguments for excluding Mexicans.

Other groups, including organized labor, demanded that employers fire Mexicans and replace them with "American" workers. Some union members introduced resolutions to require all members to be U.S. citizens. These resolutions were aimed at Mexicans, who were described as a danger to unions because they acted as strikebreakers, hindered organizing efforts, and lowered wage scales.

For the Mexican government, the events of 1921–1922 were sobering and instructive. Initially officials in Mexico City had welcomed the idea of having thousands of nationals return to their homes. Helping to repatriate Mexican nationals would accomplish the dual purpose of regaining much-needed workers and demonstrating the government's compassion for its people. Officials soon realized, however, that Mexico lacked the human and material resources and experience to carry out such an extensive plan. The arrival of thousands of destitute Mexicans along the border created enormous problems for officials in border cities. Their resources were soon exhausted, and they could do little to assist the needy. The government's colonization plans and promises of employment also failed to materialize. Upon their return many Mexicans found themselves in even more dire straits. Realizing that even fewer opportunities existed in Mexico, many returned to the United States.

After 1922 Mexican officials created government agencies to aid and protect Mexican nationals in the United States. They hoped to be better prepared to handle future massive repatriations. They also undertook an extensive information campaign to dissuade Mexicans from leaving their homeland. Toward that end, they emphasized the painful lessons of 1921 to potential emigrants, but Mexican officials ultimately failed to stop Mexicans from emigrating. The fiasco of 1921–1922 had disillusioned Mexicans about their government. It had promised them help, land, and jobs but had failed to deliver on those promises. Mexicans were therefore less inclined to believe their government's warnings about life in the United States. Lacking credibility, Mexican officials could do little to curtail the outward flow.

Sugar beet companies also learned important lessons from their experiences with Mexican workers between 1918 and 1921. The efficacy of their revised and restrictive contracts was proven: this system generated great profits while reducing risks and capital outlay in employment. The companies found that Mexicans were the best workers they had hired to date and were a readily available supply of labor. The growing number of Mexicans in towns and cities, the seasonal nature of industrial work, and the precariousness of finding steady employment in industry provided beet companies with a sizable and self-perpetuating labor pool. This pool, however, was self-perpetuating only if industrial jobs were available in the off-season. Beet companies also learned that Mexican workers were easy to exploit because they were isolated and poorly organized.

Most Mexican beet workers had entered the country illegally and were not U.S. citizens, reducing the likelihood that they would file complaints with the authorities. Their isolation ensured a lack of advocates for their cause. These circumstances allowed companies to exploit Mexican workers and expel them when their labor was no longer needed. The latter was accomplished with the help of local governments, charitable organizations, or the Mexican government. These advantages motivated sugar beet companies to recruit Mexicans in earnest from Texas and the Midwest once the depression had subsided. After 1922 the northern sugar beet industry became wholly dependent on Mexican laborers. In turn, Mexicans again used work in the beet fields as intermediate employment, a "staging area" for entering the steel, automobile, meat-packing, and other industries in the Midwest. Despite the setbacks caused by the 1921 depression, this steady flow of men, women, and children augmented the movement of Mexicans into urban areas and contributed to their geographic dispersion in the region.[74]

Mexicans themselves learned valuable lessons. They realized their government lacked the necessary resources to be of much help. This knowledge served as one impetus for creating their own organizations to handle problems faced by Mexican immigrants. Mexicans also learned they were welcome in the United States only as long as their labor was needed. The depression had amply demonstrated that employers had no qualms about firing them. Such experiences soured Mexicans on the United States. Nationalistic attitudes surged and an overwhelming majority, for a variety of reasons, opted not to become citizens of a country that judged them solely on the unfamiliarity of their language, the color of their skin, and the fluctuating value of their labor.[75]

CHAPTER 3

Housing and Labor

Almost as fast as they had disappeared in 1921, Mexicans reappeared in late 1922. Thousands had been returned to Mexico by employers who no longer wanted them. A few months later they were again being lured northward by recruiters and employers. Mexicans were understandably confused and considered the gringos an odd people. Although their employment status improved, their socioeconomic status did not. Their problems were those of the poor and the powerless: high disease and infant mortality rates, substandard housing, malnutrition, segregation, discrimination, prejudice, and blatant exploitation were commonplace. Because they were relative newcomers and many were illegal aliens, their troubles were compounded. Hazardous working conditions, urban violence, and changes in environment also took their toll.

In Indiana Harbor alone, about 400 Mexicans died between 1923 and 1929 as a result of illness, work-related accidents, and acts of violence. Because their living quarters were interspersed among a maze of railroad tracks, streets, and streetcar lines, many died after being struck by passing trains. Numerous deaths were also attributed to the dangerous environment in the steel mills, where safety precautions were virtually nonexistent. The average unskilled laborer was forced to work 63.1 hours per week, including a continuous 24-hour shift with only one day off every two weeks. These intensive labor practices and ensuing fatigue were responsible for the highest accident rates in the industrial world.[1] Despite their government's warnings, Mexicans continued to emigrate. After the 1921 depression had bottomed out, the number of Mexicans coming to the Midwest maintained an upward curve until the onset of the Great Depression in 1929.

Problems in Mexico

Mexican officials believed that nationals would gladly return to Mexico once the violence of the revolution had subsided, but they were wrong. The government lost a great deal of credibility during the economic crisis of 1921 when it failed to provide adequate assistance to the needy and destitute. Promises of employment, land, and financial and social security were unfulfilled because Mexico was still suffering from the ravages of the revolution. Even though great progress had been made in rebuilding the economy, the damage caused by years of war and corruption overshadowed any gains. Mexican leaders soon realized that the root causes of emigration were not so much the revolution as the structural defects in the Mexican economy.[2]

As the violence waned, President Alvaro Obregón and his successor, Plutarco Calles, began to redistribute land. Superficially the land distribution program looked promising: Obregón and Calles redistributed almost 4.5 million acres to 588,692 people between 1920 and 1929.[3] This policy, however, had serious drawbacks. Hacienda owners, who were loath to relinquish their lands, formed small private armies to repulse those who attempted to lay claim to *ejidal* (public land) grants. Violence and bloodshed ensued, followed by government intervention.

As long as the instability continued, farmers could not grow enough food to feed the hungry populace. Food shortages, hunger, and starvation continued to plague Mexico despite the government's efforts to import more food. "The total volume of agricultural production in the 1920s never exceeded in any given year the amount of food grown in 1910, but from 1910 to 1930 Mexico's total population, despite emigration and losses from revolutionary violence, grew from 15,160,000 to 16,553,000. As had been the horrendous case in late Porfirian times, the third decade of the twentieth century saw no respite from widespread starvation in the countryside."[4] The quality of much of the ejidal land was poor. Without sufficient resources to improve these lands, their contribution to remedying the food shortage was negligible.

These economic woes were aggravated by inflation, lack of employment opportunities, low wages, and a high cost of living. In postrevolutionary Mexico prices rose 300 percent faster than wages. Wages in rural areas were as low as 12 centavos per day for men and 6 centavos for women, $.06 and $.03, respectively, in American currency.[5] On the Central and Northern Plateaus, the origin of most immigrants to the Midwest, a family of five needed 288 pesos or $144 per month in 1926 just to live at subsistence level. The average male worker in these areas earned about 1.15 pesos per day, or 35.65 pesos per month. In American currency this was equivalent to about $17.50 per month, or one-eighth of what they needed just to survive.[6] Compared to earnings in the United States, this amount was paltry. Although Mexicans were paid less than their Anglo and European counterparts, their average wage in the United States was $3.38 per day, or $105.00 per month—six times more than what they could earn in Mexico.[7]

Wages paid to Mexican industrial workers were not much better than those paid to agricultural workers. In 1927 industrial wages averaged 1.29 to 1.76 pesos per day. Mexican economists estimated that the average industrial worker had to earn at least 5 pesos per day to provide a family with the minimum necessities. In addition to depressed wages, Mexicans suffered from high unemployment throughout the 1920s. Manufacturing, which had been severely disrupted by the revolution, did not begin to show signs of recovery until the eve of the worldwide depression in 1929.[8]

Economic motivations were not the sole reason for the rise in Mexican emigration during the 1920s; lack of personal safety also played a role. The tensions engendered by the revolution did not subside when the heavy fighting ended. Weapons were easy to acquire and visible everywhere. The lack of law enforcement and civilian authority led many people to resolve conflicts through violence. Towns, villages, ranches, and *ejidos* (public lands) were attacked by roaming bands in search of food, shelter, and other comforts. Local military chieftains continued to exercise control over the populace. The desire for personal safety and security did as much to drive people from their homes as the economic conditions. One emigrant explained, "I did not want to get shot down from one day to the next."[9]

This civil unrest was exacerbated by the Cristero revolt, which swept across Mexico between 1926 and 1929. Tensions had been building in the early 1920s between the Catholic Church and the secular government over the anticlerical articles in the constitution of 1917. When Roman Catholic leaders in Mexico openly challenged these provisions in 1926, President Calles retaliated with a vengeance. He banned all religious processions; closed church schools, monasteries, and convents; forced priests to register with civil authorities; and deported foreign priests and nuns. On 31 July 1926 the archbishop of Mexico, José Mora y del Río, declared a strike. For three years no infants were baptized, no last rites were administered, and no masses were held. Violence erupted. In the ensuing three years of bloodshed, each side committed sordid excesses.[10] Before it ended, President-elect Obregón was dead at the hands of a pro-Cristero assassin's bullet, Mexico's economy suffered further disruption, anarchy prevailed in some parts of the country, and thousands of people either lost their lives or were forced to flee Mexico for their own safety.

Some Mexicans left their country for more peaceful reasons: to meet new people, learn about another culture, see the United States, or search for adventure. One emigrant to the Midwest stated, "When my parents died in 1912, I went from my town in Michoacán to Mexico City to get work to support my two younger brothers. In 1917 I heard about the United States, so I came. I went to work on the Pennsylvania Railroad, then returned to Mexico. But I returned to the United States and went to California. I returned again to Mexico, and came back to the United States. This time, in order to get to another place, I came to Gary."[11]

Problems in the United States

Mexican emigrants quickly learned that leaving Mexico did not end their problems; on the contrary, their problems often multiplied once they had crossed the border. Although economic gains alleviated some worries, other worries replaced them. Mexican stereotypes abounded among the American populace. The revolution, Cristero revolt, and vicissitudes of U.S.-Mexican relations exacerbated anti-Mexican attitudes. The high tide of Mexican immigration occurred during the 1920s—a period in American history characterized by nativism, racism, isolationism, fundamentalism, and demands for conformity and "100 percent Americanism."[12] This decade witnessed the resurgence of the Ku Klux Klan, which expanded its doctrines of race hatred and White supremacy to include hatred of aliens, Catholics, and immigrants.[13] The growing intolerance and the anxieties that spawned it were mirrored in the race riots of 1919–1920 and in the divisive trial and execution of Sacco and Vanzetti in 1927.

The "Tribal Twenties" also witnessed the enactment of two very restrictive and discriminatory immigration laws designed to drastically curtail immigration from southern and eastern Europe. Although no quotas were imposed on Mexicans, the issue of whether to restrict Mexican immigration engendered a highly emotional debate that engaged the public for years. Both proponents and opponents used a wide array of derogatory Mexican stereotypes to bolster their respective arguments. The upshot was massive doses of anti-Mexican images from the press, political representatives, nativist groups, labor unions, employers, academicians, and clergymen.[14] Many communities became hostile to the Mexican newcomers they "suddenly" found in their midst.

This widespread nativism and xenophobia did not augur well for Mexicans. Their immigrant status, skin color, language, and Catholicism all militated against them. They were relative latecomers to the Midwest, and most refused to become citizens. Job and wage competition further fueled the hostility toward them. Mexicans were kept on the outer fringes of American society, their presence tolerated only as long as their labor was needed.

Life in the Midwest

From the outset, loneliness, despair, and deprivation posed problems for Mexicans in the Midwest. Although they were no strangers to inclement weather, the midwestern winters exacted a terrible toll. Temperatures often plummeted below zero. Immigrant dwellings were inadequate to withstand the harsh weather. Some efforts to weatherproof buildings led to tragedy: in Minnesota several members of a Mexican family were asphyxiated by carbon monoxide gas after one of them had plugged every crack in their shanty to keep out the winter cold.[15] Fuel shortages were common, forcing the immigrants to collect discarded wood along the railroad yards or steal coal from nearby factories. The heavy cloud cover that characterizes midwestern winters, along with the lack of recreational outlets, absence of women, separation from friends and family, and ever-shifting work schedules, underscored the dreariness, depression, and isolation of urban life.

Even as late as 1920 most Mexican immigrants to the Midwest were young and unattached. In Chicago 65 percent of the Mexican population consisted of single males.[16] In East Chicago, the ratio of Mexican men to Mexican women was 3 to 1, and the women were already married.[17] This was a problem common throughout the Midwest: single women were a minute percentage of the Mexican women who came to the region.

Even making friends was difficult because of shifting work schedules. Because most Mexican laborers were unable to afford apartments or houses or were denied housing owing to their ethnicity, boardinghouses, or *casas de asistencia,* sprang up in the early years of migration and settlement.[18] Roommates in these boardinghouses often did not know each other because they worked different shifts. In fact, these houses were sometimes so crowded, men used them only to sleep in while their compatriots were at work. When a crew finished a work shift, those who had slept left the premises and spent their time elsewhere until their own work shift began.[19] Pool halls became favorite places for congregating.

Even the work place isolated Mexicans from themselves and others. Workers were seldom permitted to talk on the job. This regulation was especially true at Ford auto plants, where there were strict rules against talking, whistling, or singing on the job. Employers and foremen feared that too much commiserating created a sense of unity among the workers and detracted from productivity. Some employers also tried to keep workers from discovering wage differentials. Foremen and employers, however, sometimes publicized pay rates and job arrangements to engender jealousy and resentment among workers. They also segregated workers by nationality, further diluting the chances of cooperation and unified action by the work force.

Intranational conflicts were also apparent. Many of the early casas de asistencia took on names such as "Casa Jalisco" or "Casa Michoacán" to designate that their clientele was largely from that state or region. Even in the distant Midwest, long-standing feuds or rivalries often continued much as they had in Mexico. Towns and cities with large numbers of unattached men resembled rough-and-tough frontier towns. This "wide-open" feeling was abetted by the establishment of brothels, gambling houses, poolrooms, and speakeasies that sold cheap and illegal alcohol. Pent-up frustrations and emotions often exploded in these places, and violence was common. Much of the disorder involved intragroup conflict in the form of fistfights, shootings, and knifings.

In some communities occupational divisions added to the turmoil. At Inland Steel, for example, jobs were a coveted possession because of the comparatively good pay and steady employment enjoyed by most of its employees. In Indiana Harbor steel workers considered themselves superior to other industrial workers. In turn, industrial workers considered themselves better than railroad employees. Both railroad and industrial laborers looked down on sugar beet workers. Members of each group had few qualms about letting others know how they felt. This attitude led to numerous squabbles and fights in poolrooms, cantinas, and other gathering places, which gave Mexicans an exaggerated reputation for lawlessness and violence.

The rapid growth and development of urban areas in the Midwest created problems for city governments, including pollution, noise, congestion, crime, and lack of housing. As each group of immigrants improved its economic status, it abandoned its substandard housing, which was, in turn, occupied by the next group of newcomers. The experiences of Mexicans differed little from those of their immigrant predecessors.

As early as 1906 *El Tiempo*, a Mexican newspaper published in the United States, wrote that Mexican workers lived "in the most degrading misery and were treated most shamefully." Mexicans often lived in dilapidated and overcrowded structures because of the numerous legal and extralegal obstacles that barred them from decent housing. One report from Chicago described the buildings occupied by Mexicans as "deplorable." "Stairways were worn to the point of being dangerous, and the inadequate plumbing was a serious health hazard for the tenants."[20]

Some railroads, sugar beet companies, and industries provided housing for their employees. In the Midwest, however, this was more the exception than the rule; most corporations felt no such obligation. Mexicans recruited to work in the Chicago steel mills during the 1919 strike lived in company barracks, but this housing was temporary. Once the strike ended, Mexicans were asked to vacate the units and find their own lodgings.

Almost from the outset Mexican efforts to acquire adequate housing facilities met with resistance. Real estate brokers, landlords, and neighborhoods opposed attempts to rent or sell property to Mexicans. Much of the discrimination in housing was based on unfounded and unreasonable fear concerning the character of Mexicans. This practice of excluding Mexicans or renting or selling only to "better class" Mexicans had a profound impact on the development of Mexican neighborhoods and communities.

Midwestern patterns of settlement were affected by transportation needs, location of work places, real estate practices, and existing neighborhoods. These influences isolated Mexicans and created localized enclaves, where Mexicans mingled with other immigrants.

Attitudes Toward Mexicans

Efforts to isolate and expel Mexicans from certain residential areas grew from the negative characteristics that local residents attributed to Mexicans. Some refused to have Mexicans in their area because of their alleged propensity for violence and noise. Others refused to sell or rent to them because they were considered poor housekeepers and dirty. One Chicago resident had this to say about Mexicans: "The Mexicans are very dirty. They spoil the new houses they occupy. You see that house across the way? Well, it was a pretty good house 'til the Mexicans moved in. . . . They lived like rats all cooped up. You could smell the place when you passed in front of it."[21] A Flint, Michigan, resident described her Mexican neighbors as "terribly dirty and crowded." In her opinion, "they're all bad people."[22]

Attitudes such as this forced some Mexicans to lie about their ethnic background in order to rent living quarters.[23] One early Mexican resident in Detroit recalled her first experience in renting a house:

When we moved into our house we told the neighbors we were Mexican. But some other families across the street had to claim they were Spanish to get their homes because they didn't want Mexicans. Our house was rented to us through a neighbor. When the owner of the house dropped by to collect the rent, he asked what nationality we were. And when we told him we were Mexican he said he didn't want Mexicans in his house because they were too dirty. My husband convinced him to let us prove that we were not dirty by letting us stay for at least two months.[24]

Opposition to Mexicans also stemmed from the belief that they were racially undesirable and their presence depreciated property values. A resident of the Brighton Park area in Chicago complained, "If they come in, others don't want to live there. They spoil the neighborhood."[25] One Flint resident did not like living near Mexicans. She accused the males of always staring at her. "I dislike the Mexican men very much, they're bad."[26] Color also influenced attitudes about Mexicans. "Some of them are dark, just like the niggers; I wouldn't like to live among them. I want to live among white people." Another interviewee, who happened to be of Mexican descent but considered himself a member of the "better" social class, held a similar attitude: "Mexicans . . . are a low kind of people. The color is the main thing; they don't want to rent to dark Mexicans."[27]

Mexicans were perceived as unfair competitors for jobs because they worked for lower wages and displaced other nationalities. Because of the preponderance of unattached men, Mexicans were also viewed as threats to women and potential rivals in affairs of the heart.

Throughout the Midwest residents made it clear to Mexicans that they were unwelcome as neighbors. The methods of dissuading them from settling in certain neighborhoods varied but were highly effective. Some residents used violence or threats or damaged Mexican property. Others simply refused to rent or sell to Mexicans or demanded exorbitant rents. Some communities considered imposing legal restrictions against renting or selling to Mexicans because they blamed Mexicans for "White flight" and depreciating property values.

In 1926 a study entitled "Planning for the Future of East Chicago" asked workers why so many of them lived outside East Chicago even though most were employed there. Twenty-four percent of the respondents indicated they did not want to live near Mexicans or Blacks. In the report, the investigator suggested that Mexicans should be restricted to one area of the city to assuage the fears of potential residents.[28] It is obvious from reading the report that the "future" in East Chicago was not intended to include Mexicans, Blacks, and other "undesirables." Although de facto segregation did occur, nothing came of legal efforts to segregate Mexicans because these measures were unnecessary. The enactment of such restrictions would have been redundant. The methods discussed above proved highly effective in segregating, isolating, and condemning Mexicans to living in substandard housing in undesirable locations.

Mexican Housing

Pressed for time and money and confronted with hostility from landlords and residents, Mexicans settled wherever they could. In Kansas City they lived in railroad section houses or run-down neighborhoods.[29] Some found shelter in the numerous boardinghouses that catered to them. Others clustered around the industries that employed them, not only because they needed to be near work, but also because housing around the plants was cheap and accessible. The description of a Mexican settlement on the Near West Side of Chicago could have applied to other Mexican settlements throughout the industrial Midwest. "The colony centers around Halsted between Harrison and 15th . . . a community which has some of the poorest housing in the city. Here where rents are cheap, where employment agencies are near at hand, and where numerous industrial plants are within easy reach, is a natural place for the immigrant to begin his life."[30]

Yet there was nothing "natural" about the conditions under which the immigrants lived or the exploitation they suffered. Landlords in one South Chicago neighborhood routinely charged higher rents to Blacks and Mexicans than to other nationalities "because fewer units were open to these two groups."[31] An apartment was rented to an Irish family for $21, whereas an identical apartment in the same building was rented to a

Mexican family for $27.[32] A Mexican living in East Chicago in the late 1920s complained that Mexicans were at the mercy of the landlords. "They charge us more rent than other people; we have to live somewhere and we pay. They only rent the poorest houses to the Mexicans."[33]

Between 1914 and 1925 rental rates doubled. On the average Mexicans paid $30 per month in rent. Unable to purchase their own homes because of the high cost, the lack of available housing, discrimination, segregation, and the belief by most Mexicans that their stay in the United States was temporary, Mexicans continued to be predominantly renters. In 1924 only 18 Mexican families had purchased homes in Kansas City.[34] In Detroit home ownership among auto workers was high (37.8 percent). In 1928, however, among the 15,000 Mexicans living in Detroit, only 100 to 200 Mexican families owned homes in the city.[35] As late as 1930, only 13 of the 934 Mexican families in East Chicago owned homes.[36] Available figures from other major Mexican enclaves in the Midwest relate a similar story.

Because even substandard, high-rent housing was in great demand, Mexicans were often forced to share living space. In Chicago, for example, 43 percent of the Mexican families in 1925 had lodgers, most of whom were transient solos or solteros. In South Chicago one Mexican family kept nineteen boarders in its five-room house.[37] In another house investigators found seventy-five people living in the basement. The basement ceiling was so low, according to the social worker, that one could not stand upright.[38] In that same year, 1926, Police Chief Reagin conducted a survey of housing conditions in the Block and Pennsylvania area in East Chicago, where the majority of Mexicans lived. His report included the following: "We went into places where we could hardly get the door open. Sometimes there would be three beds in one little room, and in one place we found 11 Mexicans sleeping." He characterized living conditions in this area as the worst he ever saw. Reagin was shocked by what he saw and told reporters the problem had been ignored in the past because of political pressure.[39] It was not unusual to find two or three men who worked different shifts assigned to the same room and bed.[40] Others were forced to take lodging in cottages, tumbledown shacks, and railroad camps. As late as 1928, 469 Mexican men, 155 women, and 372 children were living in such camps in the Chicago area.[41]

Throughout the Midwest in the years preceding the Great Depression, Mexicans remained a largely segregated population. Although some neighborhoods preferred them over Blacks, Jews, and Asians, residents nonetheless viewed them with fear and suspicion. Their areas of residence and their treatment by other ethnic neighbors indicated their low status in American society. Mexicans resented these exclusionary practices and fought back as best they could. They complained to consuls, community leaders, parish priests, and local authorities. Their efforts failed, however, because of their lack of political power, noncitizen status, and inability to organize effectively. One Anglo observer noted, "We have used little or no intelligence in helping [the Mexican immigrant] to a decent housing situation. We have given him the back alleys of our cities. We have called him 'greaser' and left him to fight his own way as best he can. We have wondered that he does not show more enthusiasm for becoming Americanized."[42]

Mexicans and Employers

From the outset, Mexicans were relegated to the lowest occupational levels, which meant they often worked in the dirtiest, most dangerous, and least desirable jobs that paid the lowest wages. Even when they performed the same jobs as their American and White ethnic counterparts, Mexicans were still paid less. Employers rationalized that Mexicans were less skilled and less able to perform difficult assignments because of their rural antecedents. This conception, of course, was inaccurate, especially in the Midwest. Although most Mexicans came from rural backgrounds, many had worked as wage laborers, craftsmen, and small businessmen in Mexico.[43] Many who eventually found their way to the Midwest already had work experience in the industrial sector. Moreover, employer surveys found Mexican industrial labor satisfactory.

In his survey of fifty-one employers in the Chicago area, Reverend Robert McLean found that forty-nine were satisfied with the work of Mexican employees, thirty-six thought that the work of Mexicans was about equal to that of other nationalities, and nine thought the Mexicans' work was better. In describing the work of Mexicans, railroad, sugar beet, steel, meat-packing, cement, foundry, and other industries used such terms as "industrious and energetic," "hard workers," "steady and methodical," "resourceful," and "diligent." The few negative comments described limitations due to physical stature or an inability to understand instructions in English.[44]

Employers were not always the ones responsible for discrimination. In large industries Mexicans seldom came into direct contact with upper-level management. Employers and managers left the day-to-day job assignments to foremen, who preferred giving the better jobs to members of their own nationality. Foremen were also gruff, abusive, and heavy-handed in dealing with Mexican employees. They often assigned them to the hardest work or subjected them to daily harassment. This interaction with foremen, which sometimes led Mexicans to quit or provoke acts of resistance and defiance, helped shape their consciousness as industrial workers.[45]

This underlying racism was fueled by stereotypes held by members of other ethnic and immigrant groups. Such negative attitudes manifested themselves through conflict in the work place and community, as residents accused Mexicans of lowering wages, depriving "Americans" of jobs, and being scabs. Unlike their experiences with inferior housing practices, Mexicans found ways to combat discrimination and unfair treatment in the work place.

Mexican Resistance in the Work Place

Employers attributed this characteristic to their Mexican workers: docility. Whenever called upon to defend their stand on the importation of Mexican laborers, employers argued that Mexicans constituted a highly malleable work force. Once their work was finished, employers argued, Mexicans happily returned to their homeland. The image of the docile, obedient, and tractable peon was not created by the employers, but it was they who most exploited the idea.

Reports, studies, surveys, and employment records present a far different picture of the Mexican worker. Contrary to popular perceptions, Mexicans did not passively accept wage differentials, the abuses of foremen, difficult working conditions, and discrimination in the work place. Instead, what emerges is a picture of individuals who, because they lacked personal guarantees and could not mount collective action, battled the system through a variety of methods.

A Mexican living in Chicago denied that Mexicans came to the United States to work for less pay. "He would work to make an honest living and to eat and clothe himself and his wife and children, but not 'for less.' He goes from place to place, first where there is work, then to where the work pays best. That is not working for less."[46] A railroad agent who was in charge of labor said this about Mexican workers: "You can't cuss the Mexicans out or call them down in front of the others or they may quit and take the whole gang with them. It is best to take them aside and tell them their work is not satisfactory. When we began employing Mexicans we sent a man around to the foremen to advise them how the Mexicans should be handled."[47]

An employment manager stated that most of the Mexicans discharged from his plant were dismissed because of "smoking, incompetency, or disobeying instructions."[48] Another employment manager, after praising the work of the Mexicans, said that Mexicans did not "jump when the foreman talks to [them]," and he liked that lack of subservience.[49] One steel mill superintendent stated that Mexicans were not as "servile as some Europeans. If I go out in the mill, they may look at me and say good morning, but they don't cringe and curry as some of the Europeans do." That is why he liked Mexicans, because he admired "men who can stand on their own feet."[50] A Mexican track laborer told an interviewer he preferred railroad work to factory work. "There is one good thing about working on a railroad section. On most of them you can puff a cigarette once in a while, but if you work in a factory, it is 'No Smoking' all over the place. I don't envy those at the packing houses or steel plants even if they have steady work. I like a little liberty."[51]

Mexicans often quit if they were dissatisfied with the job, working conditions, or treatment. One employee said he left the stockyards because of the terrible odor. He preferred his job at a candy factory, where it was hot but clean. At a tannery, an employment manager said turnover among Mexicans working in the hide rooms and other wet jobs was high. "They didn't like it and stayed only a short time."[52] To one Mexican, the issue was not the work but the foreman who assigned the work.

"All the nationalities have to work hard, but it seems to me that we Mexicans get more than our share of the grief and abuse. The foremen know that we know very little or no English. They make us work extra hard and we get the hard jobs. Then they curse us more than the rest, because they think we do not understand. But they make a mistake; we resent it deeply."[53] Another Mexican was more specific about foremen: "They are hard task masters and drive you all the time. I do not mind working but I will not be servile to them."[54]

Mexicans reported abuses to employers. Occasionally this led to disciplinary action against foremen, their transfer, or even their dismissal. When unable to achieve any satisfaction, some Mexicans resorted to violence against their tormentors. Plant records indicate that Mexicans were dismissed for insubordination, fighting, refusing to work, and using bad language against their supervisors. Some Mexicans were also fired for instigating work stoppages or slowdowns or for intentionally breaking machines and equipment. A Mexican employee at the steel-stamping plant in River Rouge, Michigan, was dismissed after he deliberately broke a punch press and angrily told his foreman that he quit. Another Mexican auto worker refused to sweep the floor because he was "too good to sweep." When told he was fired, he responded by stating that "he would find a job elsewhere."[55]

According to Zaragosa Vargas, who conducted an in-depth analysis of Mexican auto workers in Detroit between the years 1918 and 1935, high turnover was a serious problem among Ford employees. This "was principally caused by dissatisfaction with working conditions," which included "oppressive technical control and bureaucratization of work." To Vargas "the monotony and routine of machine production, speedup, higher piece rates, job instability, and the authority wielded by management, work supervisors, and foremen was countered by Ford [Mexican] auto workers with chronic absenteeism, voluntary quits, five-day and ten-day quits or by mere walking off the job."[56]

The anger and surprise that employers expressed over this behavior reflect how little they understood the people they hired. Influenced by prevailing stereotypes of Mexican docility, employers and foremen failed to recognize the forces that had brought Mexicans to that distant place. Mexicans who made the trek northward, regardless of the reason, did so with certain expectations, including a better way of life and a better job. Laborers in Mexico had bridled against the oppressive practices of their employers and patrons; they reacted the same way in the Midwest.

Mexicans who came to the Midwest were also more determined, aggressive, and independent than the average campesino. Such qualities helped them reach their destination. It was unreasonable for anyone to expect them to discard these qualities simply because they were given employment.

Employers tended to overlook or discount previous work experience when judging the character of their Mexican laborers. This disregard proved to be a serious oversight because previous jobs had taught Mexicans some hard lessons about exploitation, wages, and status that some resolved never to repeat. Some Mexicans simply accepted their lot in life, but others were unwilling to trade their dignity or pride for money or work.

Unemployment, Underemployment, and Wages

Although work in industry was more stable than in agriculture, that stability was a matter of degree. Between 1900 and 1930 the American economy experienced serious fluctuations that affected the need for foreign labor. When times became difficult, employers customarily released Mexican workers first, contributing to the high mobility among midwestern Mexicans. Many returned to the beet fields, especially Detroit auto workers, many of whom had come to the Motor City from Michigan's beet fields.[57] Others ventured into nearby cities in search of work, especially in the diversified economies of cities such as Chicago.

Even those fortunate enough to retain their jobs found that wages and hours fluctuated dramatically during hard times. Although Mexicans earned higher wages in the United States than in Mexico, the higher cost of living diminished those earnings. Mexicans in the Midwest incurred higher costs in housing, food, clothing, transportation, taxes, entertainment, and winter fuels. Massive layoffs, firings, production changeovers, reduction in hours, and repatriation schemes caused major disruptions in the social and economic well-being of the Mexican community. The idea of stable employment at good pay was not realized by most Mexicans in the Midwest.

When Mexicans did find steady employment in the Midwest, they tended to earn better wages than workers in the Southwest. In the Southwest, Mexicans working in agriculture earned between $.20 and $.35 an hour at harvest time. On railroads and in factories, Mexicans in the Southwest earned between $1.75 and $2.00 per day. Railroad maintenance workers in Kansas earned an average daily wage of $2.50 to $3.00. Similar employees in the Chicago area averaged $.35 to $.41 per hour, or $3.50 to $4.10 per day. These wages are based on eight- to twelve-hour work days. Iron and cement workers in Chicago earned as much as $5.00 per day in the mid-1920s, although most averaged $4.75. Meat packers were paid $.43 to $.47 per hour. In Kansas, laborers who loaded sides of beef from refrigerated cars to the plant or vice versa earned $.85 to $1.00 per hour. It was back-breaking work, however, and earnings were offset because laborers were hired daily and seldom worked more than three days per week.[58] Mexicans working in other industries averaged $4.00 per day. Mexicans who worked in the steel blast furnaces of Indiana Harbor and South Chicago earned $35.22 in 1924 for a 59.7-hour work week. By 1929 the work week had increased to 60.7 hours, but wages had gone up only $.01 per hour, raising weekly earnings to $36.48 per week, or $.60 per hour. During the 1920s, the average wage earned by the 30,827 Mexicans employed in the midwestern industrial sector, excluding the automobile industry, was $4.56 per day.

Mexican Workers at Ford

The highest paid employees among Mexicans were the Detroit auto workers, who had been drawn to the area as early as 1913, when Henry Ford introduced the $5.00 work day. In 1926 the starting wage at Ford had risen to $6.25 per day in jobs other than custodial work.[59] By the late 1920s Ford auto workers earned $.90 per hour, or $7.20 per day. The 400 Mexicans employed by the General Motors foundry in Saginaw, Michigan, received a daily wage of $4.50 in 1929.[60]

Although Mexicans in midwestern industries were paid higher wages than those in either Mexico or the Southwest, they still earned less than their White ethnic counterparts because of the prevailing practice of wage discrimination. The only exception to this practice occurred in the Ford plants, where Mexican employees were paid the same starting wages as Whites and received the same timed wage readjustments.[61]

Higher wage scales and increased job opportunities encouraged chain migration to the Midwest after 1921. In fact, during the 1920s chain migration accounted for the largest percentage of Mexican migration to the region, superseding the numbers brought in by recruiters and drift migration.

Chain migration was common in Detroit, where Mexican auto workers regularly sent for friends and relatives after they had acquired a place to live and sufficient funds to pay for their trip north. Ford employee cards indicate that many Ford employees had relatives who also worked in the plants. More often than not, these individuals had been hired on the recommendation of a friend or relative already working for Ford. These people generally lived in the same house or in the surrounding neighborhood, which helped ease the adjustment to the Midwest.

When jobs became scarce in Detroit, Mexicans left the city and traveled to Flint, Highland Park, and Saginaw auto plants and foundries in search of work. They also returned to the beet fields if they could not find work in the cities. If they found employment, they sent for those who had remained in Detroit. Mexicans also left their families in Chicago, the Calumet region, Kansas City, Toledo, Cleveland, or New York while they went to Detroit to find work in the auto plants. Once established they arranged for their families to rejoin them in Motor City.

Mexicans who had not brought their families with them made frequent trips back to Mexico or the Southwest for visits because the border was only a two- or three-day train ride. Mexicans also returned to Mexico to get married, baptize children, or arrange for the move of loved ones to the Midwest. To make these trips, employees in the auto, steel, rail, and meat-packing industries commonly took unpaid leaves or quit their jobs temporarily. A typical ploy that Mexicans used was to "rent" their work identification badges during their absence.

Work identification badges were issued to employees to facilitate bookkeeping and job supervision. Foremen used them to keep track of workers in their departments and to maintain records on attendance, productivity, and other job-related activities. For the employer the badges represented a means of control. For Mexicans working in large departments, these badges were valuable commodities, allowed greater personal freedom, and symbolized their pride in being Ford employees.

During the 1920s production schedules and rigid discipline on the floor made it difficult for employees to take temporary leaves to visit relatives or friends whom they had left behind. Most Mexicans averaged one or two return trips per year, taking advantage of layoffs or production changeovers. Although the job market in the Midwest during the 1920s was erratic because of slowdowns, seasonal model or production changes, and downswings in the economy, midwestern industries after 1922 entered a period of continued growth. This surge led to work speedups, longer hours, and greater demands on workers to meet production schedules. The result was more rigid supervision and adherence to company rules. Workers who failed to heed or meet production requirements were quickly dismissed.

Mexicans found themselves in the difficult situation of wanting to reunite with loved ones but facing dismissal and the loss of good wages. The advantages of working in large groups soon became apparent to Mexican employees. They knew that most foremen were not readily familiar with all of their workers. Personnel managers also found it difficult to maintain proper records on the thousands of employees because of the numerous departments in each plant, staggered work schedules, and huge turnover each month.[62] This weakness in the system facilitated the efforts of Mexicans to find temporary replacements while they took a much-needed break from the rigors of the job. When an employee wished to take some time off, he could "rent" his badge to another Mexican, usually an unemployed friend or relative, who took his place until he returned. A Mexican worker typically arranged for a relative to come to the Midwest and assume his job while he traveled home. In return, the replacement agreed to pay the worker a percentage of his earnings for the use of the badge. Both parties benefited financially, while reducing the risk of lost wages or employment.

Coworkers usually aided this practice by showing the replacement the ropes to ward off suspicion by the supervisors. Because most Mexicans worked at unskilled jobs, the replacement often required little training. In the Ford plants during the early 1920s, 43 percent of the jobs could be learned in one day, 36 percent in one day to a week, and 6 percent in two weeks. Only 14 percent of the jobs required one month to one year to learn.[63] This cooperation among coworkers enabled others to take vacations when their turns came. The replacement was often hired by the plant on a full-time basis, upon the recommendation of the friend or relative. The experience he already accrued served him well, not only in getting a job but also in helping him adjust to the rigors of industrial work.

Renting badges also helped Mexicans offset erratic work schedules and layoffs and supplement incomes. The prices of the badges depended on peaks and lulls in hiring periods. Paul Taylor, an economist who conducted research on Mexicans in the United States, reported that they sold work badges at Ford for $10 or more. These badges had been acquired by men who had gone to the Ford River Rouge plant and applied for work several times using different names. This practice was especially common whenever the job market shrank.[64]

Employers and supervisors were aware of this practice, but it was so widespread, it was difficult to control. In the Detroit plants, those caught renting jobs were discharged.[65] Records show, however, that such dismissals constituted only a small percentage of the Mexican work force. A similar situation existed in the steel mills of South Chicago. "The Mexicans have a custom of selling or lending their numbers to other Mexicans when they wished to leave work. Sometimes they sold the number outright, and again they charge a fee for their use while the rightful owner makes a trip to Mexico or tries his luck in other employment. The foremen do not seem to be aware of this practice. Perhaps all the Mexicans look alike to them."[66]

Renting badges and jobs stimulated chain migration, as relatives and friends traveled to the Midwest with greater assurances of employment. This movement created enclaves of people from specific locations in Mexico. Emigrants from the state of Jalisco composed almost 20 percent of the Mexican population in the Chicago area, and most of these came from the city of Guadalajara. More than 21 percent of Mexicans in the Chicago area came from the state of Guanajuato, whereas Michoacán provided almost 26 percent.[67] In Topeka, 60 to 70 percent of

Mexicans came from Guanajuato, most of whom were from the city of Silao. Thirty-four percent of Mexicans in Kansas City, Kansas, came from Michoacán. Many residents who lived in the Argentine barrio of Kansas City emigrated from the city of Tanganciuaro. These "Tangas," as they referred to themselves, had been brought over by friends and relatives, who helped them find jobs in the railroad shops.[68] After 1926 a large number of pro-Cristero Mexicans came to the Midwest from west-central Mexico, forming a powerful group that clashed with less ardent Catholics.

Unlike auto workers, railroad employees found it difficult to leave their jobs because they worked in smaller crews under the supervision of foremen who knew their employees. Their only recourse was to apply for release time or wait until the off-season to return home. Seasonal layoffs did not always occur, however, and for some Mexicans the loneliness and isolation became too much to bear. One employee in Kansas City, Kansas, had not seen his family for years. He failed to get the release time he requested and also lacked the funds for a rail pass to Mexico. Not to be deterred, he decided to drive to Mexico in a locomotive, which he had been trained to operate while moving engines in and out of the shops. One day he quietly walked into the yard, boarded an engine, and pulled out on a southbound track. As he reached the edge of the yard, he was spotted by some engineers. A mad dash ensued, resulting in the man's capture. Because of his good work record, his employer did not press charges or dismiss him. Instead, he granted the leave and provided the employee with a train ticket to the border after he promised to return and repay the debt. News about the incident quickly spread through the Mexican neighborhoods in Kansas City, and newcomers were regaled with stories of his exploit. He became a local folk hero, and at least one *corrido* (popular ballad) was written in his honor.

Return Migration

The figures concerning return migration between 1923 and 1926 reveal its magnitude. According to U.S. immigration estimates, approximately 21,000 Mexicans returned home. Mexican estimates for the same period, however, place the number at 336,685, or 315,685 more than U.S.

estimates. The discrepancy lies in how both countries handled the issue of immigration and emigration. Mexico's figures are more accurate for several reasons.

From 1923 to 1926, despite unemployment in the Midwest, Mexicans in the region enjoyed the highest level of continual employment and good wages. These opportunities greatly reduced the number of Mexicans who returned home permanently. The figures cited above reflect the large movement of Mexicans across the border to visit their homes and families and the increased prosperity that allowed them to bring their families into the United States.

Most of those who returned to Mexico registered willingly with Mexican authorities along the border. Mexican law required them to register as they left or entered the country, but U.S. immigration law required them to register only upon entering, something they assiduously avoided. The purpose of Mexican immigration law was not to restrict movement, only to gauge its extent. Mexican nationals were therefore willing to adhere to its requirements. By doing so they could also avoid a great deal of difficulty and expense when they returned to the United States. Mexicans registered because failure to do so placed them in danger of being labeled revolutionaries or enemies of the government. Furthermore, registering involved no fee or delay: the only requirement was filling out a simple questionnaire. Following this simple procedure could save Mexicans the difficult, costly, dangerous, and unnecessary need to cross illegally through points far from the ports of entry.

These figures also indicate the magnitude of illegal entry into the United States. According to U.S. estimates, 890,747 Mexicans lived in the United States in December 1926. Mexico reported that 557,718 Mexicans had returned to their homeland and 329,269 left for the United States between 1920 and 1926. If these numbers are correct, 228,449 more individuals returned to Mexico than had actually departed. "In other words, during this period of six years, 329,269 Mexicans departed for the United States, and—surprising fact—in the same period not only that number returned to Mexico, but 228,449 more." The reason for the discrepancy is that these 228,449 had entered the United States illegally.

Although they did not bother to register with U.S. authorities upon entering, most did register with Mexican authorities upon returning.[69]

Factors Affecting Wages

Although the promise of higher wages, more stable employment, and kinship networks helped promote immigration to the Midwest, the real earnings of midwestern Mexicans were adversely affected by several variables. Mexicans continued to experience unemployment and underemployment because of economic downturns, retooling, or changing production schedules. Recessions and depressions in 1919, 1921–1922, 1927, and 1929 dealt severe blows to Mexican employment and earnings and resulted in many leaving the region for lack of work. During the severe depression of 1921–1922, for example, more than 80 percent of Mexican workers in Detroit Ford plants were laid off or dismissed. Mexicans working in other industries also experienced widespread dismissals or radical cutbacks in hours and pay.

Even during the so-called boom times, Mexican workers did not enjoy full and uninterrupted employment. In the auto industry several fluctuations in sales resulted in reduced earnings. Many employees worked only forty-six weeks per year and commonly only two or three days per week. Between 1923 and 1928 the average monthly employment for workers in the auto, auto parts, and auto supply industries did not exceed 83.3 percent of the annual maximum monthly employment. The average monthly employment in 1924 was only 78.7 percent.[70] Earnings in the auto plants were reduced in 1925 when Henry Ford adopted the five-day work week to cut losses due to increased competition from General Motors, which had begun to offer its customers a wide selection of models, styles, colors, and prices. Ford, who had chosen to ignore consumer demands and once said that Americans could have any color Ford they wanted as long as it was black, soon found himself outpaced by the innovations introduced by the founder of General Motors, William C. Durant. By 1925 Ford auto workers were earning $4.21 per week less than the auto industry average. In 1928 Ford had closed the gap to $1.37 as his products became more competitive.[71]

Like other Mexican industrial workers in the Midwest, Michigan auto workers had to pay more than their southwestern counterparts for food, heating fuel, clothing, housing, and transportation costs to visit those left behind. They also were sick more often because of the inclement weather, unsanitary living and working conditions, and poor nutrition, which further reduced hours and earnings. Mexicans paid higher rents than their White ethnic counterparts: $21 to $25 per month for a house, compared to the non-Mexican rent of $17 to $20 per month.[72] Solos and solteros, who lived in boardinghouses or rented rooms in private houses, paid $6 to $10 per month, excluding meals and laundry fees.

The chronic shortage of housing in many cities inflated costs even further and relegated Mexicans to some of the worst housing. In 1919, for example, Detroit had a housing shortage of more than 33,000 units, and 165,000 people lived in housing that was inadequate, run-down, or condemned.[73] There and elsewhere several hundred Mexicans and their families were forced to live in boxcar communities.

Another factor that affected wages among Mexicans was the lack of opportunity for promotion, even though employer surveys reflected widespread satisfaction with their work. This satisfaction was clear from the large numbers of Mexicans employed in the railroad, steel, meat-packing, and sugar beet industries. A group of railroad officials reported in 1928 that they employed more than 61,000 Mexicans, primarily as track laborers or repairmen.[74] In some railroad companies, Mexicans constituted as much as 90 percent of the labor force. The payrolls of every company that belonged to the Association of Railway Executives showed that at least 50 percent of employees were Mexican nationals.[75] Mexicans employed as road maintenance workers in Chicago and Gary on sixteen railroads composed 4 to 80 percent of the labor force. Those railroads employed more than 4,000 Mexicans.[76]

Inland Steel, a major employer of Mexicans, reported in 1926 that it had 2,526 nationals on its payroll. This figure represented about half of the Mexicans living in South Chicago at the time. The Inland Steel complex in South Chicago was the largest employer of Mexicans in the Midwest throughout the 1920s. Of its 7,000 employees, 30 percent were of Mexican descent.[77] A survey of fifteen different industrial plants in Chicago and Gary in 1928 revealed that they employed more than 7,000

Mexicans, which represented anywhere from 3.7 to 29.9 percent of their work force.[78] A 1927 study by the Bureau of Labor Statistics found that sugar beet companies in Michigan, Ohio, Indiana, Iowa, Minnesota, and the Dakotas employed 15,000 Mexicans. This number increased to more than 40,000 when women and children were added. Estimates held that Mexicans composed 75 to 90 percent of the beet workers in these seven states.[79]

Despite employer satisfaction with their work and employer preferences in hiring them, Mexicans continued to occupy the dirtiest, most hazardous, and lowest paying jobs in the Midwest. Surveys indicate that between 80 and 90 percent of the Mexicans in the Midwest were classified as unskilled workers. Only 1.6 percent and 16.6 percent of Mexican workers in seven large plants in Chicago and the Calumet region, respectively, were classified as skilled and semiskilled.[80] In Gary and South Chicago, 19.9 percent of the Mexican steel workers were semiskilled and only 1.8 percent were skilled.[81]

Reasons cited by employers for not promoting Mexican workers or for concentrating them in unskilled jobs included (1) lack of requisite skills in English, (2) inability to make the transition from a rural to an industrial work environment, (3) illiteracy or lack of sufficient schooling to qualify for supervisory jobs, and (4) noncitizenship. As a result of these misguided, inaccurate, and prejudicial attitudes, Mexicans were denied promotions, training, and equal pay. Closer scrutiny of the historical record shows that employers and detractors were largely mistaken in their views about the background and abilities of Mexican laborers.

Mexican Literacy and Proficiency in English

A review of employment cards and records of Mexican auto workers at Ford plants found that of 1,024 Mexicans tested for English proficiency, 934, or 91.2 percent, spoke English.[82] Those same records indicate that many of these employees had previously worked in other midwestern industries.[83] A survey by Paul Taylor of Mexicans in Chicago and the Calumet region revealed similar findings.[84] Yet even at Ford, where Mexicans did not experience discrimination in wages or wage adjustments and where they demonstrated English proficiency, promotions and upgrades remained minimal. Mexican promotions were horizontal, not vertical.

The ability to speak and understand English was not unusual among midwestern Mexicans. Many had already been in the United States for several years and had previous industrial experience. By the time they arrived in the Midwest, many Mexicans had already adjusted to the demands of industrial work and had even begun to share the same attitudes toward work and working conditions as non-Mexican laborers. The long and circuitous trip of many solos and solteros had not only tested and steeled their mettle and determination but had also required them to use their wits, intellect, and survival instincts to overcome dangers and obstacles. Lessons and skills were quickly absorbed and adopted, and one of the first was the need to communicate. Put in this perspective, it is not surprising that Mexicans had developed the language skills needed in areas where Spanish was not spoken. Yet the ability to speak English was not sufficient to satisfy promotion requirements. This was the case in 1925, when the Santa Fe Railroad reported that 80 percent of its Mexican employees were literate. To qualify for an apprenticeship or job as a foreman, employees needed at least an eighth-grade education, the level achieved by the average American citizen in the early 1920s.

The assistant supervisor of safety and labor at the United Portland Cement Company reported that 97 percent of the 450 Mexicans employed by his firm could read and sign their names. This represented the highest literacy rate among all foreign-born workers at the plant. An Inland Steel survey found that 933 of the 1,030 Mexicans employed by the company spoke English. Representatives of the Illinois Steel Company in South Chicago stated that 60 to 75 percent of their Mexican employees spoke English. Employers in the Chicago and Calumet region reported that most of their Mexican workers knew about 200 to 300 words of English.[85]

The existence of higher literacy rates and greater English-language proficiency among midwestern Mexicans is corroborated in other ways. The numerous Spanish-language publications that circulated between 1914 and 1932 attest to a readership large enough to support them.

Although most were in print only a short time, their demise was usually due to undercapitalization, poor business practices, inadequate staffing, internal squabbles over editorial policies, or severe fluctuations in the population caused by economic downturns. Other major newspapers from Mexico and the Southwest, including *La Prensa* from San Antonio and *La Opinión* from Los Angeles, also circulated their publications in midwestern cities with large concentrations of Mexicans.

Numerous letters to the editors of English- and Spanish-language newspapers from Mexicans who took exception to their views or reporting also show a readership that kept abreast of events in the community and the world. The presence of many middle-class Mexicans dispels the idea that the colonias contained only those from the lower socioeconomic strata in Mexico. Midwestern Mexicans generally came from communities of 2,000 or more inhabitants in Mexico and were more urban than rural in their outlook, experiences, and backgrounds. That most had to work at unskilled jobs is not so much evidence of their lack of ability as it is a reflection of the discrimination they encountered within American society.

Background and education generally counted for naught. Even a willingness to adopt American mores and values was not sufficient to change the status of Mexican workers. One example of this inequality is the experience of Mexican and other Hispanic students who attended the Henry Ford Service School in Detroit between 1917 and 1928.

The Henry Ford Service School

To expand his operations in Latin America, Henry Ford opened a corporate training school for members of the Latin privileged classes, who would serve as managers of his new enterprises in the Southern Hemisphere. After receiving training in all aspects of production, management, and marketing, trainees would be returned to their respective countries and placed in charge of franchises. In its eleven years of operation, the school enrolled 117 students. The enrollees were selected from some of the best families in Latin America, including Mexico. All of them were well educated, averaging 12.6 years of schooling. They were also fluent in English, articulate, and highly motivated. Under the tutelage of corporate instructors, these young men received classroom instruction as well as experience in its practical application. In the process Ford made certain they were imbued with the "proper" American values and mores. Most of the students eagerly embraced the capitalist ideology and corporate ideals that were part and parcel of the school's curriculum.

Ultimately, however, their backgrounds, education, abilities, training, and acculturation were not enough to bring them the success and advancement promised. During their apprenticeships they were subjected to the same abuses and mistreatment accorded other Mexican employees by unscrupulous foremen and supervisors. Many of them withdrew from the program in anger, frustration, and disillusionment. Those who completed the program (about 39 percent) and who remained in the United States, did not fare very well. Most were relegated to the assembly lines or to performing menial work in the plants.[86] The oft-heard argument that Mexicans would be accorded better treatment and achieve greater success if they learned to speak English, adopted American work habits, and took advantage of educational opportunities had proved specious. Even possessing a non-Indian appearance was of no import in determining the fate of Ford trainees.

Mexicans in Business and the Professions

Not all Mexicans worked as skilled or semiskilled laborers or for an employer. A small percentage, approximately 5 percent of the population, found employment as skilled professionals or operated small businesses.[87] Most were relative latecomers to the Midwest who arrived after the depression of 1921. They had traveled to the United States to escape Mexico's economic problems and the continuing strife that had also adversely affected the middle and upper classes. Once here, they encountered sizable enclaves of Mexicans who were in need of their skills and services. By the mid-1920s Mexican-operated businesses began to proliferate in the region.

Indiana Harbor, with more than 4,500 Mexican residents, contained several Mexican-owned and Mexican-operated businesses, including 40 restaurants, 6 pool halls, 6 barbershops, 5 grocery stores, 2 chocolate factories, 1 print shop, and 1 clothing store. These businesses employed about 125 people. The community also had the services of 2 druggists, 4 printers, 2 music teachers, 1 priest, and 1 midwife.[88] In Gary Mexicans operated 30 restaurants, 20 pool halls, 15 barbershops, 10 tailor shops, several boardinghouses, and 1 print shop.[89] In 1928 Chicago had a total of 113 Mexican business establishments.[90] In 1929, 27 such businesses regularly advertised their products and services in Detroit's *La Prensa Libre*.[91]

The larger cities in the Midwest also attracted Mexican physicians, lawyers, dentists, engineers, teachers, ministers, musicians, journalists, publishers, scholars, and government officials. Many of them found employment with American firms in need of highly trained professionals with Spanish-language skills. Companies in Chicago with overseas interests employed more than 400 young Mexicans in white-collar jobs, including two cartoonists on a major newspaper and several clerks in the export divisions of large corporations.[92]

Young, single, and marketable, many of these professionals earned better wages and enjoyed a higher standard of living than other Mexican workers. Emanating from the upper and middle classes in Mexico, they were well educated, fluent in English, and well schooled in the social graces. They also tended to be more noticeably White than other Mexicans, which served them well in their search for employment.[93] Living apart from the rest of the colonia and adhering strictly to their own class, they tended to acculturate quickly. Their style of dress, speech, mannerisms, and tastes reflected those of the "hip" generation. Many of them imitated their cult hero Rudolph Valentino. One observer left this description:

> Because Chicago is known as a great city it has attracted a large proportion of handsome young Mexicans, termed "sheiks" among themselves, who wear expensive ultra-fashionable clothes, learn English rather well and have a "big" time. Many of them wear "patillas" or short pointed side whiskers, in imitation of Rudolph Valentino. . . . Not only have these better-looking young Mexicans, many of whom are from

good families in Mexico, won a degree of welcome among the motley population of Chicago, but they have found openings into the more refined channels of employment.[94]

Some organizations viewed the growing number of businesses and professionals as a promising sign that Mexicans were adjusting well to their new environment. "As an agency which has watched the coming and adjustment of many different national groups," wrote a member of the Immigrants' Protective League, "[we] can justly say that no immigrant group has made a more rapid adjustment in Chicago than the newest group of all—the Mexicans."[95]

The progress and stability of many Mexican enterprises, however, remained tenuous because they often lacked the capital to continue operating. Many Mexican businesses were financed by savings and wages earned in the factories. Layoffs, shutdowns, changes in production schedules, retoolings, and economic downturns often resulted in a lack of capital and the loss of clientele.

A few Mexican-owned businesses managed to survive hard times and shifting fortunes. One was El Fénix bakery, which operated out of an "attractive store" on Pennsylvania Avenue in East Chicago. A contemporary described it as " a Mexican institution having a wobbly delivery truck . . . and a profitable and rather extensive business."[96] Such ventures, however, were more the exception than the rule. Even attempts to organize proved unsuccessful. In Chicago, for example, Mexican businessmen discussed the possibility of forming their own chamber of commerce to promote development. Unfortunately nothing ever came of such efforts.

Mexicans welcomed businesses that catered to their tastes and provided them with familiar foods , home remedies, music, books, and other items from Mexico. Their presence in the community also evoked pride and optimism. "It was not long ago," wrote the editor of Chicago's *La Noticia Mundial,*

> maybe no more than two years, that there was not one commercial establishment on Halsted Street . . . that had a sign printed in our beautiful language. . . . Now, after three

years . . . everything has changed. We now have amongst us first-class establishments that attest to the diligence of the Mexican, the businessman and the enterprising man everywhere. In walking the streets along Halsted, one can read dozens of signs advertising this and that business. It is a street traversed night and day by uncounted Mexicans, especially after work.[97]

Mexicans and Unions

Unionization promised a way to remedy problems in the work place but was not without obstacles. The labor union movement in the United States suffered severe setbacks after World War I. The wave of postwar strikes and charges that they had been inspired by radical elements polarized public sentiment against the unions. Many employers had successfully suppressed union activities by using strong-arm tactics. During the business-oriented 1920s, there was little government support for unionization. Even if the union movement had proved successful, Mexicans would not have benefited; most unions would have excluded them because they were considered scabs and strikebreakers.

This hostility was especially evident in Chicago and the Calumet region, where Mexicans had been imported as strikebreakers during the bitter and prolonged steel strike of 1919. The ensuing depression in 1921 hardened attitudes, as competition for jobs between Mexicans and non-Mexicans intensified. Many Americans attributed the hard times to Mexicans, who were accused of lowering wage scales and depriving Americans of jobs. These attitudes led to union demands in 1921 that employers fire Mexicans and replace them with American citizens. The AFL passed resolutions on this matter during its national conventions and strongly advocated restricting Mexican immigration throughout the 1920s.[98] Mexicans were excluded from the AFL because it catered only to skilled workers.

In Detroit unionization efforts suffered, partly because of Ford's introduction of the $5 work day in 1913, his corporate welfare programs, and his incentive plans. An expanding job market and higher wages among auto workers in the 1920s also proved detrimental to union organizing. By 1925, for example, the auto industry ranked first nationally in its yearly wages.[99] Because of these disincentives, it remained one of the least unionized industries in the country.

Despite these barriers Mexicans remained interested in labor issues and organizing. Their discussions were nurtured by their shared work experiences and by a history of labor activism in Mexico. At the Youngstown Steel Works during the 1920s, Mexicans walked off the job to protest the unfair calculation of hours worked.[100] In Detroit Mexicans organized around labor issues in 1927. Meetings, discussions, and information about their activities were clandestine because of company spies. Los Obreros Unidos Mexicanos (United Mexican Workers) was organized by about forty or fifty steel and auto workers in Detroit. As an organization they sponsored English- and Spanish-language classes, helped fellow Mexicans who were looking for work, and opened a café in southwest Detroit that they ran as a cooperative. Also known as the Sociedad Obreros Libres (Society of Free Workers), their politics were leftist but their programs and approach were aimed at the wider Mexican working-class community.[101]

Mexicans also joined the union movement in the 1930s, participating in marches, demonstrations, and strikes, and risked their jobs by undertaking covert organizing activities in Detroit's auto plants. The Ford Service Department carefully monitored union activities and reported anyone involved in, or suspected of being involved in, union activities. Despite this repressive atmosphere, Mexican workers continued to organize and demonstrate. One auto worker recalled how he and other coworkers had marched in a Labor Day parade wearing masks to avoid being identified by company spies.

Union perceptions about Mexicans were unfounded and mistaken. Although Mexicans were recruited as strikebreakers, their employers often concealed this fact. Employers typically spirited Mexicans onto company grounds late at night and sequestered them in company barracks because employers realized that most Mexicans would refuse to work if they knew they were being used as scab labor. This attitude was confirmed during the steel strike of 1919 and in numerous later strikes. When the Mexicans brought to the Chicago region learned of the strike, many refused to work. Some even joined the picketers and were among the injured when company goon squads and the police broke up the strike.[102] This behavior is not surprising when one considers that many Mexicans had supported the union movement in Mexico and had carried those unionist sentiments across the border. Their desire to join unions stemmed not only from grievances shared with other working-class people, but also from increasing frustration over discriminatory practices that relegated them to the least desirable jobs.[103]

On several occasions Mexicans organized their own strikes, slow-downs, and walkouts against employers who remained indifferent to their complaints and demands. Although most of their protests failed, they nonetheless demonstrated their willingness and ability to organize around labor issues. American unions eventually opened their doors to Mexicans, but this acceptance did not occur in the Midwest until the 1930s. In the meantime, because of their highly mobile nature, their precarious job status, exclusion by unions, and discrimination by employers, most Mexicans remained at the lowest rungs of the labor force. By the beginning of the Great Depression, the economic progress that most had hoped for and strived to achieve had not materialized. Described as "intelligent and indefatigable workers" and as "reliable, serious, and quick of comprehension" by many employers and supervisors,[104] Mexicans did not receive the rewards paired with such praise.

The overwhelming majority of Mexicans who traveled to the Midwest came in search of a "Mexican Dream" rather than an "American Dream." They sought to earn enough money to ensure themselves and their loved ones a better life in Mexico. Ironically it was they who helped create much of the wealth and progress that made the American Dream a reality. Most of them, however, failed to reap the same benefits. "Mexicans were not poor because they lacked industry or economy, but rather because they were victims of American industry."[105] Mexicans were victims of a society that readily accepted the misguided images it had created of them. As a consequence, Mexicans were only allowed to experience the darker side of the dream.

CHAPTER 4

Women and Work

Mexican women played important and varied roles in midwestern communities. They made essential contributions to the economic survival of the working-class family and the community at large. Their arrival in increasing numbers led to the development of more stable communities and the creation of a more diverse social environment. Both organized and informal community life depended on the interpersonal abilities, social networks, and organizational skills of women. Their vital contributions to the economic well-being and social dynamics of the community, however, remained largely unrecognized and unrewarded by their contemporaries. Women encountered prejudice, discrimination, exploitation, poverty, and insecurity in the work place and the home. Sex and gender established and circumscribed the world in which they lived and worked. That they were women of color only exacerbated the problems they experienced at the hands of the *macho* and *gabacho*.

All women worked. They labored in a variety of occupations both in and outside the home. Most Mexicanas were engaged in domestic work and personal service. Agriculture, manufacturing, and light industry constituted the second largest source of employment for women. About 2.6 percent of the women in the labor force were clerical workers, 8.9 percent were employed in trade industries, and 3.1 percent were classified as "professionals." Less than 1 percent of the Mexican women in the Midwest owned or operated businesses such as restaurants and boardinghouses or served as midwives and *curanderas* (women knowledgeable about folk medicine and herbal remedies). Some operated brothels or were involved in the manufacture and distribution of bootleg alcohol. In Detroit an important bootlegging center was located in the home of Ms. Trini. Described as "a Mexican woman of humble origin, but of great intelligence," Trini's operation employed many people. Her profits were sufficient for her to spend one or two months each year in Miami.[1] Another woman illegally sold alcoholic beverages to a large clientele. Eventually this 80-year-old woman was arrested for violating the Volstead Act.

Mexican Women in Agriculture

The subservient status of women was evident among those who worked in agriculture. Mexican women first arrived in the Midwest as part of family units that sugar beet companies recruited to work in the fields. As noted in a previous chapter, beet companies preferred to hire families because they usually cultivated more acreage. They also helped guarantee a year-round work force, thus saving employers additional recruiting costs. Families were assigned a certain number of acres per season. On the average, one adult cultivated ten acres of beets, which meant that during the 1920s two adults earned between $500 and $800 in a season.[2] A family of six or seven earned up to $2,600.[3] In Michigan and other beet-producing states, more than 90 percent of the field work was performed by families.[4]

Male heads of households considered large families an economic boon, yet the system in which they labored exploited not only men but also women and children. Children six years of age and older were pressed into service. In 1941, Carey McWilliams, in testimony before the Tolan Committee in Detroit, stated that the documentation about the widespread abuse of workers by the beet industry was "voluminous." It contained, he said, appalling revelations about "low earnings, miserable health and housing conditions, child labor, sickness and disease."[5] Much of this abuse emanated from the labor contracts described in chapter 1.

The highly seasonal nature of sugar beet work required employers to find a way to restrict the movement of Mexican workers. This need to ensure a cheap labor supply led to the institution of the contract labor system. The contracts this system engendered contained labor controls that created a complex and interwoven web of exploitation and oppression.

Central to this web was the family system of contract labor, which involved paying workers based on their contracted acres, holding pay until workers completed certain jobs, and forcing workers to perform contracted tasks even though conditions beyond their control made the work more arduous and exacting. Workers forfeited their holdbacks if they failed to perform the specified operations.[6] This system precluded workers from abandoning the fields and seeking other employment, thus guaranteeing the companies and growers a seasonal supply of labor. Recruitment of a surplus labor supply and the isolation on beet farms also thwarted organized activities to protest wages and working conditions.

The laborer's cost of living did not enter into contract wage calculations. Workers often lacked the funds to move at the end of the season and were thus forced to accept whatever assistance the employer offered. The family wage and the need to rely on credit forced Mexicans to seek supplemental work during breaks and the off-season. Many sought work in nearby cities, planted their own gardens, or worked at menial tasks. The onerous nature of beet work also convinced workers to seek industrial employment.

The ability of Mexicans to leave the beet fields permanently was often frustrated by other factors outside their control. Industrial jobs, for example, became scarcer as the population increased. Cities such as Detroit and Chicago always had a large surplus labor pool. Production changeovers and seasonal layoffs also reduced job opportunities. The poorly paid beet workers were further constrained from moving because of the cost of relocating their families to a town or city. Even if they had the wherewithal to pay the transportation, severe housing shortages in the larger urban areas made housing expensive. Moving to the city also meant the number of income earners decreased. Whereas women and children worked in the fields, employment opportunities for them were scarce in industry.

Furthermore, male heads of households were loath to let their wives and daughters work in industry. Men feared that their loved ones would be led astray by exposure to "American" values. They also believed urban living made women more difficult to control. They did not want "their women" exposed to "liberating influences" that made them more outspoken and independent. Male sexual insecurity also entered into the formula. Mexican women were not numerous in the cities, and competition for them among men was keen. Men feared that allowing their mates to enter the work force would result in their meeting other men and running off with them. Their status as providers was also threatened. They believed that having their wives work would reflect badly on them as heads of the household. Among working-class people, having one's spouse work outside the home was tantamount to a tacit admission that the family was poor.

The decision to remain in agricultural work was not solely based on economic considerations or the desire for control. Although men openly acknowledged that rural living was lonely, isolated, and difficult, they also believed it provided salubrious benefits such as fresh air, open spaces, no crime, and few temptations to lead family members astray. These were some of the same descriptors used by company recruiting agents to lure unsuspecting workers into the fields. Agents promised recruits "beautiful homes in the country," "good pay," "clean, fresh air," and "easy work." Those who had seen the urban tenements in which many of their compatriots lived had no desire to subject their loved ones to that sort of life. Their perception of urban life was very similar to the one held by agrarians, fundamentalists, and other adherents to the Jeffersonian tradition. These and other considerations convinced them that their decision to remain in the country was in the best interests of their families. What they did not seem to realize was that it condemned their mates, their families, and themselves to an oppressive and never-ending cycle of poverty and despair.

The provision of housing helped perpetuate the labor contract system. When employers realized that replenishing the labor supply on a yearly basis was expensive, they encouraged workers to settle in nearby rural locations in makeshift company towns. Companies also provided workers with off-season housing as an inducement to remain. Some Mexican workers willingly accepted offers of housing and credit to avoid the added costs of relocating or returning to Mexico. Families remained to tend garden plots while heads of households traveled to nearby towns and cities in search of temporary work.

The nature and quality of the housing varied. Some companies built standardized units, usually twelve by sixteen feet in size. These units, disparagingly called "hunky housing," were placed on wheels to allow easy movement from field to field. Whether moveable or not, housing was provided to workers during the off-season for free or a minimal charge and was usually located away from population centers.[7]

Most housing was inadequate and of very poor quality. Beet workers typically lived in cold, drafty shacks with no toilet facilities. The water supply was often contaminated or distant (sometimes several miles) from the house. Usually the unprotected wells, brooks, or ditches were located fifty yards or more from the dwellings, to which the women hauled the water.[8] The inadequate or nonexistent sanitary facilities, overcrowding, and primitive housing added to the already heavy burden of women.[9] One company, well aware of housing conditions but more concerned about community opposition to Mexican neighbors, located its beet colonies "where the residence of Mexican people would be least objectionable to people prejudiced against them."[10]

The family contract system and the field work reinforced the subservient status of women. Their subordination and exploitation were perpetuated because of the family labor contract, the isolation of the labor camps, and the manner in which wages were paid. For example, women seldom received direct compensation for their work. Their wages were paid directly to the male head of the household, whether he was the father, husband, brother, or oldest son. This practice, plus high rates of illiteracy and inability to speak English, kept women dependent on men. The Catholic tradition, the belief that large families provided parents with an economic buffer when they grew old, and the increased earnings that large families promised subjected women to numerous pregnancies. In essence, women were the "breeders" of a labor supply for spouses and employers.

The demands of field work, numerous pregnancies, and the strains imposed by large families took their toll on women. Many women worked throughout gestation and commonly until parturition. Studies by personnel in the Department of Labor reported that women "worked in 'the beets' up to within a few hours of the birth of the baby" and that they frequently did not have adequate rest after confinement. "One mother," wrote an observer, " was out thinning and blocking [beets] two weeks after her confinement; another began to pull and top one week after her baby was born."[11]

Women worked nine to fourteen hours per day in the fields, performing tasks that were brutally demanding. This was especially true of sugar beet work, which was considered the most difficult and onerous among agricultural laborers. Women often lamented that "beet work is no work for a woman."[12] The end of the workday brought little respite for those with families to care for and households to manage. It was a routine that was unrelenting. "I have to work in the field from 4 o'clock in the morning until 7 at night," one woman said, "and then come home and cook and bake until 12 and 1 o'clock." Another woman stated, "In order to get my work done before going to the field I often have to get up at 3 o'clock. I bathe the children and prepare food before going out. Then at night I must bake and clean house, so that there are many nights when I do not get more than 3 hours' sleep. The work is too hard for any woman. By the time you have worked 12 or 13 hours a day bending over you don't feel much like doing your cooking and housework."[13]

Some women, unable to maintain the heavy regimen of field work and housework, waited until the weekends to perform household chores. "I have little time for housework during the week in the beet season, and I must do it all Saturday night and Sunday. I generally work . . . all night Saturday washing and cleaning house, and on Sunday I iron and bake. I get very little sleep those two nights."[14]

Children, especially very young ones, presented serious problems for working women. The long hours of field work required during the busy seasons prevented women from devoting much time to caring for children or attending to household duties. Many mothers had little recourse but to take their children into the fields with them. Shelter for infants could consist of a canvas tent, but that was more the exception than the rule. Most children spent the day with nothing to protect them from heat, sunlight, and insects. When asked what she did all day in the fields while her parents worked, one little six-year-old responded, "I sit in the sun and wish to myself that I could die."[15]

Those who did not take their children to the fields left them at home, either to fend for themselves or under the care of "older" children, many of whom were under seven years of age.[16] One can but imagine the emotional and psychological stress experienced by women as they saw their children suffering from heat, cold, inclement weather, insect bites, and lengthy separations from their toiling parents. Sadder still was the realization that these conditions, which deprived their children of adequate nutrition, education, and other basic necessities, would condemn many of them to a similar way of life.

Mexican Women in Urban Areas

Women living in urban areas encountered similar problems. City women, however, remained a numerical minority throughout the period under study, whereas the male:female ratio was more balanced in the fields because of the emphasis on hiring family units. The cities attracted mainly single or unattached males who had left their families in Mexico, the Southwest, or small towns and agricultural communities in the Midwest.

During the early 1900s the ratio of men to women in midwestern cities was 100 to 1, whereas in southwestern cities it was approximately 100 to 116. Even as late as 1930 the male:female ratios in most midwestern cities remained imbalanced. In Chicago, for example, it was 170 to 100; in Detroit, 179 to 100; in Flint, 149 to 100; and in Indiana Harbor, nearly 2 to 1.[17] The scarcity of women, as will be discussed later in this chapter, made men even more determined to exercise suzerainty over them.

Urban women worked in a variety of occupations in and outside the home. In the early 1900s women labored in the meat-packing plants, railroad yards, and sugar beet factories of Kansas and Missouri. Largely employed on a daily or as-needed basis, they earned $.425 to $.50 per hour, or half the wage paid to men. In the rail yards, women performed a wide variety of back-breaking, low-paying jobs, including hostler helpers, coach cleaners, engine watchers, wipers, car men, boiler washers, fire builders, pitmen, painters, carpenters, cinder laborers, and shop laborers.[18] The low pay and unpredictability of work schedules forced many women to take in laundry or work as domestics to supplement their incomes. The number of women who worked in all of these industries never exceeded 3.7 percent of the Mexican female population. Even as late as 1930, only 175 out of 4,758 Mexican women living in Kansas classified themselves as laborers.[19] This figure does not include women who worked in agriculture, where the percentage was much higher. Those figures are difficult to obtain because many of the women in agriculture considered their work and wages as supplemental to those of their spouses and thus did not classify themselves as employed.[20]

These small percentages belied Mexican women's economic importance to their households and community. Although men employed in the industrial sector earned higher wages than their counterparts in agriculture, their total earnings were adversely affected by recurring periods of unemployment and underemployment. Income was further diminished by a higher cost of living and additional expenses such as heating fuel, higher rents, and winter clothing. Better pay did not translate into a higher standard of living for most midwestern Mexicans.

Male Resistance to Outside Employment for Women

Despite the need for additional income, many men were loath to have spouses and mates work outside the home. Men repeatedly argued that self-sufficiency among women led to greater desertion rates. "Mexican husbands don't want their wives to work, they would meet some other men and would go away with them; I would not blame my wife, I would blame myself, because I have control of her. She would meet a man and go away with him."[21] Some men believed allowing women to work undermined their status and authority as the primary breadwinners. In their opinion working women made poor wives because their financial independence made them sassy and difficult to control.

Familial priorities, tradition, and employer preference for hiring young, unattached women kept many married women from working outside the home. A working married woman generally represented a tacit admission of poverty, defeat, or family crisis, compounding the stigma for her husband.[22] In this regard the experiences of working-class Mexican women were not very different from those of other working-class women in the United States. The attitudes of those opposed to women in the work force mirrored the social consensus that the first responsibility of women was to bear children and maintain the home.[23]

During the 1920s, when the Mexican population in the Midwest reached its predepression peak, the average annual income for steadily employed, unskilled and semiskilled workers of all ethnicities in Chicago was between $800 and $2,400. In a 1927 study Leila Houghteling found that about two-thirds of Mexican households in Chicago earned less than this.[24] Although men strongly opposed the idea of their mates working, economic necessity led other family members who were old enough into the work force. In Chicago nearly 88 percent of the children sixteen years or younger from unskilled, working-class families worked. Among skilled, working-class families, 85 percent of those under sixteen worked.[25] Parents often acceded to the necessity of having older daughters in the work force.

Married female workers were atypical. Women were more likely to seek employment if they were single, widowed, or older daughters. These women typically worked in low-skilled, low-paid jobs with little security and no mobility. Many jobs were seasonal, and employers usually based wages on piecework. The sex-segregated nature of their jobs reinforced their subordinate role to men and underscored the conservative aspects of their socialization.

Working Conditions for Mexican Women

Most Mexican female workers were daughters who lived at home and whose earnings supplemented the family's income. They often toiled in factories, where the work was physically taxing and governed by a harsh, even abusive, style of regimentation. Regardless of the work they performed, their wages were half of those paid to men. Most were paid for piecework, "which like the family wage . . . was an effective means of perpetuating poverty."[26] In Chicago female confectionery workers were paid piece rates and earned from $12 to $40 per week. In the meat-packing industry, women started at $.30 to $.35 per hour, whereas men were paid a starting wage of $.45 per hour.

In addition to the dual wage structure, women encountered other problems on the job that affected their earnings. Most women were concentrated in seasonal jobs. In many industries female employees were required to pay employers for work materials, tools, or special clothing used on the job. Women were concentrated in the labor-intensive industries, where male employers and supervisors exercised strict control and severe discipline to increase output. Rebelliousness, outspokenness, tardiness, and lack of cooperation usually resulted in fines or penalties against women, further reducing their wages.[27] Repeated offenders were summarily fired.

Adding to their distress was the work environment itself, which was characterized by overcrowding, noise, poor lighting and ventilation, hazards, and excessive temperatures. Women in the meat-packing industry worked in dim, chilly rooms while standing in pools of water.[28]

The shrinking wages of women reinforced their subordination and dependence on men and "encouraged the retention of feudal attitudes in Mexican communities in the United States."[29] This was reflected in the experiences of older daughters who entered the work force.

Working Daughters

Like their mothers, working daughters were subjected to exploitative wage practices. Although sons were required to contribute only part of their paychecks to their families, daughters had to give all of their earnings to their parents. Few daughters appear to have questioned this practice or complained about the small allowances their parents allotted them. They considered it their filial duty and a way of showing respect. This is not to say that tensions over social freedom and money did not exist between parents and daughters. They did. Mexican daughters, however, largely followed the patterns of other working-class girls—they surrendered their wages, adhered to norms of behavior within the family, obeyed their parents, and lived at home.[30]

Families came to rely on the earnings of older daughters, not so much because of the amounts, but because the paychecks represented a continuing source of income. The meager wages that employers paid to women made life outside the family economically precarious. Sons, on the other hand, were more likely to earn enough money to leave home if parents demanded too much of their income. Women were also deterred from leaving home by the prevailing social climate in many working-class communities, which frowned upon the idea of young women maintaining separate residences.

The contributions of working daughters to the family income strengthened the bonds between them and their mothers. Both recognized that their work made it possible for families to weather economic hardships and enjoy a few luxuries. Exploitation in the work place made some daughters more sympathetic to the hardships endured by their mothers. Appreciative mothers openly praised the contributions of their daughters. One mother described her daughter as "the best daughter that a mother ever had. . . . She never thinks of buying anything of importance without first consulting me. . . . There are not many daughters like mine. The girls at the factory where my daughter works tell her that she is silly for giving me all her paycheck; that they go out on Saturday afternoon and have a good time on the money they earn. But my daughter never does."[31]

Mothers often rewarded their daughters' adherence to filial responsibilities not only by praise, but also by greater trust and relaxation of norms. One young woman had her mother's permission to buy and use makeup as long as she kept it out of her father's sight. Another daughter, who regularly gave her entire paycheck to the family, was told by her mother to keep some money for herself. When the daughter refused, the mother set aside some of the earnings for her. Later she used that money to buy her daughter a phonograph.[32]

Despite the long hours, unhealthy conditions, and poor wages, many young women preferred working to staying at home. Their jobs were often located in the immediate neighborhood and were typically acquired through friends or relatives who worked there. Jobs offered increased opportunity for socialization with friends away from the watchful eyes of parents. Work in the neighborhood among familiar faces also provided a modicum of comfort and security to working-class girls. Their sheltered lives and the inability of most of them to speak English added to the importance of neighborhood ties at work. Of course, this restriction meant they were relegated to the lowest paying jobs and poorest working conditions in the marginal industries that proliferated in working-class districts. Few, however, were willing to venture away from familiar surroundings in search of better opportunities. Most daughters took jobs near home to avoid the cost, time, and inconvenience of using the public transportation system.

The Benefits and Problems of Employment for Young Mexican Women

Jobs not only increased women's opportunities to socialize with others of their own age, they also provided a measure of independence. Mexican women relished the opportunity to work and earn their own money. "Women like to work here," said one woman. "At home the man is the boss, but not while you are at work."[33] An Italian social worker stated that newcomers to the job quickly overcame their timidity after they had been shown the ropes by experienced workers. She also observed that these women, especially those who were single, found new social outlets within the work place. "If single, the Mexican women like to remain at work; they learn English and like the independence."[34]

Others were far less enthusiastic about the increased independence that working women supposedly enjoyed. This disapproval was largely grounded in the close association between work and "Americanization." In the minds of some Mexicans, work, independence, and Americanization were interrelated. They believed that the practice of working outside the home was not only the first step toward the erosion of male authority but also a sure sign of acculturation. "Mexican men don't like the freedom of women," a parent of a working daughter complained. "It is all right for the Americans but not for the Mexicans. They don't want their wives to work."[35]

Although Mexican men disapproved of the freedom women enjoyed in the United States, they nonetheless acknowledged that it was "all right for the Americans to let their women work." A few even agreed that it was acceptable for Mexican women to work, but only if they had been born in the United States. When a young Mexican man was asked if he approved of his two sisters working, he responded he did, but only because they "had been brought up here." He remained adamant, however, about not permitting his wife to work.[36] Most Mexican men preferred to marry or cohabitate with women who adhered to traditional values. "The Mexican girls in the United States are like the American girls or worse," a young track laborer grumbled. "It is best to get a girl from Old Mexico when one wishes to marry."[37] A Mexican high school student observed, "The Mexican men here say that the Mexican girls of the United States have too much liberty. They want to marry girls newly from Mexico." He also noted, however, that Mexican girls in the United States preferred to marry Mexicans who had been in this country for a while because they were supposedly more liberal in their outlook and values regarding women and work.[38]

Fears and concerns stemming from these views resulted in fathers attempting to exercise even more control over their daughters. Yet the idea that working outside the home increased their daughters' independence was not accurate. The work place, with its male-dominated supervisory positions, tended to reinforce the subservient and inferior status of women. Low wages also kept them dependent on men in their household and made life outside the family economically unfeasible. Their experiences in the work place, by reaffirming the ideas of dependency and passivity among women, directed Mexican women toward the pursuit of traditional roles and expectations regarding marriage, family, home, and adherence to the women's sphere. Although the social circles that single women joined in the work place may have encouraged their independence, most women in those circles, whether Mexican or "American," still pursued traditional goals.

Those goals were apparent in women's conversations and in their views that employment was a temporary measure that would either provide them with the opportunity to meet eligible men on the job or allow them the economic freedom to pursue a more active social life aimed at meeting eligible men. According to Leslie Tentler, "The typical women's work community . . . was a youthful, sex-segregated social world where important conservative values about femininity were reaffirmed by women themselves. Among their peers, young working women were encouraged to seek future security and mobility through marriage rather than employment. They learned to accept a work world that defined women as dependent and marginal employees."[39]

This outlook was even evident among Mexicans who took a liberal view about permitting young girls to become socialized according to standards in the United States. In an article appearing in *La Noticia Mundial,* a Spanish-language newspaper published in Chicago during the 1920s, Esther Margo argued there was nothing wrong with Mexican women embracing American customs. She encouraged parents to allow their daughters more freedom to pursue social outlets and to refrain from imposing values and norms that differed from those in the United States. If they wanted their daughters courted according to custom, she wrote, then they should return them to Mexico where those customs were still observed. Adhering to those practices in the United States, she cautioned, could doom their daughters to spinsterhood. Of course, she concluded, once the girl was married, she should behave accordingly and drop all notions of liberation and women's rights.[40]

Nonetheless, the perception that allowing women to work outside the home eroded patriarchal authority and traditional values persisted within Mexican communities in the Midwest. Men and women were vociferous in expressing their views on the subject. Traditional-minded women considered the practice an outrage. "A woman has enough to do in the house," complained an elderly woman of Mexican descent. "If she is going to keep a happy home and a happy husband she has enough to do to stay at home and take care of cleaning the house, cooking, and looking after his needs. How would you like your wife to work? You can't serve two masters, and one of them [*sic*] has to be your husband." A young mestizo echoed these sentiments. Men, he said, were the heads of households, and that is the way it should always be. In his opinion women in the United States dominated their men, and this was wrong. "The place of the woman after marriage," he asserted, "is in the home taking care of the children."[41]

An editorial in a Chicago Spanish-language newspaper lamented the declining status of men in the United States, and cautioned that the same fate awaited Mexican men if they were not careful. "I have an American friend who can't even open his mouth to order a couple of eggs in his own home," sneered the writer. "She shoves him out to a restaurant because, according to her, she did not get married to be a cook for any Tom, Dick or Harry, and that included . . . her husband."[42] Another man declared he had not married yet because he considered Mexican women in this country "unrestrained" in their behavior and attitudes. "They are the ones who control their husbands and I nor any other Mexican won't stand for that. [They] take advantage of the laws and want to be like the American women. That is why I thought it better not to marry; and if I get married some day it will be in Mexico."[43]

Women, Casas de Asistencia, and Boarders

During the early stages of Mexican migration to the Midwest, rail and steel companies hired women to cook, clean, and wash for the men living in the camps and boardinghouses. In Detroit, Kansas City, and other cities with large numbers of solos, women worked in or operated their own casas de asistencia. Unlike the boardinghouses, these casas served more as dining and laundry establishments. They generally catered to men from particular regions in Mexico by serving food native to those regions. Another attractive feature was that familiar dialects were spoken by both the clients and the operators, bringing an element of home to lonely men far from their families. Recent arrivals or individuals who had returned from a trip to Mexico brought news and letters from home, reinforcing the practice of patronizing a given establishment. Men had little difficulty in identifying which house catered to which region because they bore names such as "Casa Jalisco," "Casa Michoacán," or "Casa Morelos."

Women who worked in these places usually earned $7 to $8 per week during the 1920s.[44] For those meager wages they prepared meals for twenty-five to fifty men each day, as they catered to shifting work schedules and twenty-four-hour shifts. Working conditions for the owner-operators were no different. They proved demanding and onerous for all concerned, exacting a heavy toll on those responsible for the cooking, cleaning, and washing.[45] Because of the demanding work and the expense involved in keeping a business in operation, there was a high rate of failure among the 1 percent of Mexican businesses (mostly restaurants, boardinghouses, and casas de asistencia) owned by women. The experiences of Mexican businesswomen did not differ markedly from their male counterparts, who also suffered from a high rate of failure. There were, however, a few success stories. In Chicago Mexicans repeatedly voted El Povenir Restaurant, owned and operated by Flora Miranda, as the best Mexican restaurant in the city. In newspaper polls, patrons remarked that the food was delicious, the prices reasonable, and the premises clean and pleasant.[46]

Women, especially those who were married, faced almost insurmountable obstacles in gaining employment outside the home. They confronted not only strong opposition from men, but also problems involving the cost, quality, and availability of child care. Because most families were nuclear and had recently arrived in the Midwest, women could not turn to their own mothers or other female relatives for help in caring for young children. This situation further curtailed the scope of women's activities. For many women living in cities, the absence of child-tenders tied them more closely to home. When a recalcitrant husband told his wife she could not work because the children needed her, she responded, "I think that I could get some good woman to stay with the children for about $5 a week and I could make $20 to $25."[47]

The need to care for very young children, social constraints against working outside the home, limited skills, low wages in the work force, and necessity for supplemental income all made boarding the dominant income-earning occupation for Mexican women. In the Midwest a large percentage of Mexican families took in boarders. During the 1920s almost 40 percent of Mexican families in East Chicago had one or more boarders living with them.[48] A 1925 survey in Chicago found that 43 percent of one-family Mexican households had lodgers.[49]

Although boardinghouses were common in the Midwest by 1916, after 1920 their numbers proliferated. After the depression of 1921, migration to the Midwest increased significantly. For many solos, rents were prohibitive. The sudden influx of Mexicans also created housing shortages. Furthermore, the food served at non-Mexican boardinghouses was alien, of poor quality, and expensive. Although men were disinclined to allow women to work outside the home, they had few qualms about letting them cook, clean, and work for boarders. The money paid to boardinghouse operators or male heads of households for the work done by women was a welcome and necessary supplement to the family income. During the 1920s, each boarder paid between $13.50 and $17.50 every two weeks.[50]

Money earned from boarders helped working-class families survive periods of unemployment and underemployment. The additional income made it possible for them to purchase a few luxuries, including phonographs, better clothing, automobiles, and jewelry. Among Mexican men gold watches were coveted as status symbols because they were considered evidence of a family's affluence. The extra funds were also used to finance trips to Mexico, augment savings accounts, or help other members of the extended family. The income earned by women who took in boarders made it possible for Mexicans in the Midwest to weather the downturns that plagued the American economy between 1919 and 1929. Ultimately this income helped families survive periods of adversity and reduced the need for frequent uprooting to seek new employment opportunities.

The Rigors of Boardinghouse Work

Boardinghouse work was tedious, onerous, exhausting, low-paying, and seemingly endless. Cooking, for example, was continuous because of the twenty-four-hour shifts of some factories. Women commonly prepared six to nine meals every day of the week to accommodate their families and tenants. The lack of indoor plumbing and hot water added to the tedium and labor of doing laundry. Women made countless trips up and down stairs to draw the water necessary to perform most chores. The work was largely manual because few could afford electrical appliances. As one woman noted wearily, "Women's work is . . . the same all over the world. They work all the time and are never done. Yes, I work all the time—from morning until night."[51]

Like their counterparts in agriculture, women who worked at home or in boardinghouses did not receive direct compensation for their labor. The male head of the household collected the rents and then provided her with operating expenses. Even if a woman did receive compensation, that money was usually earmarked for household expenses. Unlike the male breadwinners, women did not enjoy the luxury of taking money from the pay envelope to buy liquor, cigarettes, or a night on the town. For many women life was fraught with personal and economic sacrifices.

Exploitation and tedium were not the only problems encountered by women in boardinghouses. The preponderance of single men and the dearth of women promoted sexual harassment and abuse. Women, willingly and unwillingly, were used as prostitutes by husbands and mates. A Mexican reported that "in three boarding houses the husbands of Mexican women live there, and know that their wives accommodate the boarders."[52] Investigators in Chicago uncovered similar practices in the boardinghouses they visited. They also found that some women, unwilling to subject themselves to this kind of abuse and exploitation, walked out. One said she left because "the men make too many advances to women here because there are so few women."

Although life in the boardinghouses might not result in commercial prostitution, it could result in lower morals. One social worker in Chicago stated, "The conditions in Mexican boarding houses are not so good. . . . The women become common property."[53] Some boarders forced women into having intercourse with them by threatening their families. When spouses or mates learned about it, they took the law into their own hands and exacted retribution from the offender. The keen competition for women added to male insecurities, increasing jealousies, suspicions, and violent confrontations. Some men blamed the women for the attacks against them, failing to recognize that the women had been the victims of an unprovoked brutal assault. It was not unusual for these men to send the women back to Mexico or to desert them completely.[54]

For some women prostitution was a conscious choice because they saw it as a means of obtaining greater personal and financial freedom. Usually they worked as independents or in boardinghouses operated by widows. Two women, for example, operated a restaurant and bordello near the employment district on Madison Avenue in Chicago. Social workers reported that some men solicited business for their mothers, wives, daughters, or sisters at dance halls and poolrooms. Women also visited the dance halls in search of customers. Prices ranged from $2 or $3 if the services were performed in the women's homes to $10 if they were required to go elsewhere.[55] Some Mexican prostitutes encouraged other Mexican women to adopt the same occupation. To strengthen the appeal, they would say, "You don't need to work or suffer if your husband drinks. You are in the United States and do not have to do it."[56] They also pointed to the greater freedom gained by earning one's own way.

Women's Responses to Abuse, Neglect, and Exploitation

Women who found life intolerable expressed their disaffection in several ways. Some turned to settlement house workers and local authorities for help or advice. Others left abusive partners for another who promised them a better life. Still others simply returned to their original homes and families. A few, preferring to suffer the scorn of their compatriots rather than continue to live as chattels, filed for divorce or sought protection from the courts. To the more conservative and reactionary elements in the community, this did not augur well for Mexican society. Again the Spanish-language newspapers, which remained the bastions of male conservatism and chauvinism, sounded the alarm. "Let us avail ourselves of divorce," trumpeted an editorial in Chicago's *Mexico*, "and see that it is nothing but the first step that a woman takes toward her own perdition; for with the same ease that today she changes husbands, she can do it tomorrow and the next day, until her life is a succession of 'husbands' only comparable to the lives of those unfortunate ones who are called 'prostitutes.' "[57]

The editorial failed to mention the conditions that had driven women to such decisions. It was also mistaken in ascribing the increasing rates of divorce and desertion among Mexican women to capriciousness and loose morals promoted by life in the United States. Women finally had greater recourse to legal means to escape hapless or intolerable marriages. "The women here have more freedom than in Mexico," a divorcée said. "Here if you are injured you can go and tell the jail [court], or if your husband wants to desert you or beats you. In Mexico if your husband deserts you or beats you—well it's your husband."[58] A Mexican social worker stated that women were no longer willing to tolerate abuses or excesses from their spouses.

> The husband spends the money on wine, or gambles, and does not take his wife and children out to theaters, etc. [If they complain] some husbands . . . beat them with their hands and fists to try and shut them up. They say, "If you don't like to have me control you, you can go to the street." In

Mexico under such circumstances the wives would say they
made a mistake, and would carry their cross; here they want
their rights.[59]

Many women chose to forego the formalities of seeking legal separation or divorce and simply walked out. In the Midwest, desertions
were more common than in the Southwest because of the paucity of
women and the greater availability of public services. Another reason
was that the long, circuitous, and demanding journey north had tested
and steeled their resolve, further strengthening their sense of independence and self-reliance. They tended to have higher expectations in their
search for a better life.

Other factors also gave Mexican women more independence. The
availability of jobs for women meant they no longer had to be dependent on male heads of households. Of course they faced serious
problems on the job, but to some, working represented a noticeable
improvement in the way they lived. They were also able to turn to
women's organizations within the Mexican community for assistance.
Some local consuls provided funds for women and their families to
repatriate. In time, however, consuls refused to help because of a shortage of money and the belief that the practice encouraged women to leave
their spouses.

How deep the disaffection was and how many women actually left
are difficult to ascertain. Most Mexican women appear to have stayed
with their families and mates. They too, however, found ways to express
their views, grievances, and attitudes about their plight and relationships. At times those expressions manifested themselves through open
defiance or the give-and-take present in even patriarchal relationships.
They also assumed more subtle forms such as humor.

Some of that humor, fortunately, survives in written form and
shows how women perceived men and their behavior. One story involved an exchange between two lovers: Man: "Tell me, if I were far away
from you, would you still love me?" Woman: "What a question! I am
convinced that the farther you are away from me, the more I tend to love
you." Another man inquired of his mate, "Say, Matilda, if for some

reason I could not come home for dinner, should I write and tell you?" "Don't be ridiculous, Ramon," was the response. "In going through your trousers I found the note already written in one of your pockets." In an exchange between a mother and daughter, the mother cautioned, "Don't delude yourself, my daughter. Men prefer an ignorant woman to a woman who is educated." "But do you believe that all men are like father?" asked the daughter.[60]

Regardless of the kind of work Mexican women performed, they encountered the same problems faced by most working women. That they were women of color only added to their exploitation. In addition to receiving less pay, Mexican women were segregated from workers who were not of their own nationality. They encountered racial discrimination, sexual oppression, and class exploitation. They were victimized by cultural practices that emphasized a subservience to patriarchal authority. Adding to their travails was a religious, social, and economic value system that made them breeders of a labor supply.

Whether women worked in agriculture, industry, the professions, or the home, they played a vital role in the economic life of the household and community. Their roles and contributions, however, were largely ignored and overshadowed by the male-dominated society in which they lived. For those women who settled in an urban environment, the chances of achieving independence were greater because of the loosening of patriarchal authority, the existence of more educational opportunities, and their increasing participation in industry.[61]

Ascertaining the percentage who took advantage of these opportunities is difficult. During the 1920s, Mexicans in the Midwest expressed growing concern about the deleterious effect that Americanization was having on women and youth, suggesting that changes were in fact afoot. These changes and the reactions of the Mexican community to them are discussed elsewhere in this study. Of special note is the irony surrounding the experiences of Mexican women. Men might boldly assert that they were the masters of the household and the breadwinners, yet the reality was otherwise, and women proved it daily. Men complained bitterly about the exploitation, discrimination, and oppression they encountered at work and in society. They demanded respect, good wages, improved working conditions, and to be valued as human beings, not commodities. They failed to understand that women were being exploited and discriminated against because of their sex as well as their color and nationality. Mexican men remained insensitive or indifferent to the plight of women, inflicting on them the same wrongs for which they so vehemently condemned others.

CHAPTER 5

Mexican Consuls

Although wages, housing, legal and civil rights, education, discrimination, and other issues concerned all Mexicans, most action on them before 1916 was taken by single individuals or by the Mexican consuls. Mexican communities in the Midwest before World War I were unstable because of high mobility, the predominance of single and unattached men, recurring cycles of unemployment and underemployment, and the forced repatriation of Mexicans during severe downturns in the American economy. Stabilization occurred as Mexicans found steady work, as more women and families moved to the Midwest, and as the Mexican population in the United States increased from continued migration and a rising birthrate.

The Issue of Emigration in Mexico

Mexicans from all walks of life expressed concern about the high rate of emigration and its effect on Mexico's future. This chord was struck as early as 1907, when a recession in the United States forced many nationals back to Mexico. Their return not only demonstrated the proportions that Mexican emigration had reached, but also revealed the government's unpreparedness in helping the thousands of desperate repatriates who crowded into border towns.

Opponents of emigration criticized the government's do-nothing policy and forced President Porfirio Díaz (1876–1911), who wanted to avoid a potentially dangerous issue, to order his staff to develop strategies that would address the problem.[1] A major strategy involved a strident propaganda campaign that emphasized the negative aspects of emigrating to the United States. When Francisco Madero became president in 1911, he continued Díaz's policy of disseminating notices warning would-be emigrants of the unfavorable conditions awaiting them in the United States.[2]

The issue of emigration was vexatious for Mexico's leadership. Officials realized that Mexico needed the work of its people if it was to prosper as a nation. Some officials considered the Mexican people the country's greatest natural resource. That resource, however, was being siphoned to help build the economic fortunes of the United States. Emigration was also a source of embarrassment to Mexico, especially to revolutionary and postrevolutionary regimes. The mass exodus was undeniable proof to the world that the "new" Mexico could not take care of its own. Various groups exerted pressure on government officials because they viewed emigration as detrimental to their own interests as well as those of Mexico.

Revolutionary nationalists argued that emigration undermined the country's economic growth. It impaired Mexico's agricultural development and weakened its industrial development because of the exodus of much-needed technicians. The nationalists criticized their countrymen for deserting Mexico in its time of need and exhorted their government to undertake greater, more sustained efforts to stop the draining of Mexico's lifeblood.

Mexico's leaders, however, did not view the exodus as catastrophic. They believed certain benefits accrued from the emigration of Mexicans. The money emigrants sent back to Mexico went directly to the neediest sectors within Mexican society. As the number of Mexicans working in the United States increased, so did the amount and number of remittances sent back to friends and relatives in Mexico. Remittances directly helped Mexico's ailing economy. Emigration also served as a political safety valve: disaffected and unemployed persons were dispelled, enticed by opportunities across the border. Although officials continually issued optimistic statements about Mexico's growth and development, the reality was otherwise. Leaders of the revolutionary era knew that Mexicans had taken up arms to ensure themselves a better way of life and would not hesitate to do so again if promises remained unfulfilled. Rebuilding the economy would take time. Emigration, even with its evils and problems, was one way in which officials could buy that time. Nonetheless, they remained sensitive to the idea that "any government which accepted the mantle of revolutionary legitimacy had to deal with migration in such a way that Mexico's vital national interests were given primacy."[3] Consequently, between 1907 and 1921 the Mexican government pursued ambivalent and oftentimes contradictory policies attempting to stop emigration, while believing that it should and must continue.

Consuls and the Problems of Emigration

The Mexican government's dilatory policy concerning emigration severely tested those entrusted with the protection and welfare of Mexican expatriates. The records are replete with letters, reports, and other correspondence from Mexican consular officials beseeching their superiors to implement more effective measures against emigration. In 1913 the consul in Galveston, Texas, proposed that emigration be stopped because of "the poor treatment accorded Mexicans." He believed that the suffering experienced by so many workers was largely due to "the ill-will people have against them, to their exploitation by men without conscience, and their ignorance which prevents them from defending themselves—ignorance born from their lack of experience and the difficulty in learning English."[4] He urged his superiors to impose high fines on anyone emigrating and institute a campaign to discourage emigration. Failure to do this, he warned, carried dire consequences for both the emigrants and their government. His superiors disagreed. They believed that the emigration of Mexicans was only a temporary phenomenon and thus no cause for alarm. The stream of complaints from Mexican officials in the United States indicated they were mistaken.

Consuls expressed a growing concern about the ever-widening path emigrants were following and the problems they encountered in faraway places. A report from the consul in Philadelphia described the wretched condition of his countrymen, many of whom lacked work, shelter, and clothing. Without resources, he complained, he could do nothing to help them. The consul urged his government to study the matter immediately. He cautioned that "so long as we fail to resolve our economic problems and one dollar is worth twenty-five or more pesos in Mexican currency, the decision to leave will not prove difficult for Mexican workers and tradesmen. . . . [T]he exodus of Mexican laborers to this country is such that it may profoundly damage our country, impeding our development." He suggested that agencies be established in Mexico to help place workers in the mines, industry, and farms of Mexico and that the government assume the costs of providing free transportation to these areas.[5]

By late 1916 Mexican officials realized that emigration was not a temporary phenomenon. Inundated by calls for help and at the behest of border state governors, President Venustiano Carranza instituted an intensive campaign to warn would-be emigrants of the prejudice and exploitation that awaited them north of the border. The publication of news items, government reports, and broadsides describing unfavorable conditions in the United States continued until Carranza's overthrow in 1920.

The attempts at moral suasion by the various regimes were ineffective in deterring Mexicans from leaving their homeland. Many Mexicans were illiterate and thus unable to read what was disseminated. Furthermore, many already knew about the poor treatment accorded Mexicans in the United States, having learned of it through the "grapevine" or from friends or relatives who had already been there. Because this knowledge did not discourage them, it is unlikely that even the ability to read such warnings would have had much effect. Mexicans also mistrusted their government and listened to its advice with skepticism. Many assumed there was more to fear from their government and its agents than from employers and officials in the United States. Staying entailed greater risks than leaving because in Mexico they faced hunger, starvation, exploitation, violence, and death. In the words of one consul, the "representations made by Mexican authorities made very little impression on Mexicans of the laboring classes. At San Luís Potosí, especially during the year of 1918, I examined hundreds of Mexican applicants for passport visas. . . . Nearly all had friends in the United States. . . . [They] told me that they placed no reliance whatsoever on representations made by their own government officials, and that they felt assured of good treatment in the United States."[6] Mexican officials failed to recognize that as long as their citizens questioned their veracity and sincerity, their efforts to discourage emigration would fail. No greater testament exists to this fact than the continued growth in the numbers who emigrated.

Mexican Government Initiatives vis-à-vis Emigration

The economic depression of 1921 in the United States; the overwhelming number of appeals from consuls, braceros, and charitable organizations; and the thousands of destitute nationals whose presence wreaked economic havoc on border cities ended the government's complacent attitude. Again Mexican consuls led the call for action.

In a report to President Alvaro Obregón, the consul general in New York, whose area of responsibility included the Midwest, wrote about the suffering the depression brought to Mexicans. He urged his government to heed his pleas to seriously study the matter of emigration and develop effective plans to deal with it. "The jails of the United States are filled with Mexicans who, driven by hunger and desperation, steal and kill and are condemned to prison or are executed. This is the sad fate which awaits those who, in search of a better life, come, ignorant of everything and without resources, to this inhospitable country."[7]

Another consul argued, "To date, the massive number of Mexican emigrants to the United States, which represents a total of about two million people, or approximately 14% of the Republic's total population, is not only a loss to the nation but a source of considerable cost, as well as a source of constant international difficulties." The loss of manpower, he opined, threatened the well-being of the nation and deprived Mexico of a natural resource it could ill afford to lose. "From an economic viewpoint," he wrote, "each time the United States experiences an economic crisis, the Mexican government is required to make considerable expenditures to financially assist or repatriate those who are abandoned without protection in our neighboring republic." Mexico's interests, he suggested, were better served by paying more attention to the needs of expatriates.[8]

Although the unpleasant realities of 1921–1922 convinced Mexican officials of the need for more effective methods to help Mexican nationals in the United States, they did not change the prevailing belief that halting the exodus was not in the best interests of the country. Presidents Alvaro Obregón, Plutarco Calles, and Emilio Portes Gil continued to believe that the economic and political benefits derived from emigration outweighed the disadvantages.

Emigration was also a countervailing influence in the government's struggles with the Catholic Church. Because of the deepening religious controversy in Mexico, Obregón and Calles needed the support of returning nationals. Mexican leaders considered the Catholic Church an impediment to progress, industrialization, and modernization. They believed that the exposure of Mexicans to American Protestant society was beneficial because it would instill in them the work ethic and more secular views. They hoped that Mexicans would return with more anti-Catholic sentiments and support them in their struggles against the church.[9]

The decisions that Obregón and his successors made to address the question of emigration were fueled by several considerations. Firstly, they did not actively discourage emigration because of the economic, political, and social benefits they attributed to the process. Secondly, the crisis of 1921 embarrassed Mexico because it clearly demonstrated that the much-heralded promises of the revolution remained unfulfilled. People still left Mexico in record numbers, and when the need arose, the government failed to help them. Mexican officials were determined not to be caught unprepared again. Their plans and policies thus manifested a new intensity and overall purpose. Thirdly, Mexican leaders recognized that emigration was not a temporary phenomenon. Because of this, the new emigration policies and programs were geared toward harnessing emigration for the benefit of Mexico. Finally, because emigration had become a way of life and contained certain benefits for Mexico, programs emphasized assisting the large Mexican community already in the United States. Efforts were concentrated on expanding the functions of consular representatives and providing them with greater support in carrying out their responsibilities. The new programs proved difficult to implement and met with mixed results.

Consuls in the United States

Some of the consulates had been active in championing the causes of Mexicans in the United States, even though consuls were hamstrung by bureaucratic regulations and inadequate financial support. Regulations expressly prohibited consuls from meddling in the political affairs of their assigned country. Consuls were directed to maintain good relations with the authorities, particularly those involved in business and commerce.[10] The primary responsibilities of

> all agents and employees of the consular corps [were] to make every effort to establish favorable commercial relations between the Republic and the respective countries assigned them; provide protection to Mexicans residing or traveling in them; defend the good name of the Republic; inform the Government when they [deemed] it necessary about such matters; and form good relations with those authorities and residents who [were] primarily engaged in commerce in their respective districts.[11]

Consuls were inconsistent in carrying out their duties and selectively ignored or adhered to the regulations. For consuls in the United States, the first three decades of the twentieth century held numerous challenges because of the oppression and discrimination experienced by Mexicans. Some became staunch advocates for their communities, working long hours to help nationals in any way they could. Others simply ignored the problems in their districts and concentrated on developing stronger commercial relations.

Consuls in the Midwest

Consuls rendered a wide variety of services to Mexicans in the Midwest. Initially the main concern for consuls was assisting Mexicans who had been arrested in the United States. Like their counterparts in the Southwest, they investigated complaints about the lack of due process and the violation of civil rights. Another major responsibility was mediating disputes between Mexican nationals and their employers.

Disputes often arose when companies failed to pay wages or disability insurance to workers or their families. Consuls were also asked by local communities or individuals to help in repatriation.

Mexicans were no more inclined to criminal tendencies than any other group in the United States; however, their unfamiliarity with ordinances and laws and their inability to speak English exacerbated problems with law enforcement agencies. Mexicans were victimized by prejudiced policemen or judges who applied harsh sentences for minor infractions. Because many Mexicans were not U.S. citizens, they were often denied due process or fair trials. Some who were arrested did not even know what charges had been filed against them.

Unable to defend themselves or to afford proper legal advice, Mexicans turned to their consuls for help. Unfortunately, consuls were limited in the measures they could take. They were permitted to provide funds for lawyers, yet such funds were finite or nonexistent. They could investigate and, if they found irregularities, could appeal to the court's or police's sense of justice. If that failed, they had to pursue diplomatic channels through Mexico City and Washington, D.C. This often proved a long and frustrating path, which seldom yielded satisfactory results.

The records of consular activities in the Midwest before 1920 are incomplete and sketchy. The political instability that followed the overthrow of Díaz in 1911 precluded the development of a well-trained, highly organized, and professional consular corps. Because consuls were political appointees, turnover tended to be high. Reporting of activities, which was required of them, was erratic and fragmentary. Reports were often misplaced or destroyed. Inadequate funding and staffing made keeping up with the required paperwork very difficult. Before 1920, fifty-one consuls served the needs of nationals in the United States, and most of them were assigned to the Southwest.

In the Midwest the small size of the population, its highly mobile nature, and its widely scattered settlements worsened the problems faced by consuls. For example, the jurisdiction of the consulate in Kansas City, Missouri, spanned the territory of western Missouri, Kansas, Nebraska, and South Dakota. The estimated Mexican population for this area was about 25,000 in 1920, with the majority concentrated in Kansas. According to census figures, Kansas had 13,770 Mexicans within its boundaries, 5,000 of whom lived in the Kansas City area.[12] An additional 10,000 Mexicans probably lived in Kansas but were not counted in the census because they had entered the United States illegally. The jurisdiction of consuls in Chicago, Detroit, Philadelphia, and New York also covered wide areas and required them to serve large numbers of people.

Because it was a major distributing point for Mexican railroad workers, Kansas became a major focus of resettlement in the early years of migration to the Midwest. By 1914 Mexicans in Kansas City, Missouri, numbered over 3,000. It was an active and thriving community, having its own major Spanish-language newspaper, several small commercial businesses, and a consulate. The reports filed by the consuls in Kansas City were typical of those surviving from other midwestern cities. They contained information about the needs, status, and problems of the community, which included legal problems, police brutality, and discrimination.[13]

In one 1915 case, four Mexicans were charged with larceny by their employer. They were provided with legal counsel and an interpreter. After a hotly contested trial, they were found guilty as charged and sentenced to serve five to ten years in the state penitentiary. The prosecuting attorney, however, later told a fellow attorney that the defense attorneys had not "showed much interest and that he considered them a joke." Further investigation convinced the second attorney that the men had been "framed." He then informed the Mexican consul of his findings and encouraged him to seek an appeal "because if the trial is as reported to you and the prosecuting attorney used the arguments reported to have been used there is no doubt in my mind [that] the case could at least be reversed and a new trial ordered."[14] Unfortunately neither the convicted men nor the consul had the money to file an appeal, and so no appeal for a new trial was made.

A Mexican official later lamented that, because of the lack of money, the consulate was unable to help these men and others like them. For him this tragedy underscored the need for local communities to organize themselves and provide assistance when needed.[15] The four men, who might have been innocent, were forced to serve their sentence because their government lacked the resources to pay for an appeal.

Consuls toured facilities where Mexicans were incarcerated to ascertain if they were being treated properly. On such visits, which were infrequent, they listened to inmates, took down requests, and tried to cheer them up. Consuls reported that Mexicans were mostly well treated, although inmates did complain about the food and job assignments.[16] Mexicans, they reported, were generally given the harder, dirtier, and least desirable jobs. Some of the men protested their innocence or claimed that although their terms had expired, they were refused release. Three Mexicans in one prison had already completed their sentences but were still incarcerated. They told a visiting reporter they had contacted the Mexican consul, who had promised to look into the matter some time before. Since then they had heard nothing.[17]

Stories about the tragic plight of Mexicans in American jails were commonplace, and most had a basis in fact. When consuls failed to respond to pleas for relief from prisoners or their friends and families, bitter attacks ensued. People angrily declared that their government had abandoned them and cared nothing for their welfare. These complaints were a source of deep concern to Mexican officials, who tried to ameliorate the problem. One official noted the following:

> The actions of the Government should not be limited to its own national boundaries, for it has the sacred obligation to do whatever it can for the defense and protection of Mexicans who find themselves in a foreign land in dire circumstances. If their own government is not interested in their well-being, if it does not help them, and if it does not protect them, then it has no right to complain that foreign peoples and their government treat them with great cruelty, and with the deepest contempt.[18]

Some consuls were irresponsible and showed little compassion for the people they were assigned to represent. Those from the upper classes tended to look askance at their working-class countrymen. Because of their own prejudices, they willingly embraced the negative attitudes of Anglo-Americans toward Mexicans and did not feel compelled to defend them from charges or imprisonment. Other consuls were simply incompetent and often failed to follow up on investigations or promises. Some officials, however, argued that there was another side to the question about consuls and their duties.

Consuls and Mexican Nationals

In a memorandum written in 1922 on the principal reasons why consuls were unable to provide more effective service to Mexican nationals, one official noted that emigrants had unrealistic expectations about what the consul could do.

> There exists among our nationals who live in the United States the firmly vested belief that "their Consul," as they call us, has unlimited power at his disposal when one of them is the victim of violence and injustices, but when they have come to him and have learned the bitter truth, they divest themselves of their illusions and express their resentment, not against the Government, but rather against "their consul," that functionary [who has] not heard them, or who has not helped them.[19]

This resentment, he stated, was unfair. The fault, in his opinion, was not solely that of the consuls; they did the best they could under the circumstances. He posited, "the plight of Mexicans in the United States is attributable to (a) their ignorance, which is absolute; (b) their indolence in registering with their consulates; and (c) the prejudice against our people, which has greatly intensified during the past ten years, because of the propaganda of the movies and the press." These three conditions, he wrote, placed Mexican emigrants at a greater disadvantage than other nationalities. "Because of the lack of adequate legal counsel, the jails and penitentiaries of the United States . . . are full of Mexicans. . . . I could cite specific cases of Mexicans who were condemned to life imprisonment who were perfectly innocent and who attained their freedom after ten or more years of confinement thanks to the energy and tenacity of their consuls."[20] He believed the chances of gaining a new trial or the release of Mexicans who were tried and sentenced were minimal. He estimated that less than 6 percent of the inmates who sought help from their consuls were released because of the consul's intervention.[21] Indeed, the process of helping those in prison was often a slow and frustrating one that seldom netted results.

The files in Mexico City are filled with letters from friends, families, and local officials attesting to the good character and behavior of someone who had been arrested in the United States. Most letters and petitions for clemency were of little avail. The correspondence also expressed concern, hope, frustration, and gratitude from people for whatever help the consuls could provide.[22] One such letter thanked a consul for his repeated attempts since 1916 to secure the release of a Mexican prisoner. The letter, dated 12 August 1921, noted the importance of the consul's help, "especially when it seeks to alleviate the suffering of our compatriots who, unfortunately, due to the need to seek food for their children, cross the border, settling in the United States, where they are always treated mercilessly."[23]

Discrimination, acts of violence against Mexicans, and police brutality also drew the attention and intervention of the consuls. Consuls enjoyed a little more success in addressing these problems because of their ability to garner the support of the community and liberal-minded officials and citizens. They could also intercede in blatant cases through diplomatic channels.

In 1911 the Mexican ambassador wrote to the U.S. secretary of state about the shooting death of a national in Wichita, Kansas, by a policeman. In the same letter the ambassador described the wounding of a national by a policeman in Macksville, Kansas, and the assault on two other Mexicans in Ingalls, Kansas. He expressed deep concern about the "ill will that seems to prevail in the State of Kansas against the Mexicans." He asked Secretary of State Philander Knox to persuade Kansas authorities to "extend proper guarantees to the Mexicans" in that state to prevent the alarmingly frequent recurrence of assaults on Mexicans.[24] Knox informed the ambassador that his letter had been forwarded to the governor of Kansas for action.

Governor William Stubbs responded that, "based upon a very rigid inquiry," the Mexican ambassador had little to worry about concerning the mistreatment of Mexicans. "The fact is that nearly all the trouble arises between the Mexicans themselves and involves Americans only when the latter are called in, usually as officers of the law, to preserve the peace and adjust their differences." Having said that, he made this qualification: "I would not be understood to convey to the Ambassador the idea that his countrymen in Kansas are a bad set. That would be unjust, for they are not. On the whole I think they are entitled to a great deal of consideration for their conduct under the conditions of life they live."[25] In his opinion, gambling disputes were at the center of much of the trouble among Mexicans and were also at the root of the specific cases referred to him. The governor, however, was informed that the Mexican killed in Wichita had no part in the quarrel. "He was said to be an industrious and inoffensive man and the best citizens of Wichita regretted the tragedy very much." The case of the Mexican wounded in Macksville "appears to be a parallel to the Wichita case." In two of the three incidents, innocent Mexicans were shot by police, yet the governor maintained there was little need for concern. "My inquiries, as a whole, reveal strikingly satisfactory relations between the Mexicans and the Kansas people who have to deal with them."[26]

Mexicans and Local Law-Enforcement Authorities

Tense relations between the police and Mexicans prevailed throughout the era. In Nebraska a Mexican accused of killing a detective was murdered by a group of armed and infuriated citizens while the police watched.[27] In Chicago and the Calumet region, conflicts between the police and Mexicans were common. Much of the friction arose over arbitrary raids and arrests in areas heavily populated by Mexicans. One Mexican in Chicago was angered by such raids: "The police searched the Mexican's [sic] houses without warrants [during the Mexican-Polish troubles] and let the crowd hit their Mexican prisoners while they were in custody."[28] *Mexico,* a locally published, Spanish-language newspaper in Chicago, also condemned these arbitrary raids:

> In Chicago the Mexicans have been the victims more than two dozen times at the hands of the police, those abusive half-breeds who take advantage of uniforms and shining badges to perpetrate attacks on our people at the door of

the dance-hall at Hull House, simply because it suited their fancy. . . . [W]hen honorable and decent Mexicans are jailed merely at the whim of the police WE PROTEST VIOLENTLY. WE WILL NOT PERMIT SUCH ATTACKS; WE WILL CONTINUE TO PROTEST, LET IT COST US WHAT IT MAY.[29]

Another complaint from Mexicans was that the police always favored other nationalities or "their own kind" when it came to settling interethnic disturbances.

"The average policeman's attitude is still against the Mexicans, the police are largely Irish and Polish," said one Mexican who resided in the stockyards district of Chicago. A Mexican from Indiana Harbor stated: "The policemen here are hard on the Mexicans. . . . The Mexicans take a lot of abuse in this town. The authorities are always after us. . . . A Pole gets drunk and the policeman takes him home. If another white commits a crime he has a chance to get away with it; not a Mexican."[30]

Consuls and citizens alike protested the numerous shootings of Mexicans by policemen. A resident of Indiana Harbor told an interviewer, "A policeman killed a Mexican recently. Just because a Mexican is drunk they hit him or do anything to him." In Gary some Mexicans armed themselves for protection. "One reason the Mexicans carry guns is because of their relations with the police. The latter, especially in Indiana Harbor, shoot the Mexicans with little provocation. One shot a Mexican who was walking away from him, and laughed as the body was thrown into the patrol wagon."[31]

Consuls' Efforts on Behalf of Mexicans

Although some consuls were criticized for their lack of action,[32] others fought hard to end such abusive practices. The Mexican consul in Chicago, for example, was cited for contempt of court when he challenged the manner in which a man was being tried. He accused the judge of exhibiting prejudice and denying the accused man due process. Later the judge rescinded the sentence when he learned of the consul's diplomatic immunity.[33]

Consuls toured labor camps and visited companies employing Mexicans. They negotiated with employers to ensure that nationals received adequate pay for their work and workman's compensation for job-related injuries. They responded to inquiries and complaints from workers and their families about undelivered checks, discrepancies in pay, and insurance claims that had not been paid to the disabled or their survivors. Consuls also collected the belongings and money, if any, left by deceased nationals and, despite difficulties with inaccurate addresses, forwarded them to their homes in Mexico.

Consuls helped prepare and file legal documents and found people who were missing or had failed to inform their families of their whereabouts. Whenever possible they provided assistance to the needy or arranged their return to Mexico. Results varied from consul to consul, depending on his training, experience, and commitment to the job. Other factors also affected their performance: staffing; funding; personality; the extent of local cooperation, established networks, and contacts; personal attitudes and prejudices concerning their own people; the political situation in Mexico; and the amount of support they could muster from their superiors.

New Measures for Helping Mexicans after 1921

As stated earlier, the disastrous experiences after the economic slump in 1921 demonstrated to Mexican officials the need for revamping and expanding their assistance to expatriates in the United States. President Alvaro Obregón modified the existing bureaucratic structure to make it more responsive to the needs and problems of emigrants. These changes included establishing in 1921 the Department of Repatriation within the Secretariat of Foreign Relations. Consular officials in the United States were also required to establish standard procedures and budgets for assisting repatriates.[34]

Under the new directives instituted by Obregón and his successors, consuls were required to undertake periodic and exact censuses of Mexican nationals within their districts. They had to be more assertive and consistent in their protective roles, actions that some had accused them of failing to take. They were required to report accurately and promptly all cases involving denial of due process to their superiors in Mexico City. They had to file detailed reports on every national jailed in their jurisdiction. Irregularities in police practices and judicial procedures also had to be reported. Failure to give the necessary attention to these new directives carried severe reprimands and the threat of dismissal. In essence consuls were required to "omit no effort whatsoever" in aiding and protecting their fellow citizens. Precise reports on incidents involving violations of rights were crucial because they would be used to determine whether the Secretary of Foreign Relations would take diplomatic action through the consuls or other channels.[35]

The new directives required consuls to help unemployed Mexicans obtain jobs and financial aid until employment could be secured. This requirement forced consuls to familiarize themselves with the funding and services provided by public and private charities. They were also directed to continue their vigilance against acts of discrimination and segregation. To help assuage anti-Mexican attitudes, consuls were asked to combat propaganda and misrepresentations about the Mexican people. To achieve this, conscientious consuls sought public forums to educate the public about the nefarious effects of such stereotypes.[36]

Mexicans and their representatives remained sensitive to the negative images common at this time and openly criticized their perpetuation by the popular media. In Chicago and other midwestern communities, consuls worked to ban the showing of films that depicted Mexicans in unflattering terms. Some consuls asked local officials to help persuade theater operators that showing such films was detrimental to good relations between the United States and Mexico and offensive to Mexican residents. They also asked Mexican leaders in the community to exert whatever pressure they could. Some consuls succeeded in discouraging movie-house operators from showing such films. The consul in Chicago reported that he had been able to convince local officials and theater operators to stop showing a documentary on the Mexican revolution because it reinforced the idea that Mexicans were cruel, barbaric, and destructive. A few days after his pleas, the film was removed from local theaters. Another consul reported that he had worked hard to cultivate good relations with local and state officials and had persuaded them and others that they could safely trade and invest in Mexico. These same people, he noted, had been extremely helpful in suppressing films prejudicial to Mexico and discouraging their showing in local movie houses.

Newspapers were also accused of distorting events in Mexico and promoting anti-Mexican sentiments. To stem the influx of distorted and unflattering news items, consuls asked U.S. postal authorities to restrict the dissemination of false reports about the activities of bandits along the border. Mexicans contended that newspapers did not often differentiate between lawless bands and revolutionaries. One consul asserted that much of the adverse "propaganda" against Mexico came from El Paso, "a place known for its chauvinistic attitudes." There "Mexicans of questionable character and other traitors" used the press "to foment friction and controversy in our country."[37]

Consul Edmundo Martínez was referring to the stream of critical news stories printed by an El Paso newspaper, which was receiving money from sources opposed to President Carranza. According to a later report, this paper repeatedly called for U.S. intervention in Mexico in 1919. Behind these machinations was General L. T., a powerful political figure in Chihuahua, who had been divested of much of his power by Carranza. The truth came out when Mexican agents released a letter written to him by the publisher of the El Paso paper. In startling detail, the letter outlined the collusion between this man and the paper. The publisher essentially admitted to printing false news items in return for specified sums of money. He was demanding more money because these dishonest practices had caused some problems for him and the newspaper.

[W]e wish to call your attention to the fact that our exaggerated news—so evidently yellow journalism—does not produce the effect that might be desired. . . . Our attacks, systematically made in [our newspaper], upon the Carranza government, in accordance with your desires, are founded upon questionable information supplied by correspondents who obey the order to communicate to us happenings that occur on the other side of the Río Grande, carefully changed so as to ridicule the government of a neighboring country.[38]

The publisher complained that the slanted reporting of events undermined the paper's credibility. He had decided to report the news accurately, "unless the subsidy which we now receive is increased to double the present current monthly rate." He concluded, "You will readily understand that the loss of prestige is very great, resulting in a publication which, for the sake of one individual . . . changes its news . . . in order to discredit the constituted government of a neighboring country."[39] Obviously the loss of prestige could be mitigated by more money.

Consuls and Segregation

Consuls were sometimes asked by their community to investigate and protest segregationist policies against Mexicans. In Kansas City, Missouri, local Mexican residents and their newspaper complained that hospitals had assigned Mexicans to "Black wards." The paper described this as a "barbarous custom" and demanded an end to this practice. The consul first approached the hospitals without any result. He then took his case to the local press, which supported his request that this practice be stopped. Afterwards he met with the mayor, who promised he would do everything in his power to ensure that Mexicans would be treated "like the white race." The mayor kept his promise and the practice of segregating Mexicans with Blacks in Kansas City ended. *El Cosmopolita* praised the mayor and the consul for their hard work and dedication in obtaining just treatment for Mexicans.[40] It also cautioned readers that much more remained to be done and asked the consul and community to continue their fight for equality. The desire for complete equality, however, remained an unfulfilled dream because discrimination and segregation against Mexicans continued.

In 1925 Mexican school children in Kansas remained segregated. In Kansas City, Kansas, the Mexican consul persuaded his government to formally protest this practice. Mexico filed a series of protests in Washington, but failed to obtain any results. Although sympathetic to these complaints, Washington officials declared it a matter for local authorities to resolve.[41] The segregation of Mexican students continued in many parts of the United States until the 1960s.

Investigating Unscrupulous Practices

Mexicans in the United States often fell prey to unscrupulous businesses that took advantage of their trust and inexperience. Occasionally victims turned to consuls for help. Although it was often too late to help them, consuls nonetheless investigated these charges to warn others about questionable and dishonest practices.

A common complaint was the exorbitant fees that lawyers charged to clients. One consul reported that a Mr. Martínez had paid $500 for an attorney to defend him on a charge of disorderly conduct. The attorney had also taken his savings book. After he had paid $25 in bail, the accused went to see Consul Rafael Aveleyra, who patronizingly described Martínez as a "peon, ignorant and timid." Nonetheless, Aveleyra contacted the attorney and demanded that she repay Martínez $400 and withdraw from the case. He reported that he had received numerous complaints about this attorney, who "dedicates herself to exploiting Mexicans by telling them that she is their good friend." He had decided, he wrote, to gather as much evidence as possible and bring her before the Bar Association. Whether he did so or not is unknown. His inquiries and accusations, however, netted him a powerful enemy. According to Aveleyra, after the incident with Martínez, the attorney dedicated herself to undermining his credibility in the community, telling its members that "the new consul had besmirched her in a most vile manner."[42]

In another incident involving questionable practices, Aveleyra reported on the activities of a local technical school. He stated that he and the consuls from Cuba, Bolivia, Guatemala, and Costa Rica had received numerous complaints about this college. Representatives from the school recruited students from throughout Latin America, promising them a diploma after a "short" course of study and employment while they were working on their degree.

> All of this is nothing more than a deception, and the poor youths who come after making uncounted sacrifices, are

forced to work as dishwashers, bell boys, and even "peons,"
while the college, after taking all that they have, leaves them
to the mercy of their own fortunes, or denounces them to
immigration authorities so that they are deported. . . . [These
individuals] took great pains not to make themselves legally responsible and it was almost impossible to prove any
wrong-doing.[43]

The consuls were unable to do much except ask their respective governments to establish measures to prevent this college from further publicity and recruitment in Mexico and elsewhere.

That consuls had a difficult job is unquestionable. Officials from
Relaciónes Exteriores pleaded with Mexican leaders to institute changes
to support consuls. After 1920 several recommendations emerged. Some
came from Relaciónes Exteriores, whereas others emanated from the
executive level. One proposal outlined a system of stronger legal representation for Mexicans in the United States.[44] Another urged the home
government to follow the examples of Poland and Italy in protecting the
interests of its nationals abroad. According to this proposal, such a program would net Mexico not only greater good will from its people, but
also greater financial rewards.[45] Although both proposals held promise,
they were never implemented because of the high cost, lack of trained
personnel, time considerations, and inability to rally support from the
expatriate communities in the United States.[46]

Consuls and Mutual Aid Societies

A third proposal recommended making greater use of the mutual
aid societies in the United States. Although the number of consuls in the
United States rose from fifty-one to sixty during the 1920s, this increase
proved insufficient to meet the new and expanded duties imposed on
consuls by the government and by a growth in emigration. Because of
this inadequacy, the Mexican government encouraged its consuls to develop organizations that would help them serve the community. These
efforts resulted in the creation of Las Comisiones Honoríficas (the Honorary Commissions) and La Cruz Azul Mexicana (the Mexican Blue
Cross).

Members of the Honorary Commissions were appointed by the local consul, who also served as honorary presidents of their organizations. Membership was open only to men, usually the most respected members of the Mexican community. These commissions worked with the consul on behalf of resident and immigrant Mexicans. Their purpose was to serve as a conduit between the consul and the community and advise the consul on matters pertaining to the community's welfare. In areas lacking a consulate, the commissions were to report any instances of discrimination, exploitation, or abuse to the nearest consul. They were also asked to take statements concerning work-related accidents; assign representatives to visit jails, hospitals, schools, and work camps; plan and attend educational conferences; and assist in sponsoring patriotic festivals. Because they were quasi-official bodies, members received no pay for their work.

The female counterpart of the Honorary Commissions was the Mexican Blue Cross. Its role was to assist the Honorary Commissions in fulfilling their responsibilities. Its primary function, however, was to ensure the welfare of Mexican nationals and their families. The Blue Cross was asked to raise funds in the community for Mexicans who fell on hard times, including those who were unemployed, injured, ill, or without a provider. The organization could also use these funds to provide transportation back to Mexico for those who needed it.

Although the idea of using mutual aid societies to assist consuls and nationals had its merits, the results were largely disappointing. Members of these organizations were not given the necessary financial support to launch successful and sustained efforts. Membership seldom exceeded fifty, which meant that sums collected from dues were minimal. In 1930, following an extensive inspection tour throughout the United States, Enrique A. González, the consul general of Mexico, issued a report containing the main reasons for the failure of these organizations to fulfill their responsibilities. In his opinion the Blue Cross was ineffective because much of its membership consisted of women from the working class who had other obligations to meet. Housework, the need to supplement the family income, and dire economic straits did not allow them the time to perform the various duties required by the organization.

Furthermore, the Brigades [of the Blue Cross], almost without exception, have been characterized by discord, jealousy,
and disagreements in our colonias. Their existence is either
fictitious or ephemeral and its practical usefulness is relative. . . . There are many places where there are no Brigades of
the Blue Cross, in which case the situation has been found to
be neither better nor worse for the Mexicans found there.[47]

González attributed the lack of success and deterioration of these
organizations to the lack of compensation for the work their members
performed. He stated, "[T]here are few who have the virtue who will do
good for the sake of good."[48] He attributed the poor organizational
efficiency and profitability of these organizations to the low educational
level of their members. Other causes cited by González included (1) the
propensity of Mexicans to treat differences of opinion as a matter of
conceit, which gave rise to disunity and the weakening of cooperation;
(2) the efforts of the Catholic clergy to disrupt these organizations in an
attempt to get revenge against the government; (3) the tendency for one-
man rule; (4) extremely complicated rules and regulations that were not
understood by the members; (5) the lack of one director to coordinate
the activities of the other executives; (6) the high mobility of its members, who had to seek work to support themselves; and (7) the rancor
caused by political factionalism.[49]

"The major problem with these organizations is their internal
dissension. Since the consul does not have at his disposal the means to
placate or assuage them, except through moral suasion . . . there arise all
kinds of incidents which plague the Consul . . . which at times has
caused him to disband the Commissions or Brigades, given the ineffectiveness of their work or the difficulties involved in directing them."[50]
Despite these problems, González stated that the Honorary Commissions should be continued in order to assist consuls in protecting Mexicans. He called, however, for the elimination of the Blue Cross Brigades
that were not fulfilling their missions.[51]

González's comments should be placed in their proper perspective.
His reports exhibit strong class and gender biases. He attributes the
organizations' lack of success to the "low cultural levels" of the women

and to inherent defects in the Mexican people. It is noteworthy that he called for the elimination of the Blue Cross, the women's auxiliary, even though his report indicates that similar problems plagued both organizations. Certainly the Honorary Commissions, when properly funded, led, and organized, performed useful services to their communities. The same can be said for the Blue Cross. In fact, the Blue Cross provided greater and more direct aid to the community than its male counterpart by providing food, clothing, heating fuel, and financial assistance to the needy. The Honorary Commissions, on the other hand, emphasized social, legal, and patriotic programs. This clarification does not demean the latter's efforts; rather, it shows that the Blue Cross's role was just as important as that of the commissions, yet the Blue Cross was marked for eradication.

The time in which González made his tour and report must also be considered. In 1929 the United States entered the Great Depression. The large-scale unemployment that ensued, coupled with the demand for aid, overtaxed the meager resources of these organizations. The dissension, controversy, and poor management skills that González cited may have been partially due to the added stresses and demands placed upon members and leaders. In a crisis situation, weaknesses and controversies are usually magnified. González's report failed to mention the external causes of the problems that plagued these organizations, including the inability or unwillingness of the Mexican government to provide adequate guidance and support.

Consuls: An Assessment

As late as 1930 the consul general noted that Mexicans in the United States were subject to abuse, mistreatment, and exploitation. Their lack of familiarity with the language and social and legal customs of the United States only compounded those difficulties. Their lives were fraught with uncertainty. Massive emigration, however, continued and grew in the 1920s. This trend forced the Mexican government to undertake greater efforts to protect and serve the needs of its nationals. These efforts included plans to expand the consular corps's duties and responsibilities, continue the publicity campaign against emigration, and reinforce loyalty to Mexico. These programs, however, were largely doomed to fail. Like earlier programs, they consisted of mostly hit-or-miss activities or ad hoc solutions to serious problems. Like previous efforts, they were poorly funded. Attempts to pay for these programs through a head tax on emigrants met with complete failure.[52]

The inability of the government to address the problems associated with emigration in an effective manner placed great pressures on the consuls. The massive emigration of Mexicans to the United States presented them with serious challenges. They found themselves financially and organizationally unprepared to meet the voluminous requests for assistance. Their unpreparedness was partially due to the amorphous and changing nature of their roles and responsibilities. Because most consuls were political appointees, the quality and experience of individual consuls varied, and most received their training on the job. Using political appointees prevented the continuity necessary to make an impact because changing policies and administrations led to high turnover in consular personnel. Their lack of power in the host country forced consuls to rely on networks and personal contacts within their region for support. These networks often required a great deal of time and effort to develop and cultivate. Months and even years of work could be destroyed by a reassignment or dismissal. The continued problem of inadequate financing undercut most consular efforts.

Not all of the problems faced by consuls were due to external factors. Consuls also undermined their own credibility, authority, and purpose. Class differences influenced how consuls were viewed by their communities. Because consuls were drawn from the upper and middle classes of Mexican society, they tended to hold attitudes of cultural and social superiority over working-class Mexicans. This snobbery sometimes created tensions that undermined cooperative efforts between the consuls and their communities. Consuls' attitudes were often reflected in their choice of associates or appointees, who served in various ex-officio capacities. Consuls sometimes agreed with the prevailing racist attitudes in American society. Some even disassociated themselves from the very people they were assigned to protect and serve.

Mistrust and disillusion also affected consuls. Mexican officials repeatedly stressed the importance of having nationals register with the nearest consul to determine areas and extent of need. Many Mexicans, however, refused to register because they suspected ulterior motives. For example, in 1916 consuls asked people to register after informing them that hostilities between Mexico and the United States were imminent. A newspaper article alleged that the real reason behind the registration drive was to ascertain the sympathies of emigrants in case of war.[53] Registration was also viewed as a government attempt to ferret out and intimidate political exiles and critics.

The uncertainty surrounding their appointment led some consuls to focus their efforts on developing and cementing arrangements with the American business community for their own personal gain. Consuls were also accused of misappropriating funds destined for expatriates and of manipulating the internal affairs of mutual aid societies for their own selfish ends.[54]

Mexican perceptions and inflated expectations undermined the effectiveness and credibility of consuls. The desperate situation of many Mexicans and the absence of ready aid led them to view consuls as lifelines and founts of information and assistance. When consuls failed to live up to these high expectations, bitterness and disillusionment quickly set in. Mexican nationals decried the lack of attention and support from their government. Much of their ire was directed at consuls. This behavior, in turn, provoked anger and resentment among consuls, who believed that the attacks against them were unjustified.

Critics have noted the shortcomings of consuls and their overall ineffectiveness in meeting the needs of Mexican nationals.[55] Dishonest, self-seeking, and incompetent individuals were present in the consular corps; so were honest, hard-working, and dedicated professionals who served the expatriate community to the best of their abilities. In judging the overall effectiveness of consuls, one must consider both the external and internal forces that affected their performance. Consuls were often victimized and hampered by inadequate funding, bureaucratic red tape, political machinations, and just plain indifference from their superiors. The obstacles magnified either their weaknesses as administrators and human beings or their personal integrity and strength of character. Most midwestern consuls, like their counterparts in the Southwest, exhibited concern and even compassion for Mexican emigrants. At times they represented the only hope for emigrants and the only buffer between Mexicans and the vicissitudes of living in a strange country. As a result of consuls' work, Mexicans in the United States became the objects of far more governmental concern than they had ever been shown when they lived in Mexico.

CHAPTER 6

Issues Affecting
Mexican Organizational Efforts

Patterns of Mexican migration and settlement usually followed the existing railroad network. Most Mexicans who traveled to the Midwest came from the states of Mexico's Central Plateau. Initially they had traveled to the Southwest, primarily to Texas and California, in search of employment or to escape the turbulence in Mexico. There they encountered compatriots from the northeast border states who had already claimed most of the employment opportunities in the Southwest. Many of them began leapfrogging over other bands of Mexicans to midwestern locales. Because of their central location and extensive railroad connections, cities such as Kansas City and St. Louis, Missouri, and Kansas City, Kansas, became major distribution points for Mexican workers and also retained sizable Mexican populations. Chicago and the Calumet region later supplanted these cities as primary destinations, but Missouri and Kansas continued to attract immigrants, who joined the flourishing communities scattered throughout the region.

The 1920s witnessed the high tide of Mexican immigration to the Midwest, as increased prosperity in the United States and continued unrest in Mexico attracted more people across the international border. Emigration from Mexico after World War I became more purposeful and reasoned than previously because Mexicans were more informed about opportunities in the United States. Information about the Midwest came from those who had crisscrossed the country in search of employment. Emigration from Mexico had become so common that if a person had not already traveled to the United States, he or she probably knew someone or about someone who had been there. Labor agents and contractors also played important roles in funneling workers to the region. The result was that Mexicans began developing preferences about where they would work and settle. This purposefulness was an important aspect in the creation of more stable and sizable communities; immigrants settled where friends and relatives from their own pueblos, villages, or states in Mexico had lived.

Most Mexicans in Kansas came from the states of Michoacán and Guanajuato in central Mexico. In Kansas City, Kansas, many Mexicans were from Tanganciuaro in Michoacán. The "Tangas" had first arrived in Kansas in 1907 as rail workers for the Santa Fe Railroad. By 1916 many had resettled in the Argentine neighborhood in Kansas City. The size of the Tanga community increased steadily as more newcomers relocated to the Argentine barrio after friends and relatives had acquired jobs for them in the railroad shops.[1] Topeka harbored a large number of Mexicans from Silao in Guanajuato. One resident estimated that 60 to 70 percent of the Mexicans in Topeka were from Guanajuato.[2] Similar groupings were scattered throughout the Midwest as individuals from particular Mexican locales or states sought out familiar faces and customs.

At times these groupings went beyond simply working and living in close proximity and exerted wider influence in their respective communities. In East Chicago most of the leaders and members of El Círculo de Obreros Católicos "San José," an influential organization in the Mexican community, were from the state of Jalisco.[3] These developments contributed to intragroup solidarity; however, they also fostered factionalism, as groups from other towns, states, or regions in Mexico asserted their ideas and leadership in the community.

Planned migration was also bolstered by the availability of better paying and relatively stable employment in the industrial centers of the Midwest. The outbreak of World War I and the enactment of restrictive immigration acts in 1917, 1921, and 1924 curtailed immigration from Asia and Europe, forcing industry, railroads, and agriculture to seek new sources of labor. Mexico's relative proximity and its exclusion from immigration quotas encouraged employers to actively recruit Mexicans. The railroad and agricultural industries, which had long been involved in bringing Mexicans to the United States, continued their recruiting efforts, but they now faced stiff competition from the steel, meat-packing, and auto industries. Among them was Henry Ford, who began employing more Mexicans to work in the auto industry throughout southern and eastern Michigan. The automobile industry was spared the need to recruit Mexicans because they highly coveted jobs in auto work. More than three-fourths of the Mexican auto workers in Detroit had originally come to Michigan as sugar beet workers.[4]

Between 1900 and 1929 the United States was racked by a series of recessions that disrupted community development among Mexican immigrants. Increased unemployment, repatriation, and discrimination in the work place during hard economic times forced Mexicans to return home. Many were unwilling to expose fiancées, spouses, or other family members to the economic uncertainty that characterized their lives in the United States. Although the United States entered a period of sustained growth in some economic sectors, Mexicans continued to suffer from seasonal fluctuations in industry and agriculture, which threatened job security and eroded wages.

Migration to the region before World War I was not solely migration by drift. The seasonal nature of their jobs and their below subsistence wages forced Mexicans to become a highly transient work force. The youthfulness of the Mexican population in the Midwest, their mobility, and the impermanence created by this mobility profoundly affected organizational and community-building efforts in the region. Many of the problems faced by those young transients, therefore, continued to plague their lives.

A Life Fraught with Difficulty

Most Mexicans who traveled to the Midwest were young, unattached males who had left their families behind. Between 50 and 70 percent were in their twenties and thirties.[5] For many of them, life in the Midwest was difficult. In Kansas City, Missouri, public welfare officers in 1913 reported that most Mexicans lived in "plague spots . . . cursed with crime, immorality, disease and contagion, bad housing and other evils."[6]

In Gary a labor department researcher found that Mexicans lived "in a crowded condition . . . in gloomy basements, . . . alley houses, . . . tenement houses and in the second and third stories of store buildings." Lacking sunlight and dissatisfied with the high rents, Mexicans also dreaded the coldness of the region.[7]

Living in overcrowded, substandard housing and relegated to the most menial and tedious jobs, Mexicans eagerly sought social outlets that offered some escape from their daily routine. They quickly discovered, however, that segregation and discrimination stringently restricted their social outlets. Restaurants, barbershops, public baths, and movie houses denied them service because of their ethnicity. These restrictions forced them to congregate on street corners or patronize less desirable places such as pool halls, speakeasies, and brothels. Although Prohibition was in effect, bootleg alcohol was easy to obtain, and alcohol fueled fears, frustrations, differences of opinion, and hostility. These pent-up emotions often erupted into violence involving shootings, knifings, and fistfights. At times communities such as East Chicago took on the atmosphere of a frontier town, replete with speakeasies, gambling casinos, and a reputation for lawlessness.

George Edson of the Labor Department reported that conditions in Indiana Harbor were just as bad.

> The lack of merry sounds of birds and breezes is supplied [*sic*] by the shrieking and clattering of passing trains, and a pall of smoke from steel mills spreads eternally over the landscape. The two blocks where these three avenues intersect Michigan Avenue are known as "the bucket of blood" because of the fights and murders that have occurred in that unhallowed district. Mexicans are not the only ones who have been responsible for the spilling of blood, for Indiana Harbor has a mongrel population.[8]

Reports about the amount of violence in Mexican neighborhoods were exaggerated by the press. One headline in a local paper read, "Drunken Mexican Goes on Rampage with Gun." The article stated that a Mexican had run "amuck" after drinking moonshine, fired shots at his family, and wounded his eight-year-old son. According to the report, he had then terrorized the community. An eyewitness, however, related a completely different account. The man was celebrating Mexican Independence Day. When his wife locked him out of the house because he was intoxicated, he forced his way in. His son, who became frightened, ran and hid under the bed. The father thought the person under the bed was another man whom his wife was attempting to hide. He retrieved his pistol and shot at the alleged intruder. The bullet struck his son in the rear. Fortunately, no one was seriously injured.[9] News of these incidents spilled over to the larger community, adding to and reinforcing stereotypes that depicted Mexicans as violent and uncivilized.

Travelers to the Midwest included a core of professionals and petite bourgeoisie. This group comprised business people, political exiles, attorneys, doctors, students, journalists, skilled and semiskilled laborers, artists, performers, and people who had friends or relatives in the United States. Some of them opened businesses and shops that catered to a Mexican clientele. Because of their business acumen, education, and concern, they formed the nucleus of a leadership committed to the protection of Mexicans, the perpetuation of Mexican culture, and loyalty to the homeland. Some became involved at the behest of local consuls, who appointed them to honorary positions or sought their advice. Others, regardless of their social, economic, or educational background, emerged as natural leaders, who took up the cause of their compatriots in an alien country.

As colonias in the Midwest grew and stabilized, Mexicans were better able to launch collective and concerted efforts to address the numerous problems that plagued them. Although the Mexican government had attempted to assist them through its consuls, their numbers, needs, and demands far exceeded the talents and resources of the consular corps. Mexicans increasingly turned to their own resources, skills, and leadership to address the pressing issues that confronted them. Among the more important ongoing issues and problems were concerns about acculturation, the erosion of traditional values among the youth, police-community relations, crime, the changing role of women, discrimination, prejudice, and the need for wholesome social and recreational outlets.

A Call for Reform

Civic, religious, and business leaders decried the lawlessness and violence in their communities. They believed that such behavior deterred decent people from moving in and contributed to the discrimination and mistreatment encountered by Mexicans. An editorial in Chicago's *Correo Mexicano,* declared that Mexicans in the United States had "never been treated badly." Those who had encountered mistreatment, according to the editor, had no one to blame but themselves. "Some of our young people are the cause of their own mistreatment. Their poor behavior, their degenerate vices, their ridiculous and absurd manners and behavior in public . . . undoubtedly cause them to be seen in a bad light." The author lamented the existence of brothels, the smoking of marijuana, petty thievery, and vagrancy, which tainted the reputation of decent, hardworking Mexicans. Those who knew their "proper place," continued the editor, had nothing to fear. "The majority, 95 percent of our people living in the United States, are laborers praised for their excellent work. They possess good habits, are law-abiding, humble and respectful." He believed it was unnecessary for the community to be concerned about actions taken against "degenerates" who had no right to arouse the public over mistreatment they so richly deserved.[10] Another article in *El Eco de la Patria,* a Detroit newspaper, assailed the "widespread use" of marijuana in the streets, pool halls, and work place. It warned the community about the detrimental effects of the "pernicious weed" and asked decent Mexicans to fight its use.[11]

In reporting incidents of a criminal or immoral nature, the Spanish-language press, which largely reflected the views of middle-class elites, typically called upon Mexicans to restore order, embrace moral tenets, be model citizens, and disassociate themselves from any actions that reflected poorly on their nationality. Members of *la gente preparada* (the educated people) were especially vehement in their desire to instill Mexicans with the "proper values." They bitterly assailed what they construed as unseemly behavior by their compatriots. Through newspapers, speeches, and lectures, they exhorted Mexicans in a Progressive-like manner to practice better hygiene, seek an education, work hard, be thrifty, and avoid bad company. The reform impulse was also reflected in the goals and programs adopted by their organizations. The impetus for reforms, however, was not solely rooted in the conditions of Mexicans in the United States. The seed had already been planted in Mexico and was part of a larger plan by the bourgeoisie to accomplish their social, economic, and political goals in the postrevolutionary era.

The Reform Impulse in Mexico

During the Porfiriato, traditionalists had expressed concern about the social and economic apparatuses that the state imposed to socialize the work force. They believed these mechanisms also undermined the moral fiber of the family and, by extension, the role of the man in the household. They accused the state of usurping the traditional functions of the family to make the people amenable to its goals. Among these goals was the development of a more efficient and pliable work force. Even after the demise of Porfirio Díaz, the ideas about the role of the state continued to enjoy wide popularity and support, especially among the bourgeoisie who assumed control of the revolutionary agenda after 1915.

The new ruling elite, which included elements from the provincial elite who had supported Venustiano Carranza and the *pequeña burgesia* who sided with the Obregónistas, envisioned a new Mexico characterized by economic growth and development. To them "the entrepreneur would create 'national conditions of work,' [whereas] the school would form proper values and habits [such as] punctuality, obedience to authority, love of work, and patriotism in the labor force."[12] These were some of the same goals envisioned by the Americanization movement in the United States.

The ascendancy of Alvaro Obregón added aggressiveness and flexibility to the program. Representing "a subclass of middle-echelon technicians, businessmen, and intelligentsia," Mexican reformers favored more open political participation for the masses under their control and direction. They also espoused nationalism, anticlericalism, and "just rewards" for the victorious revolutionary leadership within the parameters of a capitalist economy and private property.[13]

Although the new Mexican leadership that emerged after 1915 exhibited populist sympathy for the aspirations of the working class and the campesino, it was a carefully calculated sympathy intended to win over the allegiance of the people. Initially the elite had planned to use the labor unions, vocational schools, and other grass-root organizations to carry out their reorientation of the masses. In Mexico programs such as the Universidad Popular, the country's first university extension program, were implemented to orient and convert workers to the constitutionalist ideology. By encouraging workers to seek socially acceptable outlets, such as joining choirs and sports teams, these programs sought to divert workers from taverns, politics, and the streets, where pent up frustrations might explode.[14] According to Mary Vaughn, "Part of this scheme involved an effort to refocus working-class life on the family as the primary unit of association and emotional attachment. This thrust deepened in the 1920s with the *Secretaría de Educación Pública*'s organization of workers' cultural centers and night schools."[15]

Women, who were considered the primary socializing agents in the home, had to be enlisted in their cause. The new order, however, did not entail instituting major changes in the lives or roles of women. In fact, the programs of the bourgeoisie sought to perpetuate the subordination of women, thus continuing the patriarchal tradition that dated back to the Iberian Catholic and pre-Columbian traditions.[16] Again the intended outcomes of these programs mirrored those espoused by proponents of Americanization, settlement house workers, and members of corporate sociology departments.

The programs formulated by the elite envisioned women as wives and mothers who would continue serving as the "subjects" of men.[17] To accomplish this goal and instill in women the "proper values and habits," they sought to make women loyal to the nation-state rather than the Catholic Church. In the process women would retain "many of the values taught by the Church (restraint, submission, obedience, and modesty)" and adapt them to "a new ideology compatible with the needs and values of a bourgeois elite which emphasized work, discipline, savings, and national loyalty."[18] This goal, according to Justo Sierra, the architect of Mexico's public school system, would be achieved through the education and training of women.

In an address to students at the Escuela Miguel Lerdo de Tejada, a vocational training school for women, Sierra stressed the important role women would play in building Mexico's future by creating stable homes. "In all Mexican schools we are forming men and women for the home; this is our supreme goal. In doing this, we firmly believe that we are performing a service beyond comparison. . . . The educated woman will be truly one for the home; she will be the companion and collaborator of the man in the formation of the family. That is what we want and that is what you are being so firmly and morally prepared for."[19]

This ambitious program of "educating" women proved largely unsuccessful because the school system did not reach into many Mexican communities. Lacking the funds to support such an extensive educational endeavor, proponents of this program pursued other avenues, including the trade unions, which remained bastions of male conservatism.

Most of the programs to promote the goals of the bourgeoisie in Mexico failed. Continued revolutionary ferment and economic instability prevented the ruling elite from mustering enough money to fund the programs. Their attacks against the Catholic Church alienated many Mexicans and created a polarization that ultimately contributed to the Cristero revolt. The inability of the ruling elite to satisfy the land redistribution requirements of the populace and fulfill many of their revolutionary promises further undermined their limited credibility and support among the people.

Feminists who had supported the revolution in hopes of bringing much-needed reform for women bridled against the pequeña burgesia's ideology regarding women. They opposed attempts by the bourgeoisie to restore the status quo and expressed their dissatisfaction through a renewed militancy within the labor movement. Of course, they encountered stiff resistance from those elements determined to establish a patriarchal, bourgeois family model among the working class.[20] Among those who supported the family model were women from *la gente decente* (the decent people, i.e., the middle and upper classes), who wanted to "civilize" poor women by instilling in them proper habits of hygiene, domestic economy, morality, and sobriety. La gente decente believed that each lower-class woman should obtain "theoretical-practical training [to] save her from undesirable practices and habituate her to fulfill not only her social obligations but also her duties as a homemaker."[21]

Failure to reorient women to these goals, warned revolutionary leaders, would result in "children abandoned to the immorality of the gutter, the filth of the factories, and the temptation of vice." From them would spring the men who would form the society of tomorrow—a society characterized by hatred, class struggle, anarchy, and incongruent impulses among the proletariat, who would seek to overthrow the established order.[22] If anyone questioned the veracity of these warnings, he only had to observe the forces unleashed by the revolution.

The realization by Mexico's ruling elite that emigration was not a temporary phenomenon forced them to examine its impact on their programs and to develop strategies to reach the large expatriate community in the United States. Mexican leaders believed exposure to American ideas and institutions carried salutary effects for both the emigrants and their government. Life in the United States would expose them to capitalist ideas and the Protestant work ethic. They would acquire new skills that would prove useful and necessary in rebuilding their country. Mexican leaders hoped that emigrants would become more secularized in their views and thus become more sympathetic, if not supportive, of the government's struggle with the Catholic Church. Reaching out to expatriates was also an opportunity for the government to win the hearts and minds of the working class by assisting them during their stay in the United States. The added visibility, leaders believed, would enhance their credibility and legitimacy in the eyes of Mexicans and thus increase the government's base of support once the expatriates returned home. As noted in a previous chapter, the programs designed to fulfill these goals met with mixed results.

Mexican Leadership in the Midwest

Although most of the responsibility for carrying out these programs fell on the shoulders of the Mexican consuls, another group in the expatriate community actively promoted these ideas. This group was part of the displaced elite who had fled Mexico when the revolution threatened their well-being and that of their families. Many had been forced to abandon their material possessions and wealth in their mad dash for safety; yet they carried with them their world views, their sense of class and status, a desire to return to Mexico, and a patronizing but sincere sense of noblesse oblige. As they resettled in Mexican colonias in the Midwest, they formed tight-knit circles of self-proclaimed leaders and guardians. Although many were forced to labor at menial tasks alongside the campesinos and urban proletariat, they never lost sight of their obligation to lead and serve as role models for the expatriate community. Like most Mexicans, they believed that their stay in the United States was temporary. They also assumed that after they returned, they would once again be Mexico's leaders. It thus behooved them to instill the appropriate values and behavior among working-class Mexicans in the United States, who would return and rebuild Mexico according to the tenets of the bourgeoisie.

The elite's attempts to fulfill these goals were by no means coordinated or completely successful. Many of their organizations, however, were based upon the philosophies of the bourgeoisie in Mexico: fervent nationalism, anticlericalism, self-improvement through education, a strong work ethic, adherence to moral principles, clearly defined gender roles, and unity. Each of these values, except anticlericalism, was integral to the organizational principles espoused by the elite.[23] How each of these goals was pursued cannot be adequately detailed in a single chapter. For illustrative purposes I will focus on the promotion of nationalism and the anti-acculturation campaign because they encompassed many of these goals.

Resistance to Acculturation

One issue that drew strong and continuing support from all sectors of the Mexican expatriate community in the Midwest was the drive against acculturation. From the outset Mexicans voiced concern about the erosive effects life in the United States had on their culture and language. They feared life in America would lead to massive acculturation among expatriates, especially the youth. As Mexicans of all ages adopted American language, customs, mores, and fashions, community members responded with programs to deter this trend. Newspaper articles, interviews, and even songs of the era attest to the dismay and even anger with which Mexicans viewed acculturation. One song, entitled "El enganchador" ("The Hooker" or "The Contractor"), protested that many Mexicans had turned their backs on their culture:

Many Mexicans don't care to speak
the language their mothers taught them
and go about saying they are Spanish.
They call me "fader" and don't work
and are crazy about the Charleston.

Another song, entitled "El renegado" ("The Renegade"), was even more explicit in condemning those who denied their ethnicity:

But he who denies his race
is the most miserable creature.
There is nothing in the world
so vile as he.[24]

The Spanish-language press in the Midwest, which largely reflected the views of la gente decente and la gente preparada, stridently attacked acculturation. Many of the regional newspapers published between 1914 and 1932 openly declared that one of their major goals was to promote loyalty to Mexico and its cultural heritage. Like their counterparts in Mexico, elites in the Midwest believed that women were central to instilling and maintaining strong cultural bonds in expatriate families. Discussion in the press about the role of women increased during the 1920s, when the number of women and families rose markedly.

Concerns about the duties and responsibilities of women were far-ranging and involved employment outside the household, acculturation, morality, and the Americanization of Mexican youth. In sounding the call for the preservation of Mexican culture, the Spanish-language press and supporters of traditional gender roles argued that women were integral to the process. The home was the bastion against the eroding influences of acculturation, and women transmitted the culture and values that would see Mexicans through their exile in the United States. The greatest service women could perform, according to the press, was to provide their families with a clean, secure, and cohesive environment that promoted loyalty to Mexico. Failure to do so, warned a typical article of the times, carried dire consequences for their children and the future of Mexico.

> There is no danger of the desertion of those who came with the ripeness of years. But those who came here as children or are born here are influenced by education, habits, simultaneous acquisition of Spanish and English, often preferably English, combined with a systematic and private campaign of Americanization. This naturally tends to make them far away in spirit as they are in body from the land of their origin. At the end of two generations, when the parents who carried the dust of their native land have died, when there are no causes for remembrance and no pretext for love, the idea of Mexico will be so flimsy and distorted that all those children who should be ours will belong to a country which offers them nominal rights of equality . . . so that [they] are always regarded with disfavor . . . and scorn.[25]

Augusto Franco, writing in *La Noticia Mundial* in 1927, made an impassioned plea to parents, asking them to teach their children the language, customs, and history of Mexico because they contained valuable lessons in honesty, morality, and determination. "It is critical to the colony that children born in the United States not forget their heritage and culture," he wrote.[26] Another Mexican noted it was bad enough the United States was depriving Mexico of its own labor. An even greater calamity, however, was the de-Mexicanization of its children, who were "being educated in protestant schools by teachers who instill in them American ideals and convince many of them to become citizens" of the United States.[27] One resident of Indiana Harbor lamented that Mexican children were "being educated in the schools and taught to be Americans. They will never return to Mexico now. . . . The conquest of Mexico, which could not be accomplished with a hundred thousand bayonets in a hundred years, is taking place quietly but effectively here on American soil."[28] A Mexican consul reported that "the children . . . who have been born here are, despite the patriotic fervor of their parents, losing their love of Mexico little by little, for I observed that all of the ones I saw, even those who were very dark complected, only spoke English."[29]

Mexicans were constantly reminded that they should not let themselves or their children forget that their stay in the United States was temporary, and that one day they would return to rebuild their own country. José Vasconcelos, the noted Mexican thinker and author, said this to a Chicago audience in 1928:

> Mexicans, let us never forget or cease to show interest in our country and in the land in which we first saw the light of day. For if we are here working hard and suffering, it will not always be so. We are but the Children of Israel who are passing through our Egypt here in the United States doing the onerous labors, swallowing our pride, bracing up under the indignities heaped upon us here. If we expect to return and escape all this, as all good Mexicans ought to, then we should show interest in the affairs of our country from this Egypt of ours.[30]

To bolster patriotic fervor among women, newspapers published numerous articles, editorials, features, and literary works praising and glorifying feminine virtues. Stories about the courage, loyalty, patriotism, and sacrifice of women during the Mexican revolution became commonplace. Articles openly exhorted women to continue the supportive role played by the Adelitas during the revolution and thus contribute to rebuilding a stronger, better Mexico.[31]

Columns focused on the supportive role that mothers, wives, and daughters could play by being good homemakers. Women were characterized as the "heart" of the household, whereas men were the "brains." Women were charged with instilling the correct values and attitudes in their children because they were considered the guardians of the moral values of the community. To help them in this important endeavor, newspapers carried information on moral standards, hygiene, and Mexican history; tips on saving; and directions about proper dress, etiquette, and social behavior. Articles such as "La mujer y el amor" ("Women and Love") advised women to be virtuous, get married, and be good mothers and obedient wives.[32] "Como deben ser las mujeres" ("How Women Should Be") suggested women "should be like sand, delicate and cool; but should not be like the sand, which cannot serve as the foundation for weak structures. They should be like wine, which is full of spirit, but they should not behave like the wine which muddles the senses of people."[33] Throughout the 1920s Spanish-language newspapers included items written by women on nutrition, child care, housekeeping, grooming, food preparation, and manners in order to support women in their work.

Newspapers also used humor, sarcasm, and scathing attacks against feminism and acculturation to convey their message. Editorials and stories criticized and ridiculed women's liberation in the United States, often attributing the lazy, domineering, and capricious behavior of American women to their new-found freedom. They expressed shock and dismay over the antics of the flappers and their outlandish styles. This permissiveness, they warned, had encouraged women and youths to drink, smoke, and indulge in highly suggestive dancing. Such behavior, they concluded, often resulted in moral degeneracy for women. They also preached that modernization and feminism were responsible for the rise in promiscuity, divorce, and desertion in the United States.

In an article entitled "Las mujeres que fuman" ("Women Who Smoke"), acculturation and immorality were linked to smoking because it constituted the first step in attracting women to modern ideas. "The woman married to 'modernization' is a calamity," wrote Juisca. "She neglects her children. She drinks cocktails. She smokes to the point of asphyxiation. When she reaches fifty, she spends all morning on the streets. She dances like a sprout of twenty years. She detests the home. And where will it end? What will be the fate of this generation with mothers such as these?" In Juisca's opinion, "drinking can be stomached because it is detrimental to the consumer and their pocketbooks, whereas smoking causes friends to cough, irritates the eyes, and impregnates the hair and clothes." Juisca concluded by stating that she was twenty-six and still single because she had been raised in the "old fashioned way." She refused to adopt modern standards just to attract a man. "I prefer to live alone rather than in bad company."[34]

The appeal to women, however, represented only part of the campaign to promote nationalism and anti-acculturation among Mexicans.

To fulfill their goals, the elite first had to unite and establish hegemony over a disparate, heterogeneous, and highly transient population. It was one thing to rally the community behind ideas such as opposing naturalization, staving off acculturation, or preserving traditional values; it was quite another to overcome the suspicions, mobility, autonomous impulses, youthful rebelliousness, and parochial loyalties of their compatriots.

The Roots of Parochialism in Mexico

To understand the relative strength of parochial loyalties over national loyalty, one must look back to Mexican political history in the second half of the nineteenth century. The development of Mexico as an integrated nation was arrested, retarded, and even undermined after the conclusion of the Mexican War in 1848. The war not only cost Mexico half of its territory, it also exacerbated the deep divisions within the body politic. These divisions manifested themselves in several ways, including the failure of the Mexican people to rise up en masse against a foreign invader.

The succeeding years (1850s to 1860s) witnessed a bitter struggle between two factions, the monarchists and the federalists, which deepened the division and acrimony plaguing Mexico. After the victory of Benito Juárez's forces over Maximilian and the Mexican royalists, a semblance of unity and direction began to emerge as the Indian-mestizo heritage assumed ascendancy. Although the Juáristas' tenure was a troubled one for the people of Mexico, the troubles were insignificant compared with what followed during the Porfiriato (1876 to 1911). The needs of Mexico and its people became subverted to those of the ruling oligarchy and its foreign allies.

Porfirio Díaz and his Positivist advisors tried to subvert traditional Mexican culture, which they deemed backward and barbaric. They intended to replace it with a European and American culture that would make Mexico part of the commonwealth of modern nations. Accordingly the modernizers, who were interested in progress and order, attempted to shunt the old Mexico by regulating, if not ending, popular festivals and rituals such as the Day of the Dead, Carnival, and Judas burnings.[35] Bullfighting was also prohibited under Díaz in an effort to change Mexico's image as a cruel and primitive nation. To replace this ritualistic activity, baseball, horse racing, bicycling, and other "civilized" activities were promoted by the ruling elite.[36] Mexicans embraced some of these new pastimes but also clung tenaciously to their cultural traditions. As Indians and mestizos continued to suffer under Díaz's discriminatory policies, they were forced to turn further inward to survive. Local and regional ties and loyalties were reinforced, fostering what Arturo Rosales has termed a *patria chica* mentality. In essence, Mexico remained a series of island communities.

Luís González alluded to this in his study of San José de García, a village located in northern Michoacán, the home of many Mexican emigrants in the United States.

> We can be sure that those who lived here before 1861 knew each other very well but had hardly any knowledge of human beings or events anywhere else. At the turn of the twentieth century not much had changed. On the eve of the revolution [of 1910] their lives were beginning to be affected by nationalistic sentiment, an interest in politics and an awareness of the outside world . . . but the majority were unaware of the move toward nationalism, or even toward regionalization.[37]

For those who traveled throughout Mexico and later the United States in search of work and safety, the patria chica mentality began to dissipate. As they met and interacted with people from other areas of Mexico, they learned more about each other. They became more aware of their commonalities as Mexicans and the forces that had propelled them from their homeland. They heard different dialects, listened to regional music, and learned about the foods and diets of others. In the United States their shared experiences expanded, through work and discrimination. Their collective identity was shaped by these experiences, many of which were negative.

Nonetheless, elements of that patria chica mentality were maintained and even reinforced. Mexicans in the United States continued to seek out members from their place of origin, practice chain migration, and take trips back to Mexico to visit, get married, or attend to family matters. Combined with suspicion of the elite and high mobility, the patria chica mentality led to fragmentation and lack of ethnic cohesiveness among Mexicans in the Midwest.

Organizational Efforts by the Elites

The elites recognized the importance of organizing and uniting the disparate elements in their respective communities, not only to address the plethora of problems that plagued Mexicans, but also to accomplish their own goals. The question was how. Part of the answer lay in harnessing and directing the nascent but burgeoning nationalism within the expatriate community. To foster that nationalism, the elites used rhetoric and symbols that underscored the idea of a common cultural, linguistic, and historical heritage.

Both the rhetoric and the symbols, which focused on the Indian and mestizo, were drawn from a wide variety of sources and images. They emphasized the mythic proportions of the indigenous cultures such as the Aztecs; the heroic Indian-mestizo qualities embodied in Benito Juárez and his followers; and the ideals, principles, and personas of the revolutionary era. The goal of the elites was to forge a nationalistic mystique, the symbols of which stressed the uniqueness and grandeur of Mexican culture. Like their social and intellectual counterparts in Mexico, the expatriate elites attempted to define and re-create nationhood among Mexicans. It was not only a question of reshaping people's politics but also of using selected history to promote social awareness and self-knowledge.[38]

Stock symbols of Mexican identity—the nopal or cactus, the eagle, and the serpent—as well as an emphasis on the Indian-mestizo aspects of Mexican culture, were carefully used and manipulated by the elites to promote Mexicanidad. Stories and features in the Spanish-language press extolled the virtues and accomplishments of Mexico's past and current leaders. The fervid holiday celebrations on Cinco de Mayo and Mexican Independence Day kept the symbols and images before the community. During these celebrations, broadsides and the local Spanish-language press published lengthy articles about Mexican heroes and history: Ignacio Zaragoza, Benito Juárez, and their deeds against the French invaders; Father Miguel Hidalgo y Costilla; and El Grito de

Dolores, the Mexican cry for independence in 1810. Orations at these events focused on the grandiose exploits of Mexican heroes, the tremendous accomplishments and changes wrought by the revolution, and emotional appeals on the need to unite and the importance of retaining ties and loyalty to the homeland.

Throughout the year Mexicans were reminded in a myriad of ways that patriotism was a civic and moral responsibility. Literary works romanticized Mexico and its heritage. Editorials filled with patriotic fervor and rhetoric defended the homeland against detractors or intruders and glorified the revolution. Even the names of many of the organizations established in the Midwest manifested acceptance and pride in being Mexican. Organizational names such as La Sociedad Benito Juárez, La Sociedad José María Morelos, La Sociedad Mexicana Cuauhtémoc, and La Sociedad Ignacio Zaragoza reflected a conscious effort by Mexicans to identify with their Indian, mestizo, and Mexican heritage. Religious symbols also strengthened nationalism: many midwestern churches erected by Mexicans bore the name of the Virgen de Guadalupe in honor of the dark-skinned virgin who appeared to the Indian Juan Diego in 1531.

To ensure the cultural integrity of their own organizations, bylaws prohibited the induction of individuals who had become naturalized citizens of the United States. Leaders also worked through broadsides, articles, speeches, and peer pressure to discourage members of the local community from becoming naturalized. In an article typifying those that appeared in the Spanish-language press, the publisher exhorted Mexican organizations to unite and combat the destructive influences of acculturation in their community: "Unfortunately, we cannot deny the fact that there is an enormous number of us who completely ignore not only the prosperity and greatness of our country, but even lack culture to the extent that there are many of us who have not had the most rudimentary teachings in our language." The editorial concluded by stating that many Mexicans "feel ashamed of their origin and deny their country either by changing their citizenship or by making up their mind not to return [to Mexico]."[39] Another newspaper accused those who "change their names, . . . deny their nationality, . . . and are embarrassed to speak [Spanish] in front of Americans" of being unpatriotic.[40]

A scathing satire poked fun at those who became American citizens. The essay noted that the United States drew untold numbers with its promises of work and opportunity and that the continued exploitation of these newcomers made it one of the wealthiest and most powerful nations in the world. Yet it was these poor unfortunate souls who were immensely grateful. This misguided gratitude often led them to renounce their cultural heritage and become naturalized citizens. Such was the case of one Mexican, who not only became a U.S. citizen, but also changed his name from "Pila" to "Washington." (The word *pila* means "sink"; hence, the rough translation to "Wash-ing-ton.") The folly did not stop here, wrote the satirist. Washington also made his wife anglicize her name by changing it from "Nieves" to "Ice Cream Studebaker de Zamarriga." He then "affiliated himself with a pentecostal group, quit smoking and began chewing tobacco because he believed it would help him speak English better, bought businessman's clothes, and placed a picture of [President] Washington at the head of his bed." He opened a restaurant, which he continued to operate until Prohibition agents closed it after they caught him using beer to make his very popular soup. "Freed at last, the downhearted [Mr. Washington] again registered with his local consul and took back his original name. . . . [H]is wife refused to speak English any more. Disillusioned [they], along with their brood, [set off for Mexico] . . . in a small Ford without tires—convinced that 'Yankeedom' was not agreeable with those of Aztec lineage."[41]

If the efforts of the elites are judged by the number of Mexicans who sought citizenship, they were very successful. According to naturalization figures, only 22,732 Mexicans became U.S. citizens by 1920—about 4.8 percent of the 478,383 Mexican-born persons living in the United States. By the end of the decade, the percentage of naturalized Mexicans had increased to about 5.8 percent, making them one of the least naturalized groups in the country.[42]

A Growing Sense of Community

The development of a stronger nationalistic identity and the low rate of naturalization within the expatriate community in the Midwest, however, cannot be credited solely to the efforts of the elites. In fact, the nationalistic impulses among Mexicans were largely shaped and promulgated by other forces in the United States. Common experiences and problems, including poor working and living conditions; prejudice and discrimination; the need to coalesce to address these concerns; the strained relations between the United States and Mexico; and the accentuation of national consciousness by the immigration process created a sense of community among Mexicans in the Midwest, regardless of their previous social and economic status in Mexico.

Migration imposed a broad social leveling among Mexicans. Like their compatriots, members of the middle and upper classes did not speak English. Licensing restrictions, lack of money, and language barriers prevented many professionals from pursuing their practices and careers. Regardless of their social or economic status in Mexico, emigrants were collectively referred to as "Mexicans," which was a racially loaded and derogatory term among most Americans.[43] These factors and their status as newcomers relegated even the elites to the least desirable jobs and places of residence and virtually reduced them to the same level as all Mexican emigrants.[44] The inability of Anglo-Americans and other ethnic groups in the United States to recognize class differences subjected members from the elite ranks to the same discrimination and humiliation as other Mexicans. This discriminatory treatment led the elites to make common cause with their lower-class compatriots.

Discrimination and prejudice were important forces in shaping and reinforcing the idea of Mexicanidad among expatriates. Newspaper stories, movies, magazines, and congressional debates on immigration restriction reminded Mexicans they were an unwelcome element in the United States.[45] An editorial in the *New York Times* concluded, "It is folly to pretend that the more recently arrived Mexicans, who are largely of Indian blood, can be absorbed or incorporated into the American race."[46]

Mexicans angrily reacted to charges they were dirty, lazy, inferior, and lawless. They resented segregationist policies and the widespread discrimination they encountered in housing, education, employment, and the legal system. The poor treatment they were accorded added to their resolve in retaining loyalty to Mexico. "The more [bad things] they say about Mexico," one national stated, "the more I love it, and the less I want to take [*sic*] my United States papers." His partner concurred. "We are scorned here."[47]

Others viewed their mistreatment as part of a continuum that characterized relations between the two countries. "We remember that the American government took advantage of our weakness to invade our country and wrest from it a large part of its territory. We know that American money has fomented revolutions in Mexico, and that the United States has interfered with our sovereign rights as a free country. . . . Now, when we were driven here by hunger and the devastations of war we figured we would have to care for ourselves."[48]

Many Mexicans eschewed naturalization: they saw little reason to seek citizenship. It "offered little of substance to the Mexican national who knew that if he became a citizen he would still be in the eyes of Anglos a Mexican."[49] In commenting upon the extremely low naturalization rate among Mexicans during the 1920s, a Labor Department official wrote this: "It is not strange, then, that the Mexicans coming here have no intention of becoming American citizens. . . . It is strange that we have shown no more diplomacy [in their reception and treatment] and that we are ready to condemn these people for not thinking more of us than they do."[50]

Another reason some Mexicans did not seek U.S. citizenship was because they knew they would no longer be subject to the protection of consuls, who were authorized to assist only those who retained Mexican citizenship. Mexicans also believed that turning their backs on their homeland would reflect poorly on their character. Anyone who became naturalized was viewed as disloyal, untrustworthy, and dishonorable. Such a person would be an undesirable citizen in any country. Mexicans believed their comportment in the United States already proved they were "good" citizens. Many argued they worked hard, paid taxes, raised families, and contributed to the welfare of their communities, as any upstanding citizen was expected to do. If they conducted themselves as good citizens, they reasoned, why must they formally apply for naturalization? Their behavior was more important than a piece of paper in measuring their value to society. A resident of Gary exclaimed he was as much an American as any "Pollack or Italian who carries a mere certificate of naturalization in his pocket. [Besides, I] was born on the North

American continent and [my] ancestors were the original owners of the land."[51]

The procedure for obtaining citizenship also deterred many nationals, who could not comprehend its bureaucratic intricacies. The process was even more difficult for those who did not speak English. One official of the Immigrants' Protective League stated the following:

> The question may be raised as to whether there would have been any United States at all, if it had been necessary in 1492, or . . . in 1607 and in 1620, as it is now, to present at the shores of America birth certificates, marriage certificates, medical certificates, photographs, signatures, official seals, reentry permits, students' permits, passports, visas, etc. . . . [T]he present gate to America is a documentary gate, which necessitates a multitude of public records and ever increasing thousands of file clerks and administrative officials.[52]

If this paper chase did not discourage some Mexicans from applying for U.S. citizenship, then their illegal entry into the United States did. To apply for their first papers, they would have had to recross the border and reenter the country legally. Most lacked the inclination, time, and money to undertake such a journey.

Mexican resentment toward the United States was widespread and served as a unifying force that bolstered patriotic fervor. Although Mexican-U.S. relations had improved markedly under Porfirio Díaz's tenure, events during the revolution and its aftermath severely strained relations between the two countries. Between 1910 and 1930 several incidents brought both countries to the verge of war. These included the invasion and bombardment of Vera Cruz in 1914 and General Pershing's punitive expedition against Pancho Villa in 1916. In the 1920s tensions remained high as the United States attempted to protect the interests of its investors, especially oil companies, from provisions in the Mexican Constitution of 1917 that granted ownership of all subsoil mineral rights to the Mexican people. Controversies were also sparked by the religious persecution of Catholics during the Cristero revolt and by the deaths of Americans in Mexico. Mexicans in the United States followed these events closely. According to consular reports, emotions ran high among the expatriates, many of whom offered their services to Mexico if and when war broke out with the United States. Edson noted, "The United States is the big bugaboo of the Mexican people, the great hobgoblin, the fork-tongued dragon." In assessing the impact of these views on Mexicans, Edson was partially correct when he wrote, "In [a] boiled down sense [anti-Americanism] constitutes the whole patriotism of the Mexican: it is the only reason he knows he has a country."[53]

Interethnic Conflict

In Chicago and the Calumet region, interethnic conflict, police brutality, and discrimination in the courts also contributed to Mexicanidad. The ethnic conflict stemmed from several sources. Mexicans started off on poor footing when they unknowingly worked as strikebreakers during the steel strike in 1919. The unions, which had a large European membership, attributed the strike's failure to the use of Black and Mexican scab labor. During the 1920s the size of the Mexican population in the region grew dramatically. Increasingly Mexicans found themselves competing with White ethnics for jobs, housing, and neighborhood sovereignty. The continued weakness of unions, low wages, and recurring economic downturns of the era were mistakenly attributed to the presence of Mexicans. The poor relations between Mexico and the United States, negative stereotypes about Mexicans' propensity for violence and lawlessness, their refusal to become naturalized citizens, and a hostile press that reinforced antagonisms exacerbated tensions in many of these communities. Interethnic fights, shootings, knifings, and murders involving people of Irish, Polish, and Mexican descent became common occurrences in many neighborhoods.

Mexican representatives in the press and the affected communities decried the escalating violence in their neighborhoods. They counseled moderation and forbearance and urged their compatriots not to take the law into their own hands or to carry weapons. Good behavior would help promote greater justice toward Mexicans, they advised. "When we act accordingly then we can protest the wrongs against us and the law will listen. So let us not protest against the rigor of the Yankee law but against the vices and shortcomings we possess."[54]

Intraethnic violence involving Mexicans was also frowned upon, regardless of the circumstances. Not only was it considered a tragedy when Mexicans committed violent actions against their own kind, but such behavior also placed the entire colonia in a bad light among Anglo authorities. "Of what good is it that the majority of Mexicans conduct themselves accordingly, proving they are honest men who respect one another [when the authorities seldom acknowledge it?]," asked an editor rhetorically. In reality, he continued, they only paid attention to those incidents that confirmed negative suspicions and prejudices about Mexicans. "All Mexicans are judged by the actions of one or two individuals; that is the way that Americans treat . . . outsiders. . . . The law in this country is inexorable regarding the foreign element, and [violence and lawlessness] . . . only make the situation much worse [for all of us]. That is why it is imperative we avoid such regrettable incidents in the future."[55]

Not everyone attributed the problem to the behavior of Mexicans. Oftentimes the most vitriolic criticism was leveled at police authorities, who were accused of corruption, mishandling the situation, and discriminating against Mexicans. In 1926 and 1927 tensions between Poles and Mexicans in Chicago erupted into several violent outbreaks and confrontations. Although members on both sides were responsible, the arrest rates for Mexicans were much higher. The Mexican community accused the police, many of whom were of Polish descent, of favoring their own nationality in enforcing the law. After a Mexican woman shot a Pole in self-defense,[56] Mexican representatives questioned the motives and actions of the police. Although they lamented the growing violence between Poles and Mexicans, they believed the police exacerbated the situation. Investigations by the Mexican community revealed that most of the attacks against nationals had been provoked by the Poles. In many cases Mexicans had acted only in self-defense. The police, however, failed to investigate the incidents, arrest the guilty parties, or discourage further assaults. Mexicans leaders deplored "the lack of action and indifference with which the police authorities in Chicago . . . treated these matters" because of their detrimental effects on both the victims and the community. They wondered if this inaction by the police was due to their prejudice against Mexicans. If this was indeed the case, they asserted, then the police were guilty of inflaming the situation and alienating those who were adversely affected.[57] Paul Taylor, an economist from Berkeley who studied Mexicans in the United States during the 1920s, suggested that police–ethnic-European collaboration did exist because "the police in the districts inhabited by Mexicans were often first or second generation of the very nationalities which feel themselves in competition with the Mexicans."[58]

Mexicans also complained about police corruption. They believed mass roundups and arrests were intentionally designed to harass them or to get bribes. According to a resident of East Chicago, Mexicans who operated illegal gambling houses were forced to pay protection money to high-ranking police officials. "When they failed," he stated, "their places were raided." He called the treatment that police accorded Mexicans "shameful."[59] An investigation into corruption in Lake County, Indiana, disclosed that Mexicans paid extortion money to the mayor and other city officials in Indiana Harbor so they could continue to operate their speakeasies.[60]

Most Mexicans distrusted law enforcement authorities and held them in low esteem. Mexican resentment at discriminatory actions by the police and the belief that they were corrupt bolstered Mexicans' resolve to fight for their rights. When one Mexican was asked why so many of his compatriots owned guns, he responded, "One reason . . . is because of their [poor] relations with the police."[61] In the Chicago area conflicts with the police were so common, Mexicans believed they were under siege and could not expect justice within the American legal system. Even the courts seemed arrayed against them: judges tended to hand down more convictions and harsher sentences against Mexicans.

Editorials in the Spanish-language press assailed the police and the courts, charging them with discrimination, corruption, and insensitivity. One newspaper editorialized that "those charged with enforcing the laws contribute to lawlessness."[62] Others noted that Mexicans could not expect justice in the United States simply because of who they were and where they came from. The idea that they were "outsiders" and foreigners suffering a collective oppression was reinforced by their experiences with the legal system. This idea also served as one more element in uniting the community and strengthening Mexicanidad.

Cynical and suspicious of their neighbors and a justice system that favored European ethnic groups, Mexicans mobilized themselves. By rallying community support behind someone they believed was unjustly arrested or convicted, the elites and other organizers appealed to patriotic and nationalistic sentiments. They argued that Mexicans were discriminated against because they were "outsiders" who exhibited no desire to abandon their homeland. They told their compatriots to expect no justice in this country. In an obvious appeal to a common linguistic and ethnic heritage, elites warned Mexicans that the mere fact that they spoke Spanish and not English militated against a fair trial. Those with dark complexions and Indian features, they concluded, faced even greater disadvantages. "To do the Mexicans justice," wrote a Labor Department researcher, "requires a certain amount of charity of heart. Their dark complexions, their submissive spirit, the odium usually felt toward a foreigner all militate against them."[63] Mexicans were convinced they were usually found guilty simply because they were Mexican.

A Mexican leader in Chicago exhorted his audience to "unite . . . to protect each other's interests. Why must we suffer this curse of disunity," he queried, "which lays us so open to the attack of our enemies?"[64] Unite they did, as Mexicans throughout the Midwest contributed their hard-earned money to defense funds and sponsored bazaars, raffles, and dances to raise money for legal fees. They also formed organizations specifically to protect the legal rights of Mexicans. Among these were La Sociedad Protectora Mexicana, formed in Gary in 1924 after the mass arrest of 400 Mexicans, and La Confederación de Sociedades Mexicanas de los Estados Unidos de America, an umbrella organization composed of about thirty-five Mexican mutual-aid societies, founded in Chicago in 1925. Although both organizations were short lived, they did provide bail money, helped pay for legal fees, and made legal services available to Mexicans.

Broadsides, newspaper accounts, poems, corridos, plays, and dramatic reenactments recounted the exploits of Mexicans who had defied the law in defense of their rights. These accounts often helped mobilize community support, especially when Mexicans were involved in shoot-outs with the police. Such events were followed with great interest and, in some cases, the exploits of the perpetrators were admired. The latter response was due to emigrant nationalism and the anger, frustration, and sense of persecution felt by Mexicans. Although the killing of policemen exacerbated the enmity between Mexicans and other ethnic groups, the colonias generally championed the cause of their own kind. Many individuals became folk heroes among Mexicans, who admired their courage, mental adroitness, resolve, and defiance—characteristics that openly challenged and discredited prevailing stereotypes about Mexicans.[65]

Mexicans were relative newcomers to the Midwest. There they encountered prejudice and limited and unstable employment. Although they were not as segregated as Mexicans in the Southwest or as Afro-Americans in the Midwest, they nonetheless remained economically and politically weak and isolated. Political, educational, economic, and law enforcement agencies were in the hands of people who were unresponsive and even hostile to their needs and problems.[66] These forces, combined with the Mexicans' recent immigration, accentuated their national consciousness. "Loneliness and an unfamiliar environment turn the wanderer's thoughts and affections back upon his native land. The strangeness of the new surroundings emphasizes his kinship with those he has left."[67] This was the sentiment in editorials of the era, which declared that it was "evident that among Mexicans, the further we find ourselves from our homeland, the more strongly we feel Mexican."[68] Both by choice and by circumstances encountered in the United States, they remained Mexican in culture and nationality.[69]

Despite their initial regional loyalties, when faced with common problems and a common label, Mexicans from all walks of life united to combat the forces arrayed against them. Conditions in the United States forged a stronger national identity among Mexicans, whereas geography, regionalization, and class prejudices had kept them apart in Mexico. The elites, however, failed to fully tap the potential of this nationalism. Although they kept the symbols of Mexico conspicuous through holiday celebrations, patriotic speeches, and cultural pride, symbols by themselves were inadequate in eradicating internal class prejudices and other divisive forces that plagued their communities. The reasons for this failure will be discussed in the next chapter.

CHAPTER 7

Mexican Mutual Aid Societies

As Mexicans entered the Midwest, they crossed into a new world, devoid of much that was familiar. Few in number, isolated, scattered, unable to speak English, confronting new situations and institutions, and lacking a support network, Mexicans quickly realized the importance of creating their own self-help organizations. In this respect Mexicans were like other immigrant groups, who formed mutual benefit associations to cushion themselves from the cultural and economic shock created by their uprooting.

Because other kinds of support networks existed, mutual benefit societies had not been common in Mexico.[1] In some communities the *caudillo* (local patron) provided assistance, whereas in other places people turned to the local parish. Mexicans could also rely on the extended family, friends, or *compadres* and *comadres* who, although they might be in dire straits themselves, were compelled by custom, practice, and desire to help their less fortunate friends and relatives.[2] No such networks, however, were available in the Midwest to the newly arrived immigrant, who often traveled to the region alone.

Efforts by the Mexican government to establish organizations for its people in the United States paled in comparison to what the Mexican people did for themselves. The most common and popular organizations were the sociedades mutualistas. Initially their purpose was to cushion immigrants from the economic hardships caused by unemployment, illness, or injury. They also helped pay burial expenses. A major concern among Mexicans was that they would die far away from home. By joining a mutual aid society, they hoped part of the cost for returning them to Mexico for burial would be borne by the organization.

The duties and functions of the mutual aid societies quickly expanded in response to new challenges, needs, and problems such as widespread discrimination, segregation, and exploitation. These societies provided more wholesome social outlets as the number of families increased. They also became the instrument used by the elites to promote their goals and ideals among Mexicans.

As stated in the previous chapter, the elites in the Midwest faced a formidable task in their efforts to unite working-class Mexicans under their tutelage. The highly transient and self-reliant immigrants arrived in the Midwest imbued with strong local and regional ties, linguistic differences, suspicion of authority in any guise, and no overarching sense of nationalism. In an attempt to steer clear of topics that would further divide the community, many organizations assiduously avoided entanglement in the political issues and controversies that plagued Mexico. To ensure adherence to this principle, the constitutions and bylaws of some societies expressly forbade members from discussing religion or politics.[3] Instead, the societies concentrated on issues of immediate concern that would unite Mexicans by appealing to their nationalistic impulses. The emphasis, therefore, was on combating acculturation, ending harassment by the police, and protesting U.S. interference in the affairs of Mexico and Latin America.

These organizations also promoted a more positive image of Mexicans in their respective communities by demonstrating that Mexicans were cultured, civilized, and progressive. Programs and activities were designed to foster adherence to traditional values espousing the importance of the family, hard work, honesty, cooperation, and love of country. By redirecting the cultural and social life of their respective colonias, the elite sought to eliminate activities that had previously catered to the "baser instincts of single men" and replace them with activities favored by people who were respectable, cultivated, and refined. This would educate and uplift Mexicans and prove to Anglo-Americans that they had unjustly condemned a whole group for the actions of a few.[4]

The Elites and Their Organizing Principles

The outlook, strategies, goals, and programs of the elites were shaped by their experiences in both Mexico and the United States. They tried to create an ideal Mexican colonia in exile based on three principles.

The first principle involved founding the "new society" on moral and Christian values. These included love of God and one's neighbor, cooperation, and order. The elites thus deplored and condemned violence, corruption, and anarchy.

The second principle was closely related to the first. The elites remained extremely sensitive to American disdain for the Mexican-as-stereotype because this view adversely affected them. They resented this guilt by association. The idea that they were linked with the very stereotypes they abhorred—violence, ignorance, laziness, and uncleanliness—was repugnant to them. They reasoned that this discrimination would cease if Mexicans "improved" themselves.

The third principle affirmed the aspiration of elites to return to Mexico. Like their compatriots, the elites considered their stay in the United States temporary. Ultimately they hoped to return home and play a major role in its rebuilding and development. They therefore tried to ensure that emigrants who returned to Mexico could assume their role by instilling in them the spirit of patriotism and a work ethic that emphasized conformity and hard work.[5]

These three principles provided the elites with a firm foundation on which to build a broad base of popular support for their programs. Ultimately, however, the inability of the elites to overcome their own class prejudice and their failure to understand the people they were attempting to lead undermined their endeavors.

Mexican Nationalism in the Midwest

Loyalty to Mexico was readily embraced by most Mexicans in the Midwest. Unlike the societies of middle- and upper-class Mexican Americans in the Southwest, which required members to be or to become U.S. citizens, many midwestern organizations established by elites restricted membership to Mexican nationals. This policy reflected their avowed purpose to discourage Mexicans from becoming assimilated or naturalized citizens. It also was a reaction to the discriminatory practices that had systematically excluded the elites from non-Mexican organizations, their discomfort with laws and values they did not comprehend, alienation fed by residential segregation and isolation, and resentment against a society that was generally hostile to their presence. Mexicans turned to their own group for relief, protection, assistance, and camaraderie, while eagerly embracing tenets that reinforced the Mexico Lindo concept.[6]

Regardless of leadership or makeup, each mutual aid society in the Midwest had similar requirements for membership. Bylaws generally required members to swear fealty to Mexico and the organization, pay an initiation fee, and contribute whatever they could afford to the treasury on a monthly basis. Membership was restricted to males sixteen years of age or older. Some societies imposed a residency requirement, a formal vote of acceptance by the membership, and a probationary period before full privileges in the organization were bestowed on new members. A few societies established formal rules that specifically prohibited Blacks from joining.[7] The treasuries of these organizations were meager because of the poor wages earned by many members, the inability to collect dues consistently, and a constantly changing membership. The lack of money made it difficult for many societies to provide the long-term financial assistance that had spurred their founding. Financial aid to members or their families was mostly limited to a one-time payment or consisted of small donations gathered from members and the community.

Of greater importance was the social and psychological support that people derived from mutualistas. They brought the community together by sponsoring dances, holiday celebrations, bazaars, cultural programs, public lectures, concerts, sporting events, and educational forums. They also cushioned the newly arrived immigrant: members spoke his language, observed traditional festivals and holidays, provided information, assisted in finding jobs and housing, and were sensitive to his fears and concerns as a stranger in a strange city.

The social life of Mexican colonias changed as more men moved out of the bunkhouses and barracks into boardinghouses and single family dwellings. The arrival of families and a more stable economic environment contributed to the development of a greater sense of community and created the need for more wholesome and planned social activities. Class differences also added to the variety of planned activities. No longer satisfied with the social and cultural life that had evolved to serve the needs of single men, Mexicans began to organize activities that were more sophisticated, culturally oriented, and appealing to a wider segment of the community. As a result Mexican communities became the centers of a highly diverse, active, and interesting social life that brought the community together, presented the more positive aspects of Mexican life and culture to Americans, and helped relieve loneliness, isolation, and boredom.

Mexican Organizations in Kansas City

Middle- and upper-class Mexicans recreated some of the more appealing aspects of Mexican society in the United States. In the twin cities of Kansas City, Missouri, and Kansas City, Kansas, lived a sizable group of well-educated and prosperous Mexicans who had fled from the terrors of the revolution of 1910. This group, possessing the necessary funds and leisure time, actively supported the commercial, religious, and cultural activities of their respective communities. Some of the refugees worked for *El Cosmopolita*, a Spanish-language newspaper published in Kansas City, Missouri, between 1914 and 1919. Among the expatriates were doctors, lawyers, and engineers who were not licensed to practice in this country. They, along with members of the displaced landed aristocracy, spent the revolutionary years in relative safety in Kansas City, where they formed a Mexican social club, El Casino Mexicano. The club boasted a membership of more than one hundred. As the revolution ended and conditions in Mexico improved, many of these elites departed, and El Casino Mexicano ceased to exist.[8]

This dissolution, however, did not signal the end of elite involvement in the affairs of the Kansas City community. In 1914, La Unión Mexicana Benito Juárez was founded, one of the earliest mutualistas established in the Midwest.[9] Although troubled by finances, internal dissension, and the lack of sustained and experienced leadership, the society remained a strong social force in the community until the onset of the depression in the 1930s. The members' attitudes and political persuasion tended to be conservative and, at times, patronizing. Although this united some members within the organization, it also led to widespread resentment and opposition. Other groups were formed by those who believed the society did not meet their needs or represent their philosophies.

Not all social activities in the Kansas City area were directed by or operated for the benefit of the elites. For many Mexicans the Catholic Church remained a powerful symbol, and it was around the church that social activities developed. One of the earliest Mexican parishes in the Midwest was established in Kansas City, Missouri, in 1914 by the Reverend José P. Muñoz. Authorized as a national parish by the Catholic bishop, the church operated out of rented rooms and a storefront from 1914 to 1919, after which the parish acquired a permanent church building.[10] In addition to providing religious services, El Templo de Nuestra Señora de Guadalupe (Our Lady of Guadalupe Church) sponsored educational classes, dances, and celebrations of religious feasts.[11]

Another organization that served Mexicans in the twin cities was the Amberg Club, organized in 1919. Named in honor of Mrs. Agnes Ward Amberg of Chicago, who had worked among Chicago's poor, it provided a wide variety of services. Staffed largely by Mexicans, the club sponsored dances, fiestas, a social club for small boys (the Knights of the Round Table), night classes for adults, and a prenatal clinic. In 1923 it began to publish the *Knight's Spear,* a monthly newspaper. The paper's purpose was "to create a brotherly feeling in the community, promote clean sportsmanship, and spread appreciation of Old Mexico." It was published by an all-Mexican staff.[12] In 1926 Our Lady of Guadalupe Church, the Amberg Club, the Mexican Christian Institute, and the Baptist Mission pooled their resources to purchase garbage pails. The pails were distributed to Mexicans in the city to comply with the city's contract, which stated that the contractor would only collect garbage that was placed in covered receptacles. Again the impetus and organization for this highly successful project was carried out by Mexicans.[13]

Mexican Organizations in East Chicago

In Indiana Harbor religion also served as the catalyst for the formation of an organization that played a central role in the social and
religious life of the Mexican community. Among the educated, middle-
class Mexicans who came to the United States during the 1920s were
refugees who had fled the growing religious conflict. Most of them came
from the Central Plateau states of Jalisco and Guanajuato, where emotions against the government ran high. Their arrival in East Chicago
profoundly influenced the mores, values, and organizational structure
of that community. Their presence was directly responsible for the creation of several mutual aid societies.[14] One of these mutualistas was El
Círculo de Obreros Católicos "San José" (Los Obreros), founded in 1925.

Although the number of exiles who left to avoid religious perse-
cution represented a small percentage of the total population of East
Chicago, their influence was significant.[15] The men who founded Los
Obreros were deeply committed to the church and the moral well-being
of their community. Individuals such as Luís Zuniga Sanchez, Juan de la
Rosa, José González, and the Figueroa brothers, Francisco, Carlos, and
Benjamin, gave freely of their time and resources to accomplish the
goals before them.[16]

Most of the leaders of Los Obreros came from the state of Jalisco.
One such leader was Francisco Figueroa who, like many of his cohorts,
was from a middle-class background. Before emigrating, he had been a
government bureaucrat in Guadalajara. He was forced to leave Mexico
in 1924 because of differences with the Obregón-Calles administration
over its policies against the Catholic Church. After his arrival in East
Chicago, he found employment in the steel mills. His exile, however, did
not dampen his religious fervor.[17]

The catalyst for establishing Los Obreros was activated when the
local priest, Reverend Octavius Zavatta, invited the Reverend José P.
Muñoz to speak to his congregation. Muñoz had been instrumental in
the construction of Our Lady of Guadalupe Church in Kansas City,
Missouri.[18] Zavatta hoped Muñoz's visit would inspire the people in
Indiana Harbor to undertake a similar project. His idea bore fruit when

members of his congregation began discussing ways to strengthen the parish. Their first step was to rent the basement of St. Demetrius Church in Indiana Harbor so that Mexicans living there would not have to travel across town to hear services in Spanish. Soon attendance at church services increased, further convincing some of the leaders of the need to build their own church. They met with Father Zavatta after church services in April 1925 to discuss strategies. To carry the project further, they founded Los Obreros.[19]

The immediate goal of this new organization was to raise funds to build a Catholic Church for Mexicans. Initially donations came from the membership. By November 1925, fifty-six persons had donated about $2,000 to the building fund. At a meeting held in January 1926, the group decided to devote its energies to sponsoring fund-raising activities such as dances, raffles, and bazaars.[20] In the summer of 1926 they had enough money to purchase a lot on Pennsylvania Avenue, near the heart of the colonia. After several years of working and waiting and with donated materials from Inland Steel, Youngstown Sheet and Tube, and the Universal Atlas Cement Company, the church was constructed. On 30 January 1927, Our Lady of Guadalupe Church was completed. A community-wide celebration marked the dedication of the building. The ceremonies featured a mass celebrated by Archbishop John F. Noll of Fort Wayne, Indiana; a parade with floats, bands, and local dignitaries; and a dance. The day, however, belonged to Los Obreros, who sat in the front pew proudly wearing their badges and banners. Thereafter Our Lady of Guadalupe Church became a focal point in the life of the community.[21]

The completion of the church project by no means ended the work of Los Obreros. From the outset the leadership had sought to foster loyalty to Mexico, promote cultural awareness, and defend the Catholic faith, especially against the encroachment of Baptist missionaries, who they mistakenly believed had converted many Mexicans.[22] Deeply committed to religious principles and to promoting the moral well-being of Mexicans, Los Obreros created wholesome recreational outlets and provided leadership in their community. Benjamin Figueroa explained,

We saw that the Mexicans were scattered here and there. [They] suffered from intolerance and were unable to express their grievances. They were getting a bad reputation. They were being exploited, and some were in dire straits; we could not stand it. We felt that something had to be done, yet none of us had the funds or time to do much. But we recognized the need of organizing the Mexicans, and enlisted in the cause others who were willing to share the toil and sacrifice necessary to improve the condition of our compatriots who had been brought here, unable to speak the language, paid scant wages and deprived of their rights by foreigners.[23]

After the completion of the church building, Los Obreros used it for their meetings and for sponsoring and promoting activities to help them meet their goals. The purpose of the organization was "to unite all Mexicans, strive for their moral regeneration, demonstrate the virtues of our people (who have been judged only by their vices) and glorify the name of our country through positive actions."[24] Los Obreros also promoted educational activities among the youth to instill in them a love of learning as well as love and veneration for their country, "whose tradition, heroes, and glories should make them proud to be called its sons." Through the erection of a church, they wanted to create "a patriotic and pious monument [to] the faith of our people." Through social action, they hoped to "tighten . . . the bonds that should unite us to that country, awakening sentiments of a true and open brotherhood that will bring us together in our joys and sorrows."[25]

To inform the community of their goals and programs, they began publishing *El Amigo del Hogar* in 1925. This weekly newspaper was distributed free of charge to more than 1,500 households in the colonia. Between 1925 and 1930 it served as a major source of information for and about the Mexican community in Indiana Harbor.[26]

To encourage residents of all ages to read about their culture, history, and society in their native language, Los Obreros established a library. They also started an organized baseball program for youths and adults to teach them about healthy exercise, good sportsmanship, and cooperation. Of primary concern to them was the education that Mexican children were receiving, which they deemed inadequate. Not only were students segregated and denigrated because of their language and ethnic background, but the curriculum of the schools was also strongly assimilationist. Parents complained that teachers were insensitive to their children. One parent stated that a teacher told his son he was not an American and did not belong here. When asked by the teacher "why he did not go back to Mexico," the boy responded, "I am more of an American than you because all of my ancestors were born in North America and yours were all born in Europe."[27] In Gary a social worker described Mexican girls who had darker skins as lonely because they were considered Black and not White.[28] To combat discrimination, stave off the eroding influences of acculturation, and bolster self-concept, organizations such as Los Obreros and other mutualistas established classes for Mexican children.

In Indiana Harbor, as in other Mexican communities, classes were usually held after school in the basement of the church. Teachers from Mexico were hired to conduct the classes, which consisted of instruction in the national language, Mexican history, and civic instruction. It is difficult to ascertain the number of students who enrolled in these classes. The numbers were sufficient, however, to require the services of two full-time teachers until the onset of the depression in 1929.[29] Classes were also offered in a small private school in the Brighton Park colonia, starting in 1924. The school was in a vacant store below a boarding-house. Enrollment was small, consisting of about eight children and six adults. The instructor, a Mr. Martínez, taught the adults English and the youngsters Spanish. The Benito Juárez society of Indiana Harbor also sponsored a school for all ages under the tutelage of a Mexican instructor in 1929.[30]

Despite their accomplishments, Los Obreros, like other elitist-led organizations, were not able to unite the community under their leadership. This failure was partly due to their own attitudes and practices vis-à-vis the rest of the colonia. Because most of the members of Los Obreros emanated from the middle and educated classes in Mexican society, they referred to themselves as la gente preparada. Although most of them were blue-collar employees who worked at Inland Steel, they did not consider themselves part of the working class. This attitude was reflected not only in their associations and mannerisms, but also in their places of residence. Several lived outside the Block and Pennsylvania area, where the Mexican community was concentrated.[31]

Like their counterparts in Kansas City and other midwestern cities, these elites strove to recreate the cultural milieu they had enjoyed in Mexico. Toward this end Los Obreros founded their own theater group, El Cuadro Dramático, which presented several plays each year. The nine productions staged between March 1927 and May 1928 were directed by J. Jesus Cabrera, a professional actor from Mexico City who had fled the revolutionary chaos. Cabrera directed the plays and provided the scripts. The casts often consisted of the sons, daughters, and wives of the most prominent members of the Mexican community.[32] Despite the influence of the elite, "community involvement in the productions was extensive. . . . Moreover, judging from the records of ticket sales, the productions drew audiences of over two hundred people."[33]

Los Obreros also sponsored exhibitions of original works by prominent Mexican artists, including those of muralist Alfredo Siquieros. Other cultural activities included cello concerts, poetry readings, public lectures, and musical reviews.[34] Another popular social activity was *El Té* (tea). These gatherings, organized by the wives, included dressing up in long, elegant gowns in colors designated by the hostesses. Men also attended these teas dressed in suits and ties. A dance usually followed, and members were expected to conduct themselves in an orderly fashion.[35] Because of its elitist nature, membership in Los Obreros never exceeded 180.[36]

Los Obreros were criticized by members of La Colonia del Harbor for their elitist nature and were accused of sponsoring activities that did not appeal to the larger community. Some Mexicans resented the society's invitation to only the "more socially acceptable" emigrants for their inner circle of activities, such as the formal teas. The decision of some members of Los Obreros to reside outside the colonia angered others, who saw it as one more example of their elitist sentiments.

Working-class Mexicans were also angered by the members' patronizing and critical attitudes. These attitudes were common among la gente preparada, who often criticized and chastised the *peónes* for their lack of education, poor hygiene, inability to express themselves in

proper Spanish, immorality, and uncooperativeness. One member from
East Chicago complained that working-class Mexicans spoke Spanish
worse than he. "I have trouble understanding them sometimes. . . .
Ninety percent of the Mexicans who come here are no good and they
come to bother those who are here, and we don't want them to come.
They give us a bad reputation and when the papers say that Mexicans are
all alike that [sic] it hurts, too."[37] The same person stated that an attempt
to unite and educate the peónes in 1926 failed because they refused to
cooperate. "Our aim was to unite the whole colony. First we learned
we needed instruction, books, etc. But the peónes didn't care for instruction. We found that they needed clean hands, clothes, etc. But the
peónes said they did not care. They said because we were clean we were
trying to be better than they. They said they did not need to be told how
to dress."[38]

Another member related that Mexican laborers refused to join the
Benito Juárez society in Chicago because they disliked the middle-class
makeup of the club's leadership. "The laborers didn't want to come in
with the doctors, lawyers, etc. They said they didn't like the principles;
that the Benito Juárez people were so high that they had no principles
[i.e., would make no efforts] to help the poor Mexicans."[39]

When Mexicans boycotted a local theater because of its segregationist policies, the operators told community leaders that any patron
wearing a button or badge that designated them as members of Los
Obreros or the Benito Juárez society would not be subjected to that policy. Although Los Obreros refused this preferential treatment, the Benito Juárez society did not. This action stirred some resentment against
them in the community. According to a disgruntled Mexican, "They
[the Benito Juárez society] are supposed to be working 'pro patria' and
should not accept special privileges."[40]

In an editorial, the publisher of El Amigo del Hogar remarked that
he was deeply disappointed by the Mexican community's moral deca-
dence and weak character.[41] Members of Los Obreros further demonstrated the ideological differences between them and the greater community when they decried the "absurd and anarchic . . . revolutionary
platform of the Constitution of 1917." They also praised the regime of
Porfirio Díaz as the only one in 400 years of Mexican history that was

prosperous and stable. They were openly contemptuous of revolutionary heroes such as Pancho Villa, whom they described as a *jefe bandido*
who robbed the people, attacked the government, and terrorized foreign
investors. The opposition to Villa and those of his ilk was echoed by
another elite member of the community, who said he refused to organize a society among the "ignorant Mexicans" because "they praised
Villa, who was a bandit." He sarcastically added, "The Mexicans become
patriotic here and they want to celebrate, but they don't even know the
Mexican national hymn."[42]

Members of Los Obreros did not advocate the interests and protection of the laboring class, even though they advertised their society as a
worker's organization. Instead of condemning discriminatory actions
against Mexicans, they usually argued that much of the discrimination
stemmed from the reprehensible way in which Mexicans conducted
themselves.

Much of the criticism and resentment toward Los Obreros was not
openly voiced; the discontent regarding their philosophical, ideological,
and social attitudes manifested itself in other ways. Other organizations were formed. For example, in 1926 La Sociedad Cuauhtémoc was
founded by Jesus García and José Anguiano. Many of its members were
Indians from Michoacán, who were proud that their membership came
from the "less educated members of the colony." In naming their society
after the last great Aztec chieftain, who died in defiance of the Spanish
conquerors, members of this organization delivered a clear message to
the elites about their ideology and politics. This society's appeal lay
with the working classes, who had been oppressed in Mexico and were
still suffering exploitation in the Midwest. Whereas groups such as Los
Obreros and the Benito Juárez society sponsored cultural events comparable to middle-class functions in Mexico, the Cuauhtémoc society
launched Mexican-style vaudeville shows and other recreational activities appealing to working-class people. The society provided an alternative to organizations that many Mexican workers considered too
"highbrow for their tastes."[43] These differences in class and ideology,
however, never led to open conflict with Los Obreros or other elite
organizations.[44]

By 1929 East Chicago and La Colonia del Harbor boasted eleven

Mexican organizations. In addition to the Cuauhtémoc society and Los Obreros, there were La Sociedad Mutuo-Recreativa "José María Morelos," organized in 1925 as an athletic and mutual aid society; one chapter each of La Cruz Azul Mexicana and La Comisión Honorífica, sponsored by the consul and the Mexican government; and La Sociedad Bautista de Jovenes Mexicanos, a Baptist society for young men.[45] Religious preferences, however, did not cause noticeable conflict in the community. Even though these organizations differed in character, most remained mutual aid societies at heart. All were created to address specific issues, problems, or needs, and many disbanded or dispersed as those problems disappeared.

Mexican Organizations in Detroit

Although Detroit's Mexican population never approached that of Chicago and the Calumet region, its community nonetheless enjoyed a varied and active social life. As elsewhere in the Midwest, Detroit's Mexican community organized a plethora of clubs and organizations to address the growing needs of its people.

Initially Mexican migration to Detroit had been small. Whereas the rural segments of Michigan witnessed an influx of Mexican laborers for the sugar beet industry, Detroit and other urban centers did not. Only twenty-seven Mexicans lived in Detroit in 1910.[46] Most Mexicans who worked for the railroads and sugar beet companies preferred steadier, year-round employment in the auto and related industries but lacked the opportunities to enter a highly competitive work force. This situation was especially true of the auto industry, where Ford had introduced the $5 workday in 1913 to reduce absenteeism, discourage unionization, and gain employee acceptance of accelerated production schedules. Mexicans did, however, enter auto work in increasing numbers when World War I and the Immigration Act of 1917 created a labor shortage. One Detroit paper reported, "During the industrial boom of 1917 to 1918 hundreds of Mexican laborers came to Detroit, bringing their families with them in many cases."[47] Those who brought their families probably came from the beet fields. By late 1920 Detroit's Mexican population had grown to 8,000.[48] The depression in 1921 drove many of them back to Mexico or to the beet fields, reducing the Mexican population in the Motor City to less than 2,500.[49] By late 1922 and early 1923, however, a new wave of Mexican laborers arrived in Detroit to work in the Ford plants. This influx continued unabated until 1928 and increased Detroit's Mexican population to about 15,000.[50] Many of these Mexicans were also highly transient, seasonal laborers who traveled to the Motor City from the beet fields.

The development of civic and social organizations in Detroit differed from that in other cities. Whereas the impetus for mutualistas and other organizations in the Midwest generally emanated from the elites, the Catholic Church, consuls, or disaffected Mexicans, in Detroit the stimulus for organizing arose from a very unlikely source—Henry Ford himself. Although Ford had no intention of fostering the kinds of Mexican organizations that emerged, his work among Latino students led to the creation of the first vital Latino organization in Detroit.

Henry Ford believed that capitalist penetration into Europe and the Third World would increase his profits and bring other nations greater economic and political stability. As a corollary to this economic expansionism, other peoples would be exposed to the glorious tenets of American civilization. This exposure would imbue them with the necessary values to become good producers and consumers. Ford's goal was to build plants in other countries that would be operated by native people whom he trained. That was the motive behind the establishment of the Henry Ford Service School, where carefully selected students from abroad were trained in all facets of industrial operations.

As mentioned in chapter 3, the Henry Ford Service School recruited youthful, well-educated, and well-connected students, most of whom were from the middle and upper classes.[51] Hundreds of Latin Americans became trainees, the majority of whom were Mexicans. The training period, which averaged slightly less than three years, consisted of much individual instruction geared to the needs and capabilities of each student.[52] The school was established in 1917 and continued to operate until 1927, when increasing competition from other domestic auto makers and falling profits forced Ford to curtail spending and scrap many of his overseas projects.

Although the hours were long and the demands great, students were also given the chance to hone their social skills. Such opportunities

were part of Ford's overall plan "to instill enthusiasm for the corporation and a love of the United States in the Latino students."[53] This was
the purpose behind the formation of the Latin American Students'
Club, founded under the auspices of Ford in 1919. The club, which met
at a local YMCA, lasted until 1923. During its existence membership never
exceeded one hundred. By instilling in its members the work ethic,
corporate spirit, and an appreciation of U.S. culture and values, the club
accomplished what Ford had hoped.[54] It also affected the larger Mexican
community in Detroit. Although some members eagerly embraced the
assimilationist tenets of the club, others remained uncomfortable with
the idea. This latter group formed El Centro Español. In 1922 El Centro
Español became El Círculo Mutualist Mexicano, making it the first all-
Mexican social organization in Detroit.[55]

The beginnings of the Círculo were quite informal, consisting of
weekly get-togethers at the predominantly German St. Mary's Church
on the edge of Greektown. Members of the community gathered there
on Sunday mornings to hear mass in Spanish and then returned in the
afternoon to socialize. At these gatherings children played and were
given lessons in language and history. The men and women played
cards, sang corridos, and discussed religion and politics.[56] After the
organization was formalized, weekly dues were assessed to help care for
the sick and homeless. Some of the money was sent to Mexico to aid the
needy or support the religious struggles sweeping across the country.
This group also provided the leadership that organized Our Lady of
Guadalupe Church in 1923, the first Mexican Catholic parish in Detroit.[57] Although membership in the Círculo never exceeded 150 people,
it became the leading Mexican society in Detroit.

Círculo meetings were held at the International Institute, with
which it maintained close relations. Most of its members were businessmen, professional people, and white-collar workers. For a short time it
published a bimonthly newspaper, *El Eco de la Patria*, in cooperation
with three other Mexican organizations: La Comisión Honorífica, La
Cruz Azul Mexicana, and El Club Progresista Tlaltenanguense. The paper contained information about community events, news from Mexico, and articles that encouraged readers to seek an education and re-

main loyal to their heritage.[58] Mismanagement and lack of subscribers brought about its demise.[59]

The Círculo sponsored numerous social and cultural events throughout the year. It was an integral unit of El Comité Patriótico Mexicano, a federative organization that promoted the celebration of Mexican national holidays. Because of its leadership and central role in the community, the Círculo acted as the representative of the Mexican community at many of the international activities sponsored by the International Institute.

Although the Círculo actively worked for the welfare of the community, some Mexicans in Detroit disagreed with its politics and elitist leadership. Some of the criticism of the Círculo emanated from its own ranks. It was from this dissenting membership that several other social and fraternal organizations sprang, including El Club Anahuac and El Centro de Cultura, both of which emphasized cultural and literary activities.

Other Mexican organizations were founded by working-class people in Detroit and the surrounding area. These included several mutual aid groups, social clubs, and youth organizations, all of which testified to the growing permanence of Mexicans in the area. In 1925 Los Obreros Unidos Mexicanos was established in Detroit. In 1928 a group of Mexicans in Dearborn formed La Sociedad Emilio Carranza. Named in honor of a young Mexican aviator who had been killed in 1928, its members came mostly from the state of Coahuila, the birthplace of this young hero.[60] The club was founded to create a sense of unity among Mexicans living in Dearborn, who found it difficult to attend the meetings of other organizations in Detroit.

Church-oriented groups appeared during the same period. Some were founded to champion the Catholic Church's cause in Mexico and the United States and to support the efforts of those involved in the Cristero revolt.[61] Other church groups, such as La Sociedad de Damas Católicas and La Sociedad de San José dedicated their efforts to social welfare and the welfare of the church, respectively.[62]

A major organization with strong ties to the Catholic Church in Detroit was the Mexican Catholic Society. One of its founders was

Father Juan P. Alanis, an exiled priest from Monterrey, Mexico. José V. Espiru was also a founder of the Catholic society. Born in Nogales, Arizona, he arrived in Detroit in 1916. During World War I, he served in the American Expeditionary Force and saw action in France. His experiences imbued him with American ideals, patriotic fervor, and a strong belief in Americanization. These attributes were further influenced and reinforced by his experiences as an auto worker. His views were widely shared by many members of the Catholic society, most of whom were middle-class professionals.

Individuals such as Espiru and Alanis were supported in their work by the Catholic Church and major employers in Detroit. For auto manufacturers and other employers, Americanization served to educate and discipline laborers with work habits that made them more productive, efficient, complacent, and eager. It also made them better citizens, which was central to the mission of the Catholic and Protestant Churches in Detroit. Outreach programs and other services that the churches provided tried to help Mexicans accommodate to life in the Motor City by helping them embrace the tenets of Americanization. Father Alanis was "confident that [the church programs] could teach them a sympathetic understanding of the laws and liberties of the Republic."[63] Espiru was even more emphatic. "Mexicans," he said, "were to adopt and cultivate American work habits, they were to express loyalty to and identity with the auto companies, and they were to aspire to the American standard of living."[64]

The culture of the Motor City and the auto plants also helped speed the drive toward Americanization. Shared work experiences; the relative lack of interethnic conflict because of Ford's hiring practices and wage structure; the comparatively low rate of union and strike activity, which had engendered bitter divisions in other industries and other cities; and the lure of the consumer culture were among the many forces that promoted the Americanization of Mexicans. Work on the auto assembly lines required a regimented work force. The hiring practices at Ford and other auto manufacturers demanded conformity and citizenship. Many of the early and influential Mexican organizations were established by students from the Henry Ford Service School, middle-class professionals, or clerics, all of whom embraced the central tenets of the Americanization movement. All of these influences made Detroit a bastion of Americanization. As early as 1920, James Devlin of the *Detroit News*, in a series of articles on Mexicans, wrote, "The unity of purpose among the Mexicans reveals . . . the infinite possibilities that are in the Mexicans for rapid Americanization."[65]

Detroit's Mexican consulate contributed its share of organizations. It helped establish one chapter each of La Cruz Azul Mexicana and La Comisión Honorífica, which, according to a Detroit newspaper, "branched out into every place where as many as 100 Mexicans were found."[66] The consul also helped coordinate the large-scale Mexican patriotic celebrations. His central role in these activities ended in 1930 when El Comité Patriótico Mexicano was formed to carry out this responsibility.[67]

During the 1920s consuls throughout the Midwest were directed by their government to form organizations that would help them carry out their expanded duties vis-à-vis the expatriate community living in the United States. Members of these organizations were appointed by the consul. Las Comisiónes Honoríficas, for example, were charged with informing consuls about issues affecting Mexicans, including discrimination, the need for legal representation, police brutality, segregation, and unemployment. They also planned and sponsored national celebrations to promote strong cultural and political ties to Mexico within the expatriate community. These organizations were usually an umbrella group that incorporated other Mexican organizations into their structures; the boards of directors often consisted of officials from other Mexican clubs, societies, and organizations. During the celebrations, Mexican consuls served a central role as ex officio leaders and featured speakers. At these gatherings consuls urged people to remain loyal to Mexico, work hard and learn new skills to take back with them, and act like responsible citizens.

Because of the numerous organizations and social events that gave the Mexican community a high, positive profile in Detroit, a contemporary newspaper account cited it as the "best organized national group among us."[68] Even the acerbic George Edson of the Labor Department was impressed by the education, tenacity, and organization of the Mexicans in Detroit. In a letter to the Bureau of Labor Statistics written in

October 1926, Edson described Detroit Mexicans as cooperative and more acculturated than other Mexicans he had visited in the Midwest. His visits to other communities had raised serious doubts about Mexican attributes and adaptability, but his visit to Detroit had led him to consider revising some of his conclusions about them.[69]

Despite appearances, there were serious divisions within Detroit's Mexican community that adversely affected their unity and cooperation. These divisions arose because of class differences, segregation, poor communication, conflicting goals, and assimilationist tendencies. Even though Detroit's population consisted mainly of foreign-born or children of foreign-born parents, discrimination against "foreigners" and minorities was still widespread. Because of their color, religion, language, socioeconomic status, and comparatively recent arrival, Mexicans were discriminated against in housing and employment. Not all Mexicans were affected, however. Those who had light skin color, possessed an education, and spoke English could, and sometimes did, pass for other nationalities.

At times the drive for social acceptance, better employment, and residence in select neighborhoods led some Mexicans to shun relations with the Mexican community and deny their heritage. Some of these individuals, who readily embraced American values, were able to achieve structural assimilation by marrying European Americans and converting to Protestantism. During his research, Manuel Gamio interviewed several Mexicans residing in the United States. One of his interviewees was José Robles, whom Gamio described as a man of thirty-two with light chestnut hair, light eyes, and a fair complexion. Robles, who was well educated, had arrived in Detroit in 1919. His interview with Gamio revealed that he had become assimilated. "I am now following North American customs in everything that I can. I married a German girl in Detroit in the Baptist Church and before the Justice of the Peace." Robles also told Gamio that he believed in sharing things equally with his wife and that he was a "strong advocate of birth control." He stated that after having lived in the United States, he now found certain Mexican customs and habits, such as child-rearing practices and treatment of women, "strange." He deemed American food "better" and "more healthful." He said when he ate at home he "digested well, but when I go to the homes of relatives and they give me Mexican dishes I am sick at night."[70]

The assimilation of some Mexicans was viewed by others as detrimental to the unity of the community. One member of Detroit's colonia stated the following:

> It is the second generation of American Mexicans who forget the land of their ancestors. These young people hate being called Mexicans. Passing as an American pleases them mightily. Why, right here in Detroit I have good reason to believe that there are one thousand people of Mexican extraction who are scattered throughout the city and who make no effort to contact other Mexicans. They are completely Americanized.[71]

Another contributing factor to factionalism within the colonia was the dismay felt by the educated and elite over the "unlettered masses'" suspicion of them. The elite decried the ignorance and unwillingness of many Mexicans to accept their leadership without question. What they failed to realize, however, was that their actions alienated Mexicans. For example, about twelve families from the elitist Círculo Mutualist Mexicano formed a small clique who entertained themselves in lavish style in their homes or at the Hotel Statler.[72] These entertainments caused them to be viewed with some derision and resentment within the wider Mexican community. Some elites also expressed reluctance about associating with members of the lower class. One young woman who considered herself and her family to be of a higher social class acknowledged that she was "friends" with people who belonged to the "peasant class." She told the interviewer that she was friends with them "because they are her people, but probably if they had remained in Mexico, her friends would be of a different class."[73]

The less fortunate but numerically larger segment of the community believed that its interests were usually subordinated to those of the elite.[74] That such tensions emerged between groups of different socioeconomic classes is not surprising. In Mexico the Detroit elites had enjoyed wealth and status as well as authority. When they arrived in the United States, they found that their training and experience served them well in their organizing efforts. As they assumed a more central role in community affairs, they developed a stronger sense of mission and leadership, which they guarded carefully. The campesinos who came to the United States also held preconceived notions about the democratic nature of this country. Many came prepared to enjoy freedom of action and choice and were loath to return to a patron-peon relationship. In their eyes some of the elite were attempting to recreate the same system they had left behind. One member of the community stated the following: "Then too there are those people who were better off socially and economically in Mexico than many of their compatriots who came here with them, and over whom they continue to attempt to lord. The heretofore lower class Mexicans resent this attitude because some of them are now in better circumstances than the would-be aristocrats who sneer at them."[75]

The reactions of Mexicans who did not come from the middle or upper class were not unique to Detroit. The campesinos who came to the Midwest were not the stereotypical, docile peons. They had demonstrated a great deal of independence and initiative in traveling so far from home. They were tenacious, individualistic, and determined to retain their sense of self-worth. Mexicans asserted themselves in the work place and had no qualms about asserting themselves in the social sphere. They bridled against anything that smacked of class or elitism. Some broke away to form organizations that were more conducive to their views and goals. Although this splintering sometimes hindered the development of a unified front, it also had its positive side: leaders and organizations knew the community would hold them accountable for their actions and attitudes.

Out of some 8,000 Mexicans in Detroit, only about 500 were active members in the various societies and groups.[76] In East Chicago, where the Mexican population numbered about 4,000, estimates placed the total number of dues-paying members in all organizations at about 500.[77] Nonetheless, a large percentage of the population often took part in the activities these organizations sponsored. Mutual aid societies and Las Sociedades Patrióticas sponsored a wide variety of programs and activities to commemorate important dates in Mexican history such as Cinco de Mayo and 16 September. These celebrations, which became more elaborate as the 1920s progressed, featured patriotic speeches by local dignitaries such as the Mexican consul, elected officials of the Mexican societies, and civic officials. In larger cities parades were held in which floats were assembled, bands played, and the mayor and other elected officials rode alongside Mexican organizers.[78] Food was plentiful, and numerous activities were scheduled throughout the day. The festivities usually culminated in a dance with more speeches and the playing of the Mexican national anthem. Attendance at these functions generally numbered in the hundreds.

Mexican organizations throughout the Midwest offered afterschool programs that taught language and history to school-age children and funded small libraries containing a wide selection of literary, religious, and historical works from Mexico and Latin America. The larger and better organized societies brought in dance and theater troupes from Mexico and the Southwest to perform in the community. They invited noted Mexican personalities, such as José Vasconcelos and Diego Rivera, to the Midwest. The themes of these public lectures and forums usually remained the same: work hard, acquire new skills, never forget one's roots, and return to Mexico to help rebuild it. Mutualistas supported bands and orchestras that performed the latest music from Mexico and the Southwest. All of these activities were designed to maintain and enhance community solidarity and a sense of national identity and loyalty among Mexicans.[79]

Internal Dissension and the Question of Autonomy

Efforts at maintaining solidarity were not always successful. Dissension was common within many of the Mexican organizations. Disagreements arose over politics, leadership, finances, and religion. Oftentimes the targets of members' criticisms were the elected officers. Members expected them to remain strongly anti-assimilationist in their personal outlook and to avoid condescension in their treatment of compatriots. Leaders were expected to model exemplary behavior, ensure compliance with the constitution and bylaws of the organization, exercise scrupulous honesty in dispensing funds, and serve as a link with other Mexican groups. When leaders failed to live up to these expectations, they were ousted. This was the case in Kansas City, Missouri, when one of the founding officers of La Unión Mexicana Benito Juárez was forced to resign.

The president of the organization was M. A. Urbina, whose family had business interests in the community. Members voted to remove him from office because he had consistently challenged the authority of the other officers at meetings; had failed to pay dues; and had written an article criticizing the working conditions, low wages, and lack of job guarantees offered Mexicans. He had also instructed Mexicans to join the railroad union to combat these injustices. Conservative members took issue with this suggestion and argued he had used his position to espouse ideas that were contrary to the wishes of the organization. Supporters of Urbina labeled the charges as "unjust and capricious."[80] Nonetheless, he was forced to step down, although he remained active in the organization.

In Gary the president and treasurer of La Sociedad Protectora Mexicana were accused of embezzlement in 1926. The president was also considered "a drinker [who] was not trusted by his people." Although both men were found innocent of the charges, "the credit and reputation of the society suffered."[81] Shortly thereafter a Spanish-speaking minister from the Gary Neighborhood House was elected president, and the society enjoyed a period of tranquility and prosperity. In Detroit the improper disbursement of funds for a building project by an official from a Mexican self-help organization caused the project to be scrapped, the official to be dismissed, and the organization to be dissolved in 1929.[82]

Throughout their existence most mutual aid societies remained highly autonomous organizations that looked askance at efforts to coalesce with other groups. In this respect they were similar to other immigrant groups, who placed a high value on local freedom, autonomy, and control over their own affairs.[83] Mutualistas sometimes cooperated with each other or with local Mexican officials but seldom confederated. Despite the consuls' efforts, they proved especially resistant to Mexican government control because they believed it undermined the apolitical posture of their organizations. For similar reasons, they also opposed efforts by discontented elements to introduce measures and ideas directed against the Mexican government.

Even though mutualistas and other Mexican-based organizations clung tenaciously to their independence, some attempted to establish confederations. Again the call for cooperation and unity of purpose largely came from the elite-controlled press and from members of la gente preparada. One editorial, "La unión y la fuerza," typified the appeals and arguments written throughout the predepression era espousing unification. It urged Mexicans to set aside their differences and suspicions and to come together for the greater good of the people.

> There are in Chicago a large number of societies, organizations and clubs who are held in high esteem by the Spanish-speaking people in this city, but, it is painful to admit that few of them serve to unite the Hispanic-Americans. . . . We must remember that they [the organizations] are here to help us realize our dreams, which is to see our people respected, as others in our community who are inferior to us are respected. . . . Let us all dedicate ourselves to promoting [our common interests] . . . and we shall see how quickly we will be more respected and no one will dare lift a hand against us. . . . Would it not be better if these diverse groups united and formed one solid, cohesive and powerful entity that would give force to what our people have to say in this city? In you, señores secretarios of clubs, organizations and societies . . . lies the responsibility of building the foundation upon which the structure will rest. . . . Let us bring to fruition that praiseworthy ideal which holds: "In Union There Is Strength."[84]

Not all appeals emanated from the elite. In an article announcing the formation of La Sociedad Ignacio Zaragoza in Chicago, a working-class newspaper published in Iowa urged its readers to support the organization. "It is important and necessary that all Mexicans join mutual aid societies, so as to present a united front against the difficult circumstances in life, by rendering mutual and fraternal help to ourselves. This is what is called forming a homeland on foreign soil."[85]

Three years later, the president of El Círculo Azteca in South Chicago warned members of the same Ignacio Zaragoza society about the sinister forces that sought to sabotage efforts at uniting Mexicans.

> Let us ever be alert to oust from our midst those who would plant and sow the discord, the ill-will, the break-up of our friendships and purposes. There are many who would join us, agree with us, to only later take hold of the reins and by disgraceful acts discredit us not only before our own people but amongst Americans. For it is to their benefit and to their advantage that we remain disunited. There are powerful interests here in Chicago and elsewhere who look with jealous eyes on our efforts to unite and better ourselves. It is more than often that their emissaries come amongst us to disorganize and disrupt us. When they do come, let us pick them out, and step on them hard and cast them out.[86]

Mr. Gomez, the outgoing president of the Ignacio Zaragoza society, echoed those sentiments when he said the following:

> In this district bounded by Canal, Madison, Ashland and 16th there are over six thousands of [sic] Mexicans. Where there exists six societies of Mexicans there should be only one. Let us unite into one strong society to protect each others [sic] interests instead of being divided as we are. Why must we suffer this curse of disunity which lays us so open to the attacks of our enemies. I am but an old man, it is up to you young people to do this. If an old man can feel this way why is it that the young, energetic blood does not bring once and for all an end to this disunion? Let it be a Mutualistic Society, a Social one, or one of both, but let us have but one.[87]

A particularly ambitious effort to unite Mexican organizations in Chicago and the Calumet region was launched in 1924. After several meetings and a great deal of cajoling by the proponents of this unification plan, La Confederación de Sociedades Mexicanas de los Estados

Unidos de America was established on 30 March 1925. It included representatives from nine Mexican societies in Chicago, Indiana Harbor, Joliet, and Waukegan. Internal dissension and personality conflicts among the representatives led to the group's demise less than two years after its initiation. Other efforts to unify societies in the Chicago and Calumet region met with the same fate.[88]

In Detroit appeals for unity proved fruitless. In Kansas City, Missouri, several efforts to form a collective organization also met with failure. Ultimately the desire for local control of organizations proved too strong. Those who advocated centralization and collectivity were unable to convince local chapters and organizations to surrender their autonomy.[89]

Mexican Organizations: An Assessment

The difficulties encountered by Mexican organizations should not detract from their accomplishments. They gave form, substance, and direction to planned activities in the Mexican community. Although limited in size, which averaged about fifty dues-paying members, they made the Mexican community more visible to the larger society through their organized events. At the same time they kept before their community the symbols of their culture, heritage, and homeland, which fostered a renewed sense of pride and self-worth. Their existence attests to the willingness of Mexicans to help those who suffered from the lack of services in a society indifferent or insensitive to their needs. The response in many midwestern communities was, to say the least, noteworthy.

Mutualistas and other Mexican organizations also protested against the injustices that plagued their communities. In addition to providing limited insurance benefits and financial assistance to those in need, they fought to end discriminatory practices against Mexicans. Although most of them shied away from the contemporary politics affecting Mexico, they did not shy away from confrontations with American society. They worked tenaciously to alter the intolerable features of their temporarily adopted country. They launched protests against segregation, discrimination, stereotyping, and oppression of Mexicans.

In Toledo, for example, several organizations joined forces to protest police harassment of Mexicans. Leaders argued with local authorities that the police commonly attributed all crimes to Mexicans. On this pretext they made wholesale and illegal arrests before identifying the guilty parties. The protests launched by the mutualistas ultimately proved successful, and the arbitrary police raids ended.[90]

In Gary Mexicans organized La Sociedad Protectora Mexicana in 1924, following an avowed police effort to run the Mexicans out of the city. The police had overreacted after a Mexican "ran amok" in Indiana Harbor, where he killed a policeman and wounded two other officers, and then fled to Gary, where he wounded a third policeman. More than 400 Mexicans were summarily rounded up and arrested. After protests were filed by community leaders with American and Mexican federal officials, the police ended their raids. The society was formed to protect the rights of Mexicans, provide bail funds and attorneys, and promote peaceful relations with the police.[91]

In South Chicago Mexicans formed La Sociedad de Obreros Libres de South Chicago to combat the oppression of Mexicans by Polish Americans determined to run them out of the area. This organization, consisting of thirty to forty active members supported by numerous sympathizers, bitterly complained that the Poles and local police authorities (many of whom were of Polish descent) were hostile and arbitrary in their dealings with Mexicans. This antagonism resulted in numerous fights, injuries, and deaths, making certain areas in South Chicago dangerous combat zones. In one district Polish residents "designated a certain street as a line which no Mexican shall pass after sunset under penalty of being beaten up."[92] The society's pressure on local authorities resulted in more police patrols, who were ordered to keep the peace and avoid favoring one group over another.

In April 1925 El Círculo de Obreros Católicos "San José" became embroiled in a battle against segregation when its leaders organized a boycott against the Garden Theater in Indiana Harbor, which was owned by a Pole. According to the owner Mexican patrons were segregated in the balcony because they wore their soiled work clothes to the movies. He also accused Mexican patrons of being rude to non-Mexican women and of being excessively noisy when those who could speak English attempted to translate for those who could not. After much discussion the management agreed to stop segregating Mexicans if they wore badges pertaining to Los Obreros. The society refused. They knew that if they accepted this condition, other organizations and members of the Mexican community would resent the preferential treatment accorded Los Obreros. Such an arrangement would only serve to divide the Mexican community. Because of this Los Obreros declined the proposal and encouraged other Mexicans to do the same. Although the boycott proved unsuccessful in forcing the theater to change its seating policies, it did result in the establishment of Mexican-owned theaters that showed Spanish-language films.[93]

Mexicans challenged employers who used dual wage structures or discriminated in other ways against Mexican workers. Some mutualistas published handbooks that advised workers about their rights under federal and state laws and, if finances permitted, secured legal assistance to help them press their claims in the courts.[94] According to Lawrence Cardoso,

> The struggle for civil rights went hand in hand with a campaign to remove economic disabilities, for there could not be one without the other. Mutualist leaders were intimately associated with the labor union movement. They invited workers to use their organizations' meeting halls. Mutual members who belonged to a union or were trying to form one naturally sought the comfort and resources of their protection organizations. When strikes were called, as they frequently were, mutual funds were often donated to strikers to help them survive the time of industrial strife.[95]

That mutual aid societies were plagued by financial difficulties and internal dissension cannot be denied. Overemphasizing their shortcomings, however, overshadows their importance to the Mexican community. Mutualistas raised the socioeconomic level of their compatriots, fostered continued allegiance to Mexico, and defended the legal and civil rights of Mexicans. They openly protested against injustices and fought to end discriminatory practices in schools, health services, police practices, and businesses that segregated Mexicans. Whereas the era of the 1920s stressed traditional values, such as individualism with its basic focus on "I" or "me," mutualistas represented a social movement that emphasized concern for one's fellowman. Welfare officials, social service workers, and those familiar with the needs of Mexicans praised the help Mexicans provided for their own people. A social worker in the Hull House District noted that Mexicans were "awfully kind to each other. Even with a house full of children they will take in another family." A Hispanic affirmed that "Mexican friends take care of Mexican men who are out of work." A charity executive in Chicago reported, "We find that the Mexicans do get on even if we don't help them. We don't know how they do it."[96] Social workers stated that Mexicans did not abuse the welfare system; they returned to self-sufficiency as soon as the immediate disability had been removed. In many ways mutual aid societies "were an extension of the informal kinship system," wherein tradition and custom dictated that they assume responsibility for those who were less fortunate.[97]

Most of the mutual aid societies were the result of private or individual efforts, and most were created to address specific issues. Although some of the mutualistas were elitist in nature and composition, most consisted of a cross section of the Mexican community. They provided common meeting grounds where laborers, skilled workers, teachers, businessmen, and recently arrived immigrants discussed common concerns. In some respects this joining of forces helped break down class differences and create a greater sense of community and purpose among society members. If the society appeared too elitist and narrow in meeting the needs of the greater community, dissatisfied members formed their own organizations.

Those critical of mutual aid societies have argued that their leaders, largely drawn from the middle class, were elitist in attitude and action. Although they sponsored a wide variety of cultural events such as dramas, concerts, lectures, and poetry readings, such events did not hold wide audience appeal.[98] Another criticism leveled at the mutualistas was that they withdrew into their own culture, choosing to exalt the past while doing little to confront the issues and problems facing their community.[99] Although both of these criticisms have valid points, they overlook the larger significance of mutual aid societies. One student of mutualistas wrote this: "The interests of society membership, leaders, and the general public were not confined to patriotic and insurance functions. Mexican immigrants were not passive onlookers who used mutualist groups as a place to lick their wounds and give each other psychic balm. Leaders vigorously challenged and attempted to change intolerable features of Anglo-American society."[100]

They accomplished this aim through organized protest, pressure on local public officials, and cooperative ventures with groups and individuals supportive of their goals. Mexican organizations served a political function by providing a forum for members to discuss local problems and strategies for solving them. They also served as training grounds for community leaders.

Many services performed by the mutual aid societies ended with the onset of the Great Depression. In the Midwest most of the mutualistas disappeared as thousands of Mexicans were uprooted from their homes during the massive repatriation drives that swept the country. Some, however, managed to survive during the 1930s and valiantly struggled to meet the objectives that had led to their creation. Although their legacy was mixed, their existence demonstrated to the larger community the determination of the Mexican people to preserve their way of life and their commitment to self-help.

By the end of the 1920s, Mexicans had established hundreds of organizations throughout the Midwest. The Chicago and Calumet region alone boasted well over thirty organizations, and Michigan, Missouri, and Kansas each had more than twenty. Dozens more were scattered throughout the Midwest, each seeking to serve the community in whatever way it could. Their widespread existence speaks well of the communities that supported them and of the Mexican people as a whole. The high tide of mutualistas in the Midwest occurred during the "Tribal Twenties," when Anglo-conformity, 100-percent Americanism, and intolerance of foreigners were at their zenith. The mutualistas and other organizations, however, openly challenged prevailing notions of assimilation and American ethnocentrism. They flaunted their allegiance to Mexico at a time when such demonstrations were derided, discouraged, and suppressed by American society. They represented models of resistance and cultural identification that inspired subsequent generations of Mexicans.

CHAPTER 8

Social and Cultural Life of Mexicans in Some Midwestern Cities

Life in the Midwest was harsh, dreary, and lonely. During the cold winters there was little to do. People stocked up on wood and coke provided by their employers. In the evenings parents taught youngsters to read and write Spanish; after that, hot chocolate, some talking, and then off to bed. Mothers led evening prayers. Most fell asleep watching the flames of the heater flickering on the walls and ceiling.[1] In Minneapolis the homes were usually overcrowded, poorly heated, and dimly lit. "The furniture is stuff that people have discarded, boxes are offered as chairs to visitors, firewood is piled up in corners with sacks of beans and stuff, old grandams [*sic*] sit humped by the stove, unkempt children tear up picture books on the floor, the air reeks with a hundred odors, and outside the atmosphere tingles at 20 degrees below zero."[2]

A Mexican described life in the Midwest thusly: "Life is more *triste* [sad] here. We don't know the language and don't go to dances and can't read the titles of the movies."[3] Another said, "It costs much to go into Chicago to the dances. It isn't *allegro* [cheerful] here like in Mexico because the *muchachas* [girls] are not here."[4]

Living in overcrowded and substandard housing and relegated to the most menial and monotonous jobs, Mexicans actively sought out social outlets to relieve the tedium of long work weeks. Few social outlets were available to them. In most midwestern cities Mexicans found that many barriers excluded them from the activities of the larger community. Restaurants, bars, and barbershops refused service to Mexicans.

Public baths were off limits to them, and most local theaters had restricted seating. Most early Mexican immigrants to the Midwest were forced to patronize places that catered mainly to single males, such as bars, pool halls, and brothels.

Pool Halls and Casas de Asistencia

Pool halls were common in Mexican communities. By the end of the 1920s, almost every colonia had at least one Mexican hall in operation. In Chicago and the Calumet region, one-third of the businesses operated by Mexicans were pool halls. More than fifty Mexican pool halls did business in Chicago alone.[5] Even though a more viable and varied social life had emerged because of the formation of mutual aid societies and other organizations, few of those activities attracted many solos, who considered many of the programs too elitist. Most young, single male transients sought recreation in the pool halls, speakeasies, or movie theaters.[6]

Some pool halls and "saloons" operated under the auspices of local political bosses. For example, the Hotel Paraíso (Paradise Hotel) in Kansas City, Missouri, was closely linked to Tom Pendergast. The powerful politico subleased the five-story brick building to a succession of Mexican managers. This "hotel," which provided its clients with hard liquor and prostitutes, was a notorious hangout. It closed in 1916 after a series of police raids, although it reopened for a short time as the Hotel Mexicano.[7]

The pool halls, described as "a social center, news dispensing agency, and mutual aid society" by one observer,[8] became favorite gathering places for Mexicans. Initially most of the pool halls were owned by people from other ethnic groups, but Mexicans eventually purchased these halls or opened their own in converted store fronts. The more respectable residents of Mexican colonias frowned upon their existence, arguing they promoted vice, encouraged sloth, and attracted undesirable elements into neighborhoods.

These biases aside, the halls served important and useful functions within communities. They provided social and recreational outlets as well as a wide variety of services. Some pool hall operators expanded their businesses to include barbershops and public baths. They served as "banks" that cashed checks or provided lines of credit. According to one observer, "the trusted pool hall proprietor often did more bank business than the bank in the Mexican district."[9] They were places where mail was delivered for those whose work required a great deal of mobility. Pool halls became centers for information about jobs, wages, and news from Mexico. Patrons caught up on the latest news and gossip, met new people, renewed acquaintances, and exchanged political and ideological viewpoints. Men often contributed a few pennies and collectively bought a newspaper so that someone in the hall could read to them. Discussions and heated exchanges over news items or editorials usually ensued after each reading. Although critics viewed pool halls with disdain, many Mexicans considered them a second home.

As part of their informal social life, Mexicans also congregated around casas de asistencia, some of which provided room and board to solos and solteros. As stated in a previous chapter, most casas only served meals and took in laundry. They typically catered to persons from certain geographic regions, as reflected in their names: La Michoacána, La Oaxaqueña, Ocatlán, or San Miguel.[10] At the casas the gatherings assumed a more personal air: regional ties, dialects, and origins brought men together to discuss common experiences and mutual friends and to meet recent arrivals who brought news from home. The casas were also sources of information about where to work, live, and socialize. New ties and friendships developed that continued even after people had returned to Mexico.

Mexicans also enjoyed gambling. It was not unusual to see anxious young men serving as lookouts for policemen. If one listened carefully enough above the din of city life, one could hear loud voices yelling in alleys or open lots as they urged fortune to smile upon them. Gambling assumed many forms, but one of the favorites was cockfighting.[11] Although this was against the law, pleasure took precedence. The screeching of game roosters, the noise of spectators, and the betting continued until there were no more cocks or until a policeman appeared. When the latter occurred, people scattered, leaving only a few tail feathers to indicate what had gone on before. The sport became so popular and widespread in the Midwest that Spanish-language newspapers carried advertisements selling game cocks. One ad boasted that its roosters were bigger and stronger and included a sketch of a powerfully built rooster challenging a smaller adversary.

Movie Theaters and the Segregation of Mexicans

Among the more socially acceptable diversions was the cinema. The movies had graduated from a novelty to a major form of entertainment. By the late teens and early twenties, great movie palaces had been built to accommodate the large audiences. Some of these movie houses were elaborate structures that resembled Roman amphitheaters, Greek temples, or Oriental palaces. Richly decorated and carpeted, they were considered great social equalizers. Everyone who paid the admission charge was greeted by a uniformed attendant and escorted to his or her seat. Once the lights were dimmed, all social differences temporarily vanished, as people settled into their chairs and lost themselves in the fantasy world created by the movies.

This was not the case for Mexicans, however. They were often forced to sit in sections specifically designated for them. "The Mexicans here are not a very good class," the operator of the Indiana State Theater said.

> They are ushered to the first aisle with the colored. . . . White people don't like to sit next to the colored or Mexican, even though [they are] clean. Many of them are not clean and we can't separate on the basis of dress, so we separate them on the basis of nationality. We used to have trouble about it the first four months, but not now. They go by themselves to their place. We have only about ten to twenty a night whereas we used to have one or two hundred. Their societies tell them not to go [to segregated theaters].[12]

About the only equality was that the movies were silent, which obviated the need to understand spoken English. Audiences, however, were still required to read the accompanying dialogue. Mexicans who read English often translated for those who could not, drawing complaints from non-Mexican patrons, who accused them of being overly noisy and disruptive. Mexicans also objected to the movie etiquette practiced by Americans. They found it too formal and straitlaced. One interviewee explained the behavior of Mexicans this way: "In Mexico [you are] supposed—that is, expected—to laugh and make noise at the movie if you like it or if you don't by whistling, etc. Here they must keep quiet and they don't like it."[13] At times the noisy reactions of Mexicans in the theaters were attributable to the unsavory images of "Latins" they saw on the screen.

In some theaters Mexicans were segregated because of their aggressive and "rude" behavior toward American girls. This aggressiveness was partly due to the lack of women but was also prompted by what Mexicans saw on the screen. Hollywood painted an alluring portrait of American culture and society, filled with images of beautiful young women, romantic escapades, and loose morals. Although film producers were increasingly forced to include messages and endings that cautioned against excesses, the effect of the caution on younger audiences appears to have been minimal. Mexicans who viewed these productions and read the movie and gossip magazines that proliferated during the era acquired a distorted and inaccurate impression of American values and society.

Like most young people, Mexican youngsters tried to emulate the behavior and mannerisms of their favorite movie stars. For many young men of the era, the person they most admired and imitated was Rudolph Valentino. His character represented a radical departure from the unsavory Latin stereotypes of the era. Dashing, romantic, and even heroic, Valentino became a role model for Latins and non-Latins alike. In Chicago and throughout the Midwest, there were many "handsome young Mexicans, termed 'sheiks' among themselves, who wear expensive ultra-fashionable clothes, learn English well and have a 'big' time," reported George Edson. "Many of them wear 'patillas' or short pointed side whiskers in imitation of Rudolf [sic] Valentino. . . . Valentino was a great hero to the Mexicans, the psychological explanation being that he popularized the Latin type in the United States."[14]

At times the efforts of Mexicans to imitate the great "Latin Lover" led to trouble. Theater owners in Detroit segregated Mexican youths to stop their amorous advances toward female patrons. In East Chicago

Mexicans were segregated because they "hugged the girls."[15] George Edson noted the following:

> I have observed that some young Mexicans have a misconception of our liberal standard. The amorous scenes in the moving pictures and the novelty of our social customs and a false impression of city life leads these ignorant bucks to think that American girls are rather fast. There have been some complaints of their attention in moving picture theaters, and plans have been considered to compel all of this race to occupy a separate division in the theaters, to which all Mexicans vigorously protest as an insult.[16]

Community leaders argued that such incidents were isolated and that theater owners simply used them as an excuse to discriminate against Mexicans. Mexican leaders also believed that many Americans had fallen victim to Hollywood's unsavory images of Latins.

Mexican Reactions to Derogatory Stereotypes

The derogatory stereotypes of Mexicans in movies, which depicted them as vile bandits, lascivious señoritas, buffoons, violent revolutionaries, and "greasers," was another source of friction and discontent within Mexican communities. Mexican representatives and government officials often expressed anger and chagrin at Hollywood's portrayals of Latins. They argued that such images promoted hostility toward Mexicans, adversely affected relations between the two countries, distorted reality, and endangered Mexico's economic development by discouraging foreign investments and trade. A Mexican resident attributed the difficulty he experienced in finding a decent place to live to the "mistrust" people had of Mexicans. This mistrust, he said, was based upon the poor "reputation of Mexicans in the papers, movies, etc."[17] At a national conference of social workers, one panelist decried the derogatory stereotypes of Mexicans appearing in newspapers, movies, and books. These, she concluded, fostered and perpetuated antagonism toward Mexicans and everything associated with them.[18]

Some journals and newspapers interested in promoting better

trade relations with Mexico criticized Hollywood producers for making such films. "[T]he moving picture men deliberately insult the Mexicans by showing them as bandits and nothing else," wrote an editor. "This has a tendency to spread the belief that the Mexicans are all of that class, but as a matter of fact they are not all cutthroats and murderers." According to this article, several major newspapers in Texas were demanding that "the government . . . take the moving picture men in hand and regulate them. They call attention to the fact that this country is now at peace with Mexico and that there is no reason our relations should not be pleasant." The editor emphasized that the United States needed Mexico's laborers and that its people would respond more favorably to proper treatment. "Their idea that we wish them ill is constantly fertilized by American writers and speakers who cover them with literary or oratorical obloquy."[19]

Mexicans and their supporters applauded the Mexican government in 1922 when it banned films that portrayed Mexicans unfavorably. To underscore its seriousness in bringing an end to this practice, the Mexican government extended this ban to include all films produced by offending companies.[20] The controversy did not end there. Community leaders and parents alike were appalled at the low morality depicted on the screen and sought to shield their children from its corrupting influences. The task, however, proved almost impossible to accomplish. Soon the combined influences of living in the United States and being exposed to its popular culture became increasingly evident in many Mexican communities.

Acculturation

Not only did young men sport the "sheik" look popularized by Rudolph Valentino, but Mexican women of all ages also wore makeup and clothes imitating those of the flappers. They bobbed their hair, smoked in public and, according to one disapproving male, behaved like "liberated women." A Spanish-language newspaper wrote about this "increasing phenomenon" among Mexicanas.

It is a common sight on many streets in Chicago, and especially on thoroughfares which attract large numbers of "raza"

[people of Hispanic descent], to see a lot of women walking
with short steps and wiggling in such a manner as to put the
flappers to shame. . . . One can see the rouge on their cheeks
and the red on their lips from as far away as three blocks. . . .
Sadder still is that some naive youths tranquilly walk along
with these thin brats, arm in arm, . . . making a public
spectacle of themselves.[21]

To the chagrin of their parents, young Mexicans began to dance
the Charleston and the Blackbottom, which were considered by conser-
vatives to be suggestive and vulgar. One editorial decried the "flapperization" of the world. The author was scandalized by the behavior of flappers, "those young girls who did nothing at work but put lipstick on
their mouths and powder their noses." Worse still, continued the editorial, were the older women, or "las viejas who emulated the behavior
of the flappers." The author also condemned the Blackbottom. "In addition to the flapperization of the Anglo women, we are now overrun with
another plague which is strange, more odious and unaesthetic: it is that
negro dance, 'the black Bottom,' which has even contaminated married
people over fifty years of age."[22]

In many cases the transformation or "de-Mexicanization" was
more subtle but no less effective or profound. Adolescents and young
teenagers, for example, were increasingly exposed to U.S. influences in
the schools, on the playgrounds, through motion pictures and radios,
on the streets, and at settlement houses. In Detroit Mexican youths
mingled with other nationalities and communicated with them in English. They played basketball and baseball on integrated teams and increasingly participated in the celebration of American holidays. In East
Chicago Mexican organizations took part in Fourth of July and Labor Day celebrations by sponsoring booths and bands. On 28 October
1928, La Cruz Azul Mexicana held a Halloween masquerade dance. That
same year, a Mexican youth won the Charleston contest at a local high
school.[23]

Hybridization was also apparent within the language as words
made up of English-Spanish combinations began appearing. For example, *baqueria* was used instead of *panadería* to denote "bakery." An

editorial in *La Noticia Mundial* remarked that "desmexicanización" was not so much evident in the children as it was among adults in their mid-twenties. The editorial remarked on this in a positive vein.

> Those who are "de-Mexicanized" here, become accustomed to visiting the doctor three times a year, to make sure that their health does not suffer. They frequent the dental clinics twice a year, even if it is not necessary, so that they can have their yellow and decayed teeth treated. They bathe every day ... and visit ... the beauty salons. ... Men are manicured and women have their nails colored red so that they can go to dances at Hull House. Those who become de-Mexicanized here learn English and, those who do not learn it successfully, forget what little Spanish they know. . . . If one can call learning to live a more civilized life de-Mexicanization, then may St. Peter come and chastise me.[24]

Despite the lamentations of the traditionalists, the old was beginning to mix with the new. This intermingling was reflected in a description of Halsted Street in Chicago, written by the missionary Robert C. Jones in 1928.

> Through the open windows of a second-story room opposite Hull House on a midsummer Saturday evening come the jazz strains of a gospel hymn lustily sung in Spanish. . . . There are other interesting things to be seen along South Halsted during the twilight hour. . . . First we pass a restaurant whose brilliantly painted murals are covered by designs reminiscent of that Indian culture which Cortéz and his followers so ruthlessly destroyed in their conquest of Mexico.
>
> In the next block we pause before the window of a music store and glance at the display of ukeleles, guitars, violins, and wind instruments. This little shop makes phonographic records of music played and sung by Chicago's finest Spanish-speaking artists. . . .
>
> Across the street a Mexican woman of middle age,

straight black hair caught up in a knot at the back of her
head, modestly garbed in a long brown skirt and green silk
waist, stands beside her husband. They are looking at the
primitive *metates* in the window of a grocery store. . . . A
well-dressed young Mexican man passes by, escorting a Mexican girl who is smartly attired in the most modern fashion.
They are probably on their way to a dance of the Azteca Club
in Bowen Hall at Hull House. The older woman gazes after
them in stern disapproval. Then she shakes her head. Such an
immodest dress for a girl to wear in public! And to think of
any young girl being out on the streets alone with her lover!
Such things are never done in Mexico![25]

Whenever possible, Mexicans treated themselves by dining at local
restaurants. Among Mexican businesses, restaurants tended to have the
longest life spans. They generally served good food at reasonable prices.
Of greater importance, especially to the unattached men who made up
the majority of the population in the Midwest, was the atmosphere
retaurants provided. People gathered at these small, cozy establishments
to read, talk, and meet friends. A visitor to the Calumet region wrote,
"The climate and outside scenery here may not be like Mexico but the
interior of some restaurants is typical. The odor, . . . the tinpan music of
a mechanical piano, colors and decorations on the wall, the Spanish
language on every tongue and voluble señoritas waiting on tables fur-
nish a setting where the frequenters may eat their tortillas and frijoles in
an atmosphere as Mexican as in their native pueblos."[26]

The informal aspect of social life continued to predominate, and
increasingly much of it reflected the effects of mass culture. Although
Mexicans generally shunned citizenship and denigrated those who acculturated, they were nonetheless subject to the influences of U.S. culture and mores. This Americanization became especially evident during
the 1920s, as communities took shape and became more stable. During
this era a wave of new leisure activities began to occupy Americans'
time and interest. Americans longed for new heroes and heroines who
underscored the country's greatness and whose actions embodied more
traditional American values such as hard work, honesty, rugged indi-

vidualism, and republican virtues. Football, basketball, tennis, boxing, baseball, and other sports flourished in interest and attendance.

Baseball and Other Sports

During the 1920s baseball became the national pastime, and the Mexican community proved no exception in its devotion to the sport. Mexicans, in fact, were not strangers to the game. During the Porfiriato, the game had been brought to Mexico by Americans. The first pickup game took place in the summer of 1882, when U.S. employees of the Mexican National Railroad played against the Mexican Central Railroad.

After the revolution of 1910, baseball made a rapid comeback in Mexico. This recovery was partly due to the new postrevolutionary attitudes about sports, which were seen as one way of diverting workers from the bars and streets. Although the goals of the reformers in education, politics, sports, and society in general were overwhelmed by renewed violence during the late teens, baseball experienced a rebirth in 1920.[27] When Mexicans crossed the border into the United States, they carried with them a fondness and understanding of America's pastime.

Sundays were baseball days for many Mexican communities in the Midwest. Players and fans alike brought their families out to the parks to enjoy the day, adding to the festive air of the games. Clubs and organizations often served as sponsors for teams, which enjoyed large and loyal followings.

Although Mexicans embraced much of the mass culture in the United States, they applied to it their own ethnic flavor. The proof that mass culture did not undermine their identity or ethnicity is apparent in their identification with Rudolph Valentino, a person they believed embodied many of the positive qualities of Latins. This retention of a strong ethnic identity is also evident in the baseball they played. Their teams, although outfitted in uniforms and equipment made in the United States, took on names such as the Aztecas, Aguilas, and Yaquis. Balls and strikes were called in Spanish, and patrons as well as players taunted, cheered, and good-naturedly yelled at the players and umpires in Spanish. Whenever possible they also named their ball parks in Spanish.

In communities where long working days and erratic work shifts hindered scheduling, other alternatives were found. Mexicans in East

Chicago added lights to their ball park so that games could be played in the evenings. Later, members of El Club Internacional erected stands for spectators at El Parque Anahuac. Initially El Parque had been an abandoned field located at the end of Block Avenue, near the heart of the colonia. After the construction of the stands in 1929, the park had a seating capacity of 500; however, attendance at games sometimes reached 3,000.[28] Unfortunately, when the depression struck, the wooden stands were dismantled and used for firewood. Later it was discovered the field had been erected over a coal yard, and denizens began digging it up in hopes of finding coal to burn. By the early 1930s nothing remained of El Parque except the memories.

Mexican baseball teams competed locally and regionally. According to contemporary accounts, the teams were fiercely competitive in both their playing and their recruiting activities. Teams in Chicago and the Calumet region, for example, recruited players from Mexico and the Southwest by offering to pay transportation costs and find them employment in the steel mills. Whenever circumstances permitted, communities fielded all-star teams, who traveled to play non-Mexican teams, including professional and semiprofessional teams from the major and all-Black leagues. In the late 1920s a Mexican baseball team from East Chicago played in the Whiting, Lake County, play-offs.[29] In 1926 a Mexican boy's team was formed by Our Lady of Guadalupe Church in Kansas City, Missouri. That first year they endured the teasing and taunts of opponents, who scoffed at them because of their ill-fitting uniforms and poor play. In 1927, however, they won the Parochial League championship, a title they did not relinquish for three consecutive years.[30]

Not all sports achieved this level of organization and interest. Much of the activity around sports was informal. Mexicans in the Midwest frequented the gyms at the settlement houses or at the local YMCA. There they formed loosely organized athletic clubs to promote a particular sport.

Boxing remained very popular among Mexicans. Their newspapers usually carried stories lauding the prowess of Mexican boxers who became folk heroes. One such folk hero was George Galvin, who had worked in a meat-packing plant in South St. Paul, Minnesota, since the age of nine. When he was twelve, he began boxing to earn extra money. In 1924 he became a professional boxer. Two years later he had won twenty-five fights, fifteen of them by knockouts. This teenage boxer, who was billed as "Little Dago," "Kid Galvin," or "Kid Peewee," fought bouts in Wisconsin, North Dakota, Iowa, and Minnesota. Whether he fought in Milwaukee, Fargo, Sioux City, or cities in his home state of Minnesota, Galvin drew large crowds of his countrymen, who wildly and enthusiastically cheered on their young hero. In 1933 he became active in the labor movement in Minnesota, and in 1934 he became a full-time organizer among packinghouse workers in St. Paul.[31]

Young and old alike emulated pugilists like Galvin and organized boxing clubs. Others turned to basketball. Teams of all ages competed against each other and against non-Mexicans. In 1924 a newly formed basketball team of school-aged youngsters entered a non-Mexican league and were ridiculed for their poor playing and physical appearance. That year they finished last. They persevered, however, and the next year they easily won the championship from teams who were much larger physically. They continued to dominate the sport until the league was dismantled because other teams did not like losing to Mexicans.

Social and Cultural Life

Mexicans with automobiles took Sunday drives or went on picnics. Owning an automobile in the city, however, was an expensive proposition. In addition to the cost of the car, there were state and county license fees. In the late 1920s those fees amounted to $28 in the Chicago and Calumet region. Some owners had to pay $10 per month for a garage to shelter their cars.[32] The number of Mexicans who bought automobiles tended to be higher in the Detroit area. Auto workers earned better wages, and Ford employees were encouraged to purchase cars through special incentive plans. Mexicans in Detroit were not as highly concentrated near their place of employment. Because many auto plants were far from the workers' homes, they were forced to find alternate modes of transportation to get to work. Oftentimes the only way to travel to the plant was by automobile. Many beet workers also needed reliable transportation and purchased vehicles from used car dealers.

In areas with public transportation, Mexicans boarded local trains and buses and traveled to nearby cities, where they took in sights or visited friends or relatives. This practice was especially common along the shores of Lake Michigan, where the transportation system facilitated travel between several colonias in the Chicago area. Mexicans also attended major sporting events to watch college and professional teams compete in baseball and football. The cost of admission, however, kept many of them away. Most Mexicans were not football aficionados, although many in the Midwest followed the fortunes of the University of Notre Dame. As one resident recalled, they rooted for the "Fighting Irish" because they were Catholic, their symbol was the Virgin Mary, and they were a small school taking on "Protestant" adversaries. A long-time resident remarked, "We have always cheered for *los de abajo* [the underdogs], and that is how we saw them [Notre Dame], much like us. I knew of people who offered special prayers and *promesas* [promises] to the Virgin to help the players out, even though they disapproved of the violent way in which the game was played."[33]

Midwestern cities with sizable Mexican populations attracted touring professional theater companies. Among the more popular forms of entertainment provided by these groups were the vaudeville shows that featured variety acts, comedy sketches, performing animals, one-act farces, and musical numbers. Many of the sketches were outrageous lampoons aimed at the pretensions of the upper strata in Mexico, the naiveté of the newly arrived immigrant, American customs and mores, and the peccadillos of human beings. These performances were often characterized by a biting satire, which derided the injustice, prejudice, intolerance, and insensitivity that plagued Mexicans in the United States. Songs of love, death, loneliness, and home unabashedly struck at the emotions of audiences. Tearful reactions during these performances were commonplace, as those in attendance were reminded of just how far from home and loved ones they really were.

Theater companies from Mexico and the Southwest also traveled to the Midwest to present their productions. For Mexicans and other Hispanics, the theater served as a form of expression, cultural preservation, and entertainment.[34] Audiences in the Midwest avidly attended performances by groups who drew their material from writers in Los

Angeles, which by 1923 "had become a center for Mexican play-writing probably unparalleled in the history of Hispanic communities in the United States."³⁵ Although many of the plays and sketches dealt with current events, sensational crimes, and the experiences of Mexicans living in the United States, their social and political criticism was couched in the lighter context of music and humor. The titles, however, clearly delineated their thrust and content: *Mexico para los Mexicanos*, by Antonio Guzman Aguilera; *En el país del Shimmy*, by Raul Castell; and *Los efectos de la crisis*, *Los repatriados*, and *Whiskey, morfina y marijuana*, by Don Catarino³⁶.

Audiences were also treated to serious, full-length original plays, such as the one based on the life of Pancho Villa. Other popular plays were Brigido Caro's *Joaquín Murietta* and Eduardo Carillo's *El proceso de Aurelio Pompa*. The first recounted the life of the famous social bandit Joaquín Murietta, who became a hero to Hispanics in California during the Gold Rush of 1849. The second was based upon the unjust trial and sentencing of a Mexican immigrant. This plot struck a responsive chord in communities such as East Chicago, Gary, and Indiana Harbor, where Mexicans closely identified with the machinations of a legal system they considered corrupt and prejudiced against them.

Mexican communities in the Midwest also supported their own theater groups. Some, such as Gary and Indiana Harbor, had several groups in operation. They included El Cuadro de Aficionados de Gary, La Familia de Arcos, El Cuadro de la Cruz Azul Mexicana, and El Cuadro Dramático del Círculo de Obreros Católicos "San José." The performances sponsored by Los Obreros were intended to provide "wholesome recreation" and raise money for the construction of their church.³⁷ George Edson attended one of these dramatic performances in Indiana Harbor. Later he recorded his thoughts about the experience.

> I was a guest of honor of the Mexican colony at the performance of "Don Tenorio" given in the Auditorium . . . and I had a seat up in front next to the vice-consul from Chicago and the dignitaries of the colony. . . . It was a brilliant occasion, and I met a lot of well appearing [*sic*] gentlemen—not

bankers or barristers or merchant princes but mill operatives in spotless attire, men whose hands have become calloused but who were bred with the courtly manners of a Catholic grandee, who would be in overalls when the whistle blew at daylight. There were enough good clothes there to tickle a Jewish pawnbroker to death. And gold watches and brooches and earrings.

The play was good, but it outlasted me. It started an hour late . . . and of the seven acts only five had been negotiated after midnight's holy hour.[38]

Although Edson's comments were both patronizing and tinged with racism, they were not read by his hosts. Mexicans in Chicago did, however, express anger and outrage at the derisive and inaccurate comments in a 1929 *Chicago Daily News* review of the operetta *Marina*. "This is the first time," began the review, "the residents of 'tamaletown' have done such a program." That same year the *East Chicago Daily Calumet* belittled a successful Christmas function held at a local Mexican Baptist Church by writing, "The Mexicans surprised everyone with their fine program."

The presentations created a sense of community and solidarity among Mexicans by touching upon ideas, events, and experiences they shared. The plays and performances informed, educated, and showcased the positive aspects of their culture and history. In the process the theater, according to Nicolas Kanellos, promoted Mexican culture in the United States and encouraged resistance to acculturation.[39]

The influence of Mexicans and other Hispanics in the theater was not limited to their ethnic communities. Even though the 1920s witnessed the continued denigration of Mexicans and other Latins in the popular media, the period also marked the arrival of the "romantic Latin," as epitomized by Rudolph Valentino. In addition to the "Latin Lover," audiences were now presented with a "new" and more positive array of Latin stereotypes, such as the grandee and nobleman, the aristocratic señorita, and Zorro the Masked Avenger (all of whom tended to be fair skinned, articulate, and European in background), as well as the vibrant, energetic singers and dancers who performed in the musicals.

Vaudeville and stage musicals, recognizing the popularity of "Latin themes," incorporated more "Latin" acts into their repertoires.

This trend was noted by J. Xavier Mondragón in his discussion of conflicting attitudes about Latins as portrayed in the performing arts. In Hollywood, he wrote, Mexican and Hispanic actors who wanted to perform or appear in films often had to anglicize their names, and if one looked "too Mexican or Hispanic," his chances of employment quickly faded. Hispanic actors were not even hired to portray themselves in unsavory roles. In Chicago, however, Paco Perafín, a well-known dancer and instructor from Mexico, operated a studio in 1925 that attracted a large non-Hispanic clientele who were dance instructors, choreographers, and directors from famous and highly respected companies. Among his clients was Mr. Pavley, of the Pavley-Oukrainsky Ballet Company. Mondragón noted there was a great demand for Mexican and other Latin dancers in vaudeville and dance companies. This popularity led Anglo-Americans and other European ethnics to Hispanicize their names to acquire employment in the productions. "On many stages in this country we see dozens of vaudeville performers with Spanish names, when in reality they are Jewish, American and even Russian."[40]

Settlement Houses

The settlement houses and the International Institutes provided numerous opportunities for social and fraternal activities. They also provided charitable support, conducted English classes and other forms of instruction for immigrants, served as mediators between the Mexican neighborhoods and the larger Euro-American community, and could be genuinely sympathetic and less culturally biased toward Mexicans than other external agencies. Settlements also strove to assist newcomers in adjusting to life in their newly adopted country and sought to Americanize them. The settlement movement showed its greatest strength in the Northeast and Midwest.[41]

Hull House and other settlements in the Chicago area learned quite by accident that Mexicans lived in their midst and were latecomers in working with Mexicans. Most of their programs did not attract Mexicans until after 1922. The first reference to Mexicans by the University of Chicago Settlement appeared in the 1923–1924 annual report.

We first began to feel crowded . . . when one of our Residents, in preparing her Thesis for her Master's degree discovered many Mexicans in the neighborhood, and invited them in for tea and to meet their Consul. Fifty of them descended upon us, and returned the next night bringing with them some of their friends to join our English Classes. Since their advent, we have had classes meeting in our bed rooms, rather than turn them out for lack of space. The Mexicans have proven an interesting factor in our neighborhood; pathetic in their inability to cope with the doubling and tripling of rent rates when trying to rent a house for themselves; interesting in the reactions of their Polish neighbors to them; and delightful in both their courtesy and abandon when frolicking at one of their fiestas, such as 300 of their number attended last week.[42]

Initially the settlements attracted Mexican men, who came to learn English or partake in athletic activities. Settlement house workers reported that the men seldom requested relief or assistance. In the early and mid-twenties, women and children began using their services. Increasingly Mexicanas became the conduits through which the settlements made the rest of the colonia aware of their programs. They informed women about agencies such as the United Charities, the Immigrants' Protective League, and other social-charitable organizations.

Settlement workers quickly learned they were dealing with a highly mobile population, and thus began undertaking neighborhood visits and canvasses to make sure they reached newcomers. They usually stopped by "to be neighborly, . . . find out the conditions they were actually facing, what the difficulties were . . . which they must understand and overcome."[43] Women found that the settlements were friendly, open places that provided warm welcomes and useful information. Mexicanas who used agencies told friends, neighbors, and newcomers. They also identified people in need for local agencies. On occasion they became actively involved in the settlement by serving as translators, social workers, and teachers.

One particularly bright and loquacious woman, Mrs. Ibañez, was asked to teach an English class for the settlement. She later recalled, "I still remember the first day I was at the Settlement. Everything was new and I was a little bit afraid when I had to stand at the corner of Ashland Avenue and 46 Street telling every Mexican I saw to go to the Settlement . . . and learn some English." She was surprised at the response. "The English class increased in attendance. At first prosperous-looking men with light faces and clean collars came. Mrs. Thompson told me: 'Tell them that they do not have to put on their Sunday clothes to come.' . . . I did, but it did no good. They continued to come and after a while it became obvious that they came not only for English classes but for social purposes. Plans for the organization of a social club were then made."[44] The club was named El Club Cultural Latino Americano.

In 1928 the University of Chicago Settlement hired a part-time worker to assist Mexicans, and a year later it became a full-time position. Much of the success of the work among Mexicans, according to the director, was "due in large part to the confidence which the neighborhood Mexicans have been able to put in Mr. and Mrs. Ibañez." Ibañez continued her volunteer work and formed a club for Mexican girls, where she taught them sewing, cooking, and handicrafts. During the 1930s she was very involved in relief work.[45]

Women, especially those who were married or had daughters living at home, were not permitted to frequent the bars and pool halls. They seldom went unescorted to the beach, public swimming pools, ice cream parlors, or movies. Females who did not adhere to these rules were regarded as morally lax. For most women the church and the settlement houses were the only socially acceptable outlets. Even the settlements, however, were often placed off limits by mates and parents, who objected to them because they were Protestant and taught about birth control. Such views were reinforced by Catholic priests. Robert C. Jones of Chicago stated that the "priests identify Hull House with birth control. Therefore they say Hull House is doing more harm than good."[46]

Settlements provided women with information on and assistance with child care, nutrition, health, employment opportunities, immigration laws and procedures, birth control, and civics. They made it possible for Mexicanas to escape the daily drudgery, isolation, and cramped quarters of their homes. There they socialized with other women of their own nationality, shared information and experiences, made new friends, and caught up on local news and happenings in the neighborhood. Women also brought new arrivals and introduced them to friends and social workers, thus broadening and strengthening community ties. At the University of Chicago Settlement, women formed the Mexican Mother's Club, which met during the day. On Wednesday evenings members went on field trips to different parts of the city. About forty women visited museums, airports, and local tourist attractions.[47]

Women generally defended the settlements and other social service agencies from critics in their community and praised their work among Mexicans. "I like the United States," declared a Mexicana. "The United States is good protection for me. If my babies are sick, the welfare takes care of them. I can go to the dispensary. The nurses and doctors come, and when there is no money we don't pay. It is better here than in Mexico."[48]

For Mexican women the settlements and social welfare agencies were important to the economic survival and well-being of the family and community. They used their services and programs to supplement and enhance the extensive informal networks that had developed in Mexican neighborhoods and colonias. Whereas men tended to conceive of American society as closed and hostile, women believed that it offered greater opportunities and services. This attitude was only natural because women made greater use of those services than men. In the opinion of a Mexican social worker,

> The Settlement has become a vital part in the life of the Mexican neighbor. . . . [T]heir contact with the Settlement will surely have an effect upon their future life. In the Settlement they have come in contact with what is wonderful in American life; have enjoyed real American kindliness and hospitality. With such experience, they will go back to their country possessed of a better understanding of American customs, and will not associate America with cold materialism.[49]

Another Mexican, who was interviewed at Hull House, said this:

I would like to tell you before I leave how much the Mexicans appreciate the help that is given them by the people and the offices of this Hull House. We hear of it even as far away as South Chicago when I first came here and they speak of it at the railroad camps outside the city. That is why my son is here and we are very grateful. . . . We remember those things more than the insults and the taunts of ignorant Americans we receive from day to day.[50]

Education

One of the more popular programs offered by the settlements was English instruction. Although some Mexicans were suspicious that learning English was the first step toward naturalization, most were forced to accede that the inability to speak it adversely affected their chances for better jobs and higher wages. "If I had known English and speak it, some of my Mexican friends who did and worked with me could have gotten me into the Union," a railroad worker said during an interview. "Once in the Union I could have gotten regular work and good work. But the Union said I must know English and so there you are. I regret not knowing it very much. The same here in Chicago. I missed some good jobs in the steel mills and other places on that account."[51]

Even the Spanish-language press, which continually cautioned Mexicans against becoming acculturated, supported the idea of education and language instruction. Again the appeals drew not only on self-interest, but also on the patriotic duty of all Mexicans to improve themselves.

An educated worker, a conscientious worker, who has known how to cultivate his intelligence, who has gone to school, who has studied and learned many new and useful things, will be sure to rise, not only intellectually but economically. . . . It is never too late to learn something and one never knows too much to learn something more. By means of an education, the Mexican worker can become great, and will be not only the pride of his hearth and home but of his beloved country, Mexico.[52]

Education for women was promoted for similar reasons. "A woman's happiness or misfortune, like that of the family, depends solely upon her education."[53] According to an editorial in *Mexico,* "to educate the woman is to educate the man; to raise the character of one is to elevate the character of the other; to extend a woman's mental freedom is to assure that of the entire community's."[54]

An official of the Immigrants' Protective League expressed both admiration and satisfaction with the enthusiasm demonstrated by Mexicans over education.

> It is pleasant also, to record his eagerness for Adult Education. He makes the most of the opportunities in the city. He goes to school in the railroad yards, in a passenger coach, by candlelight perchance, and asks if he may have a teacher not two, but four nights a week. In his periods of unemployment, he goes to school in the day time, because as he says, "Until we learn English, we know we are the last to be hired and the first to be laid off." In the total enrollment in night schools alone, the percentage for Mexicans is considerably higher than is their estimated percent in the population.[55]

In 1923, 1924, and 1925 Mexican enrollment in Chicago night schools was 303, 502, and 492, respectively. Their attendance was higher and more consistent than other ethnic groups in these classes.[56] In 1929 the University of Chicago Settlement reported that it had organized three English classes that attracted about 200 Mexicans.[57] English instruction and citizenship classes were also prevalent in Detroit and in the Ford auto plants, where employees were required to apply for their citizenship papers as a prerequisite for being hired or continuing employment. This requirement partially explains why Mexicans in Detroit and the surrounding area appeared to be more acculturated than their counterparts in other midwestern cities.[58]

Edson estimated that about 2 percent of the Mexicans in the Midwest spoke English fluently. "[A]bout 15% speak it well and about 15% can make themselves understood. The other 65% are unable to converse in the language and make no effort to learn it." He also noted that even though "the Mexicans are good attendants at classes for foreigners and they show ability and zeal equal to others not two in a hundred become American citizens."[59]

In some Kansas communities, the rates of English literacy were much higher. According to Robert Oppenheimer, 65 percent of the men over eighteen and 66 percent of the married women living in the Argentine barrio of Kansas City in 1925 were literate in English. "In Garden City 92 percent of the adult immigrants were listed as illiterate in English, but over 55 percent of Mexican and Mexican-American school-age children attended school. . . . Eighty percent of the Mexicans employed by the SFRR [Santa Fe Railroad] in 1925 were literate" (in English) because the company preferred to hire literate workers.[60]

Mexican Clubs and Organizations

In addition to language instruction, the settlements and International Institutes provided meeting space for clubs and organizations. Several Mexican social, literary, mutual aid, and athletic clubs were founded at these places. Hull House was home to several Mexican organizations, including the Aztecas and Cuauhtémoc societies. It also welcomed the Benito Juárez society, the Mexican Athletic Club, and the Mexican Art Theater.[61] Located on the Near West Side of Chicago, Hull House was at the center of the largest Mexican settlement. The numerous programs and social events drew neighborhood residents and people from as far away as Gary, Indiana, and Racine, Wisconsin. Anglo "Mexicanophiles," such as Robert Redfield, who became a recognized anthropologist for his studies of Mexican villages, also gathered at Hull House.

At the University of Chicago Settlement, located in the Back of the Yards, Mexicans established El Club Cultural Latino Americano and clubs for mothers and young people. Mary McDowell, the head resident at the settlement, intervened on behalf of neighborhood residents with the police, public health agencies, and welfare organizations. Like Hull House and the Bird Memorial Center in South Chicago, the University of Chicago Settlement offered citizenship and English classes for men and women. In 1930 the settlement's sponsors expressed satisfaction with their so-called Mexican work. The settlement, its annual report announced proudly, "has come to be an educational and social center for nearly 200 Mexicans in the neighborhood."[62]

Throughout the 1920s the activities sponsored at the settlements were neighborhood centered and ethnically segregated. Mexicans "except on extraordinary occasions, did not meet together with other ethnic groups from the same neighborhood or even with fellow-Mexicans from other neighborhoods."[63] The University of Chicago Settlement reported in 1929 that "the policy has not been to force mixing with the Polish group." It noted that "respect for the exclusiveness of each other has increased, and the animosity that always exists between old and new comers has lessened."[64]

In Gary the International Institute of the YMCA was instrumental in the formation of a Mexican women's organization. Mexicanas responded enthusiastically to Miss Bissell's suggestion in 1921 that they form their own club. However, "the night of the first meeting, most of the women sent their husbands to represent them, on account of babies, meals, lunches for boarders, etc., and in this manner the club got under way and continued."[65] La Sociedad Protectora Mexicana thus became a men's organization.

Five years later women established an auxiliary society and named it La Sociedad Naturalista Feminina. In 1928 both groups consolidated under the leadership of Miss Moreno, the president of the women's group who was associated with the Catholic Neighborhood House in Gary. This conjoining actually created a rift among members because the president of the men's organization was a Protestant. The Catholic element refused to meet at the YMCA and moved their meetings to another location.

That same year another group of women founded La Sociedad de Josefa Ortíz Dominguez, named in honor of the woman who aided Father Miguel Hidalgo y Costilla during the Mexican revolution in 1810. The club provided social outlets and benefits for members. Mexicanas also organized La Sociedad Feminina Mexicana, which affiliated itself with the all-male Benito Juárez society.[66] As in the Chicago area, many of the activities and programs sponsored by neighborhood and social service agencies in the Calumet region were segregated because of ethnic tensions.

In Detroit, Kansas City, and Minneapolis, activities were generally ethnically mixed because ethnic tensions and conflicts were not as pronounced as they were in the Chicago and Calumet region. The Mexican population in these cities remained relatively small, dispersed, migratory, and not highly visible to the larger community. Mexicans had not been brought in as strikebreakers, as they had been in the Chicago and Calumet region. Furthermore, in Detroit the prosperity of the auto industry, the availability of jobs, and higher wage scales had undermined union-organizing programs. Labor strife was relatively absent; management did not pit one group against another in order to break strikes. Most ethnic Whites in these communities did not perceive Mexicans as an economic, employment, or residential threat.

In Detroit Mexicans occupied the lowest rungs of the employment ladder, but there was no obvious wage differential based on race or ethnicity in the auto industry. Because auto plants were typically far from neighborhoods, many of the existing ethnic enclaves did not experience a tremendous influx of Mexican residents who either reduced property values or competed for limited housing. The requirement by Ford and other companies that employees apply for citizenship as a prerequisite for being hired or maintaining their jobs tended to decrease tensions based on nationalistic considerations.[67] In these communities the Mexicans and other immigrant groups often attended ethnically mixed activities sponsored by the International Institutes.

Mexicans, Settlement Houses, and the Issue of Americanization

Not everyone agreed with the mission of the settlements and institutes, nor did everyone support their activities. Some Mexicans refused to patronize these places because they did not like mingling with other nationalities. "The Mexicans think the settlement is chiefly for nationalities hostile to them," explained a Chicago Mexican.[68] Some Mexicans were uncomfortable with people from other cultural and linguistic groups. Traditionalists disliked or objected to the more liberal social mores the settlements embodied. Traditional parents did not allow their daughters to attend social events with boys. Some Mexicans also believed that the English classes were nothing more than veiled attempts by the settlements to convert them to Protestantism.[69] Edson reported that Mexicans stayed away from these agencies and their English classes because "many Mexicans have confused the idea that to learn English is to take a dangerous step toward naturalization, and the latter they do not want."[70]

Chicago's settlement houses initially offered English and naturalization classes concurrently but dropped the latter when they learned Mexicans balked at the idea of citizenship. Thereafter male enrollment in the English classes increased. Although similar classes were available to women, few attended because of the objections raised by fathers and husbands who did not want them to become acculturated or who feared that the ability to communicate in English would make them less dependent on them. Women were also kept away by mates or parents who were wary of and even hostile toward the settlements because they provided information about birth control. Men realized that the Americanization programs in the settlements and other agencies were targeted at the youth and women, which was another reason why they were discouraged from attending these programs.

The Americanization programs, which began around 1915 and gained popularity during the 1920s, did in fact attempt to instill in immigrants values, mores, and work habits that promoted the Protestant work ethic. Proponents of Americanization programs believed that if women adopted these values, the rest of the family would follow suit. Because the homemaker created the environment in which children were raised, they argued, it was important to provide her with the training, background, and outlook that would instill in her qualities such as cooperation, obedience, thrift, and hard work. Failure to socialize working-class people to these values would result in dissatisfaction and rebellion in the work place.[71] "The Americanization of the Mexican woman is as important a part as that of the men," wrote an Americanization teacher in 1923. " 'Go after the women' should become the slogan among Americanization workers, for after all the greatest good is to be obtained by starting the home off right. The children of these foreigners are the advantage of America, not the naturalized foreigners. These are never 100 percent Americans, but the second generation may be. 'Go after the women' and you may save the second generation for America."[72]

In the United States the Americanization programs failed because of their insistence that Mexicans become naturalized. Although Mexicans generally recognized the need to learn English, they had no desire to become U.S. citizens. A long-time resident of Chicago recalled his experiences in an English class in Topeka, Kansas.

> I remember when I was attending night school in . . . 1916. At the end . . . of the course they wanted all of us to become American citizens. They even put on a play depicting immigrants coming over from their countries, discouraged, dressed in rags, bent over, afraid and saying things about their country. Now there were four Mexicans who were taking out their papers and they wanted me to join them in such a scene. But I would not. The teacher asked me: "Aren't you grateful for your education, for your liberties in this country, for your living, for your good times and your prosperity?" She was very mad. I said to her, "Madam, I am not ashamed of my country. I respect the land from which I came. I love this country too but I feel that I cannot become a citizen as yet by principle. Some other time when you are not so mad I will tell you why. . . . If you insist that I take part in such a scene I fear I will leave." "Well do so," she said. And I did.[73]

Another Mexican national argued that citizenship would not alter his social and economic status in this country. "They talk to us about becoming citizens," he said, "but if we become citizens we are still Mexicans. They look at our hair, and listen to our speech and call us Mexicans. Even my boy who was born in the United States is a Mexican it seems. He has to go to a Mexican school. There is always a difference in the way he is treated."[74] Unlike the settlements in Chicago, which remained sensitive to Mexican antipathies about naturalization, those in Gary forged ahead with their plans of Americanizing Mexicans and converting them to the Protestant faith. The two settlements, Campbell

House and Neighborhood House, did not gain many converts because of these programs. Their failure was also due to their relative lateness in beginning their work among Mexicans. For example, Neighborhood House excluded Mexicans until 1925 because of fears that their presence would alienate other immigrant groups who were hostile to them.[75]

In an attempt to speed conversion and attract Mexicans, the settlements began providing social services. The health, education, and recreation programs, however, were mainly used by a small number of women and children. At Neighborhood House efforts to involve significant numbers of young girls and women in activities proved unsuccessful.[76] In assessing the efforts of the Protestant settlements in Gary, Ruth Crocker concluded as follows: "Inevitably, many immigrants came to the settlement, took what they wanted of its services, and remained untouched by its message."[77]

The inability of Protestants to sway the Mexican community in Gary cannot be attributed solely to religious reasons. The question of assimilation played a stronger role in determining the actions of Mexicans. This influence is apparent in their response to the Americanization program promoted by the Catholic Church.

The aggressive proselytizing by the Protestants concerned the Catholic hierarchy because of the inroads they appeared to be making among Mexicans. In 1920 Bishop Herman J. Alerding described Gary as "a hotbed of proselytism" and argued that "something should be done to counteract its venomous influence."[78] That same year he approached Elbert II. Gary, chairman of the U.S. Steel Corporation, and requested funding to build a Catholic settlement house. Alerding, a strong proponent of assimilation, told Gary that the funding represented a good investment because the Americanization programs sponsored by the settlement would foster loyalty and patriotism among the immigrants. These programs would not only combat the insidious forces of atheism and communism, they would also promote harmony between employees and employer.[79] Gary donated $230,000 for the project because Alerding's ideas about Americanization meshed with his. Gary and other steel company officials also decided to support the Catholic Americanization programs because they considered them more promising and realistic than the "quixotic" efforts of the Protestant agencies to convert immigrants first and then Americanize them.[80]

The Gary-Alerding House, the largest and most elaborate of Gary's settlements, was dedicated in December 1923. Under the firm hand of Father John deVille, an Austrian-born priest, the settlement began its programs of social control and Americanization. DeVille, however, quickly discovered that the Mexican community resisted assimilationist schemes, even when they were promoted by the Catholic Church.

Although he was sympathetic to immigrants, deVille's words, actions, and loyalties undermined his efforts. His programs sought to eradicate Mexican traditions and impose political conformity and religious orthodoxy. Mexicans were alienated and angered by his verbal attacks and open disdain for the "uncouth . . . peasants."[81] Not only did he consider Mexicans to be inferior and inassimilable,[82] but he also accused them of being Communists and disloyal. In a speech before the Rotary Club in 1927, he noted that the United States had excluded the European immigrant and "accepted the uncivilized Mexican in his place." DeVille tacitly admitted that the Americanization and religious programs of the Catholic Church had failed when he said, "You can Americanize the man from southeastern and southern Europe, but you can't Americanize a Mexican."[83]

Mexicans objected to deVille's accusations, arguing that he was mistaken in his views about them. In "An Open Letter to Father John B. deVille," Mr. Gallardo summed up the reactions of many of his compatriots. Gallardo wrote that, although he did not wish to besmirch deVille's reputation, he did "want to comment on [his] unfair ideas regarding Mexicans that we never become civilized American citizens." After discussing the destructive influence of the Catholic Church on Mexico's development, he chastised deVille for having labeled Mexicans as "communists." "You also judge us to be criminals," wrote Gallardo. "Criminals exist in all . . . races not just among Mexicans. No matter how great or small a nation is, they all have their criminals from those who crucified Jesus Christ to the individual who insults a race." In response to the idea that Mexicans did not become Americanized, Gallardo noted, "[W]e do not have to become Americans because we are

Americans in body and soul. . . ." He asked the priest not "to judge the cactus by its thorns but by its blossoms."[84]

DeVille's loyalty and close ties to the U.S. Steel Corporation did little to enhance his credibility among working-class people. He chided their suspicions about the motives of the company and openly espoused the view that "the loyalty to those who are responsible for the creation of Gary [i.e., the U.S. Steel Corporation] should be the first requisite."[85] Ultimately the Catholic Church's program to draw Mexicans back to the fold in Gary failed because of the settlement's strong corporate ties, the lack of community involvement in establishing the program, deVille's anti-Mexican attitudes, and the refusal of many Mexicans to desert their culture for the dubious benefits of Christian Americanization.

Most settlement house workers and social service providers were patronizing and assimilationist in outlook, yet they often proved to be more sympathetic to and less biased against ethnic and immigrant groups than the society-at-large. Mexicans were more comfortable with and responded more favorably to organizations where cultural pluralism was a major tenet, such as Hull House, the University of Chicago Settlement, the Immigrants' Protective League, and some of the International Institutes.

Even those agencies that tried to Americanize Mexicans helped them adjust to their new environment by providing a wide variety of programs and services. Through them, Mexicans learned about available resources. These agencies also served as centers where Mexicans met and formed new organizations and social networks. They helped bring Mexicans to the attention of the larger community by mediating with groups outside the colonia or by attracting people from the city's academic and social service communities to Mexican events and programs. Some of these people became important allies, who used their high visibility or positions to help Mexicans. In some instances these organizations made it possible for Mexicans and Europeans to meet each other on fairly neutral ground, allowing them to learn from one another and to begin dismantling the barriers between them. In the process they reinforced the integration of Mexicans into the White ethnic enclaves of their communities. This policy was far different from that encountered by Afro-Americans, who experienced segregation or complete exclusion from settlement services and programs. Mexicans found an open door at the settlements and International Institutes. They were not a panacea for all of the problems faced by Mexican immigrants, but they did offer some succor in an alien environment.[86]

Only about 3 to 6 percent of the Mexican population in the Chicago and Calumet region enrolled in the English courses offered at the settlements.[87] Although the desire to avoid naturalization affected enrollments, other factors contributed to this poor showing. The lack of adequate clothing kept Mexicans from going out in public for fear of being stared at or ridiculed. Self-consciousness also played a role: Mexicans did not want to embarrass themselves by making mistakes in class. Conflict with other ethnic groups kept Mexicans away. "One reason the Mexicans don't go to the public night schools is that the Slovaks and others regard the Mexicans as colored men."[88] Long hours and erratic work schedules kept many from attending classes. In 1926 Atanasio Casares told George Edson he had arrived in Gary in 1918 but had not yet learned English. "He has not learned English," wrote Edson, because "he worked every day, came home tired and spent a few hours with his family or with friends in the pool hall and had no time to learn English."[89] The high mobility imposed on Mexicans because of seasonal unemployment also adversely affected attendance.

Most Mexicans in the Midwest did not participate in the wide variety of programs and activities available to them. This noninvolvement was especially true of the young, unattached men, who often lacked clothing that they believed was good enough to wear in public. Many did not have enough money after expenses to spend on social outings. In some ways the catalyst that created more socially acceptable outlets—the arrival of more women and families—also reduced the number of people who attended these functions. The presence of mates and families helped alleviate the loneliness and boredom that had forced people to seek other diversions. Companionship and the added cost of paying for other family members at social outings induced more people to stay at home. During the winter inclement weather kept Mexicans indoors. The high rate of mobility among Mexicans and unstable employment also affected their ability and willingness to attend social functions.

Class and linguistic differences created discomfort among groups, which discouraged mixing at social events. One man estimated that 300 to 400 Mexicans living in East Chicago spoke Indian dialects and knew very little Spanish. "There are some dances but that does not help the lower classes to find amusement," he said.

> There are some *dias de campo* but they reach only about twenty percent [of the population]. The rest spend their time in overalls living in basements. The biggest part of them are ignorant. It is hard for them to go to meetings with the higher classes. . . . It is hard to go to picnic with those who can't even speak good Spanish. They go to places of vice and to pool halls. They feel embarrassed if the high class Mexicans go where they go.[90]

In spite of both Mexican and cross-cultural efforts, planned social life in the Midwest eluded the large majority of young transients.

CHAPTER 9

Mexicans and the Early Years of the Depression, 1929–1932

In 1928 the Republicans, riding a wave of prosperity, international peace, and domestic tranquility, defeated a badly divided Democratic party in the presidential election. Herbert Hoover, a man born in middle America, overwhelmed Al Smith in the electoral and popular vote. In his inaugural address he exuded extreme confidence about the future of the country. "Ours is a land rich in resources; stimulating in its glorious beauty; filled with millions of happy homes; blessed with comfort and opportunity. . . . In no nation are the fruits of accomplishment more secure. In no nation is the government more worthy of respect. No country is more loved by its people. I have an abiding faith in their capacity, integrity and high purpose. I have no fears for the future of our country. It is bright with hope."[1] This hope was dashed by the onset of the Great Depression.

Loss of Jobs

For Mexicans the depression was disastrous. As jobs became scarce, they were among the first fired and were replaced by "Whites" and "American citizens." At the University of Chicago Settlement, the staff did what it could to help those out of work. Mexicans asked to use the gym in the mornings. "We are out of jobs," one of them said, "and do not have anything to do. We prefer to play basketball than loafing in the poolrooms." M. R. Ibañez, a settlement house worker, asked a friend, "Why did you lose your job?" He responded, "Well, a 'white' man applied for a job in the place where I was working and the foreman, finding no vacancy laid me off and gave my job to the applicant." More and more Mexicans encountered this problem. "Such is the situation," wrote Ibañez in 1929. "Incidents of this nature happened before the present economic crisis came. . . . When the crisis came the Mexicans found themselves in a much more discouraging situation. They were the first ones to be laid off, and in large numbers."[2]

Competition, anger, and frustration increased anti-Mexican feelings and attitudes that had prevailed throughout the 1920s. Discrimination by employers became commonplace, as they too began to support the idea of returning Mexicans to Mexico. For Mexicans the problems created by the crash were not new. They had experienced prolonged periods of unemployment and underemployment even in the most prosperous of times. During the severe depression of 1921–1922, for example, thousands of Mexicans had been laid off or dismissed from their jobs. Their presence at that time had led to complaints that they imposed heavy burdens on local relief agencies, evoking demands for repatriation to alleviate relief rolls and make jobs available for U.S. citizens. In desperation many had turned to mutual aid societies or Mexican consuls for help in returning to Mexico. Others were repatriated by local employers or social welfare agencies. In Detroit Henry Ford had financed the return of more than 3,000 Mexicans.[3] Most Mexicans voluntarily agreed to repatriate in 1921–1922 and wait out the hard times at home. The pattern described above repeated itself after 1929, yet unbeknownst to Mexicans, this depression was to be worldwide in scope and magnitude and of long duration. The United States did not emerge from its shadows until after the Japanese attack on Pearl Harbor in 1941.

In early 1930 employers, at the behest of local, state, and federal authorities, began laying off Mexican employees and replacing them with non-Mexicans. The auto industry, as it had done throughout the 1920s, implemented wholesale layoffs. Between 1929 and 1931, 1,027 or 40 percent of the Mexicans employed by Ford lost their jobs. By the summer of 1931 Ford's labor force had fallen from 128,000 to 37,000. Unemployment in Detroit climbed to 50 percent by 1932, and manufacturing declined 54 percent. Auto industry output fell to 20 percent of what it had been in 1929. Those who had jobs worked only three or four days per week at greatly reduced wages.[4] Businesses in the area suffered from the cutbacks in production and labor force, and thus, they too reduced their work force.

Also hard hit were the steel and iron industries. Between 1930 and 1932 steel production dropped from 90-percent capacity to 15 percent nationally, and Mexicans employed in the steel and iron foundries of Chicago, Gary, Toledo, and Bethlehem lost their jobs.[5] By the early 1930s one out of every ten Mexicans formerly employed in iron and steel manufacturing was unemployed.[6] The building and trades industry cut its Mexican labor force by 15 percent. Sizable cutbacks in the railroad industry also threw many Mexicans out of work, although some employers retained their Mexican employees. In Kansas the Santa Fe Railroad shortened hours or laid off Mexicans for only short periods. Mexicans also helped each other by sharing work time with friends or relatives. In Garden City, Kansas, a rail worker and his friend each worked three days per week on a section gang. This time sharing was also done by his two sons.[7]

Mexicans, whether employed or not, found it increasingly difficult to forestall the hardship that pressed in around them. It was a time, recalled a resident of Bethlehem, Pennsylvania, "when the beans were so high, no one could reach [afford] them."[8] Adding to their travails were the statutes enacted by several states, which required all laborers on public works projects to be U.S. citizens. The implementation of such a statute in Illinois in 1931 further deprived Mexicans of employment opportunities.[9]

Mexicans composed most of the labor force employed by sugar beet companies in Michigan and Minnesota. When the depression struck, many employers discontinued providing transportation and credit and set wage structures based on acreage. They ended welfare programs that aided indigent Mexicans, forcing many to migrate to urban centers or leave the region. By 1930 signs on company doors and gates marked "Only White Labor Employed" became commonplace, as desperate European Americans willingly accepted jobs they had disdained in more prosperous times.[10]

Public Assistance

Although some public assistance was available, most Mexicans were loath to accept help from social welfare agencies. Those who stayed in the Midwest lived off savings, relied on kinship networks, worked at odd jobs, or turned to their own mutual aid societies. Many relied on a combination of these options. Mexicans who were employed often shared what little they had with the less fortunate. In Garden City, Kansas, a Mexicana provided meals and shelter to anyone who came to her door. Although the meals were meager and the table was often crowded, no one was turned away. Visitors were asked to contribute whatever they could afford, but most of the people who knocked on her door were in desperate straits and could give nothing.[11]

In Detroit Mexicans could receive assistance from private charitable organizations, city agencies, and the Ford Motor Company. Case studies from the Ford Sociological Department, however, show that the number of Mexicans who accepted any form of relief was minuscule. Accounts from settlement houses and social workers in Chicago, Gary, and East Chicago noted that very few Mexicans approached them for assistance.

In Minnesota most Mexicans refused help from local agencies. Carlota Arellano proudly recalled, "I spent one year somewhat in need. But I did not receive help . . . of any kind. I survived on my own. I owed nothing to the welfare."[12] The refusal of Mexicans to seek or accept relief is important to note because the forced repatriation drives that emerged later were largely justified on the premise that Mexicans imposed a heavy burden on welfare programs. A substantial body of evidence contradicts this premise.

Mexicans refused public assistance for several reasons. They believed in self-sufficiency and the need to assume responsibility for one's own welfare. Many had become adept at surviving hard times, having weathered numerous periods of unemployment or underemployment. Women's earnings, which had proven invaluable to the economic well-being and survival of the family, were another source of income. Furthermore, women had developed strong networks before the depression and were well informed about events and services in their communities.

Whereas men had concentrated on meeting the power structures in the community (i.e., the police, chambers of commerce, local politicians, and consuls) or on insulating themselves from the outside, women had come into daily contact with other groups and organizations that offered useful and direct assistance. They thus knew what resources were available and where to find them. In this respect they had a strong advantage over single, transient workers, many of whom remained unaware that help was available.

Many Mexicans were precluded from seeking assistance from agencies because they had entered the United States illegally. In fact, most Mexicans in the Midwest were undocumented immigrants. During the 1920s this status had not been problematic because of the lax enforcement of immigration laws. The situation changed, however, with the enactment of the Deportation Act on 4 March 1929, which declared that any alien in the country was subject to deportation on several counts, including illegal entry. The law applied to "aliens of any race" but had the most profound effect on Mexicans.[13] An untold number did not apply for relief to avoid exposure to authorities and possible deportation.

The treatment that some agencies accorded Mexicans discouraged others from seeking help.[14] Some Mexicans were promised relief only if they agreed to repatriate. Assistance from township trustees, who were responsible for disbursing relief, often came grudgingly. According to a Catholic missionary, "relief officials made applicants 'feel like something slimy.'"

In Detroit welfare workers resorted to the "cafeteria list": recipients were forced to eat at "restaurants" operated by the Department of Public Welfare. The food, consisting of veal, sauerkraut, and other items unfamiliar to Mexicans, was often poorly prepared and difficult to eat. Embarrassment, however, was an even greater concern to those who ate there. To be seen at one of these cafeterias was tantamount to a public confession that one could not care for oneself or one's family. Very few proved willing to undergo this kind of humiliation. At times case workers recommended that Mexicans be assigned to cafeteria lists to force them off relief rolls. "Family is contemplating returning to Mexico and the case worker feels they might return more quickly if they are kept on a cafeteria list rather than be given a grocery order." The Department of Public Welfare also resorted to cutting off payments as a way of reducing the number of Mexicans on its rolls. "In conference the supervisor decided to refuse to pay the rent of the family as they have refused to co-operate with the Department and return to Mexico."[15]

Voluntary Repatriation

During the early years of the depression, many Mexicans voluntarily left the Midwest. The impetus for organizing and promoting voluntary departure programs emanated from consuls, Mexican mutual aid societies, local charities, and employers. Individuals also made the decision to leave. Those who could afford to pay their own way quickly left for home. Others appealed to consuls for help in repatriating. In a letter typical of such requests, thirty-seven people wrote to Consul Aveleyra asking for transportation to Mexico. The letter, poorly typed and filled with grammatical errors, nonetheless conveyed the profound suffering and hardship many Mexicans were experiencing because they were unable to find work or relief. The situation had become so desperate that the consul represented their final recourse. They asked him to do everything humanly possible to come to their rescue before "they died of starvation and cold or were driven by hunger to turn to crime and endure the shame of it for a mere slice of bread for their wives and children."[16]

Moved by their plea, the consul immediately wired Mexico City and asked for help. The response, which came on 19 January 1931, was that the government lacked the resources to help these unfortunate people. The best it could do was provide transportation to their homes if they could make it to the border.[17] As had been the case in 1921–1922, bureaucrats and policymakers had not made plans or raised funds and were completely unprepared for the problems and demands that accompanied the remigration of thousands of Mexicans after 1929.

Government officials found themselves trapped by their own rhetoric, which had proclaimed for years their ardent desire to see Mexicans return home. Once the depression deepened, they were in no position to decry publicly the repatriation of nationals. Privately, however, they admonished consuls to do everything possible to persuade Mexicans to remain in the United States. Consuls were also urged to obtain money for the needy from Mexican organizations such as Las Brigadas de Cruz Azul Mexicana and Las Comisiónes Honoríficas. Because these organizations' resources were meager and quickly dissipated, Consul General Enrique González became disenchanted with them after his 1931 inspection tour of the United States.[18] Failing to generate much financial support from Mexican organizations, consuls cooperated with any group that organized a repatriation program. They knew that if Mexicans made their own way to the border, their government would provide rail transportation to points inside Mexico. Consuls, however, were still directed to protect the rights of Mexicans and ensure their fair treatment by those in charge of repatriation.[19]

In 1929 the consul general in New York warned Mexicans about dishonest repatriation schemes. One man pretended to represent a company that arranged transportation to the border. After collecting fares, he absconded with the money, leaving those who had paid destitute and stranded at the railroad depot. Another scheme involved bogus employment agencies that promised jobs to anyone who paid a $5 fee. One agent distributed notices of employment at the Cleveland naval yards. Those who paid the fee were promised free transportation, furnished rooms, and stoves. When the day of departure arrived, the agent was nowhere to be found.[20] Such practices led Consul General E. D. Ruiz to caution Mexicans to select leaders for repatriation efforts who were "honorable men who would not abuse the trust of our nationals."[21]

Between 1929 and 1931 most of the voluntary repatriation programs were organized by charitable groups in cooperation with Mexican governmental or community representatives. Mexican nationals also formed groups to assist in the repatriation effort. Sugar beet workers in Detroit founded El Comité Pro Repatriaciónes, which solicited help and protection from the Mexican government in returning nationals to their homeland.[22] La Liga de Obreros y Campesinos de Michigan was organized in 1932 by Diego Rivera, the noted Mexican muralist; by Luís Gasca, a newspaper editor; and by the Honduran Consul Charles Benjamin to help those who wished to repatriate. Although Rivera warned Mexicans that conditions in Mexico were much worse and "that a return [there] would not solve their problems," he helped those who wished to leave the United States by donating his own money to the program. Rivera also tried to convince the Mexican government to provide land, shelter, and tools for repatriates to use in developing agricultural colonies in sparsely settled areas of Mexico.[23]

La Liga enlisted the help of Michigan Governor Brooks, who was more than happy to publicize the campaign and encourage Mexicans to leave the state. When Brooks invited the Immigration and Naturalization Service (INS) to participate, the Mexican government asked the INS to downplay the idea that the campaign was a deportation drive aimed at undocumented workers. The government feared that such publicity would intimidate those who had entered illegally. The campaign netted about 1,288 repatriates from Michigan. Several thousand more traveled to Michigan from Ohio and Pennsylvania in order to repatriate, bringing the total number of repatriates from Michigan to about 5,000. Included in this figure were several hundred children who had been born in the United States.[24] Similar efforts were undertaken in other midwestern cities. Most of these campaigns were motivated by humanitarian reasons that sought to alleviate the hardship and suffering of those who wished to return home.

During the early stages of the depression, many Mexicans returned to Mexico of their own volition and at their own expense. They did so by purchasing rail tickets to the border or by driving their cars and trucks. Vehicles headed southward daily, loaded with all the worldly possessions they could hold. To accommodate repatriates the Mexican government allowed them to bring back their material possessions duty free. If space permitted, drivers sold seats to anyone who wished to risk the long, arduous journey in vehicles that were ill prepared to negotiate the distances. Whenever possible Mexicans formed car caravans. These images of displacement were the harbingers of scenes that came to symbolize the depression era—men, women, children, and belongings all trundled in ramshackle trucks and automobiles traveling across the American landscape in search of food, work, and opportunity.

This mass exodus of Mexicans from all over the United States converged along border points. The consul at Nuevo Laredo noted, "In crossing the international bridge each day one can always see a line of cars with licenses from nearly half the United States filled with household effects of Mexicans returning and waiting to make the necessary arrangements with the Mexican authorities."²⁵ Those arrangements were simple, requiring only an oral declaration of nationality. For people without cars the journey often proved more difficult, especially once they reached the border. There they joined thousands of others awaiting space on overcrowded trains. More often than not the wait lasted for weeks. In border towns such as Nuevo Laredo and Juárez, the increased population created shortages of all kinds and strained services that were already overtaxed. Many were forced to sell their possessions just to survive.

In addition to their desire to return home, Mexicans were drawn back by announcements of colonization projects sponsored by the government. Discussion of such projects had begun in 1930. In 1932 the National Repatriation Committee was established to create communal agricultural colonies for repatriates. Later that year the Committee directed itself to creating several colonies along the west coast.

The first two colonies opened in mid-1932: at El Coloso, Guerros, near Acapulco and at Pinotepa Nacional near Minizo, Oaxaca. The colony at Pinotepa Nacional held great promise because of its location in a fertile, sparsely populated area with an abundant water supply. Unfortunately, the project was poorly planned and administered, causing disillusionment among the seven hundred colonists. The harsh discipline, inadequate supplies, and news that the corn they raised would be fed to farm animals forced many into leaving. Within ten months of its establishment, only eight colonists remained at Pinotepa. Projects in other areas, including Baja California, met similar fates. By 1934 the National Repatriation Committee had dissolved, bringing an end to internal colonization efforts.²⁶

Forced Repatriation

As the depression worsened, governmental and private groups in the United States increasingly coerced Mexicans to repatriate. Although some pressure to leave had been exercised before 1931, forced repatriation became more common in 1932 and thereafter. The number of welfare cases across the Midwest was evidence of the growing crisis. In Detroit it jumped from 3,000 in 1929 to 21,000 by 1932. Even though that city's welfare department was one of the most efficiently operated in the country, the overwhelming demand forced it to halt relief efforts in 1933.

By 1932 Americans were asking why their government was spending limited funds on "aliens" when so many citizens were in need. Local organizations and residents began demanding the removal of undesirables and the culling of relief rolls. Hard-pressed city, county, and state officials, as well as private agencies, agreed that action was necessary. It was a matter of simple economics. "The elimination of such a large number of alien laborers and mechanics will work a tremendous benefit not only on the economic situation of the State of Michigan insofar as it concerns welfare expenditures," said John L. Zurbrick, district director of immigration in Detroit, "but will remove from the economic field a group that for some unknown reason is able to get first consideration in employment in the industries of this country and by their removal the opening in industry will be left for residents and citizens of the United States."[27]

The plan implemented by private concerns and public officials offered free food and transportation to the Mexican border. Local welfare officials and private citizens absorbed the $15 cost per ticket.[28] By this time, however, news had filtered back about the problems along the border and the failure of the colonization projects. Furthermore, many Mexicans who remained in the Midwest were U.S. citizens or had made a conscious decision to remain. "The family are very much against going to Mexico as the man has citizenship papers. Woman is very hostile to the idea," reported a case worker. Another noted, "Mary Lou (age fifteen), born in Wayne, Michigan, did not wish to return to Mexico . . . as she felt that she was a citizen and should not be asked to [leave]." A third case worker reported that "although Mr. M. had citizenship, the worker demanded that he repatriate himself in view of the dependency of his family."[29] Mexican resistance to repatriation led to harsher measures by officials and blatant disregard for the immigrants' rights. In many communities in the Midwest, Mexicans were threatened with deportation, stoppage of relief payments, or an end to rental support.

When the depression struck Minnesota, the Minneapolis–St. Paul area was not as affected as other cities. In fact, the Twin Cities weathered the winter of 1929–1930 rather well. The unemployed and those in need turned to the Family Welfare Association, the largest cash-assistance private agency in Minneapolis, as well as to other charitable organizations. The Union City Mission took in more than 1,000 homeless and jobless men nightly during the cold wave that struck the city in 1930. Many of the privately funded charities and welfare groups, however, found themselves hard pressed to meet the growing needs of the unemployed, which had climbed to 35,000 by January 1931.

The relief issue was exploited by Minnesota politicians, who used it to gain support and undermine opponents. The crisis intensified during 1932, as limited funds dwindled and Minneapolis voters elected conservative Alexander G. "Buzz" Bainbridge as mayor. During the election he had campaigned on a platform that espoused a compulsory work program and the complete reorganization of the relief department. A month after his election, Bainbridge proposed "that the relief department's entire investigative staff of fifty-seven social workers be abolished." Ostensibly presented as an economizing measure, his proposal was in truth designed to harass those on relief, especially "outsiders." This objective became apparent when he argued that the police department was better equipped to handle investigations of relief applications. He charged that the relief department's "paternalistic policies" toward the unemployed had driven up welfare costs by making the city a haven for "floaters from all over the country." Bainbridge proposed that all aid to nonresident transients end by 1 October 1933.

Melchior U. S. Kjorland, who had become the superintendent of public relief in October of that year, adamantly opposed the mayor's proposal. Their battles raged for the next year, attracting a great deal of attention from the public and press. By 1934 Bainbridge's fulminations had quieted somewhat, and the city adopted a more moderate stance on relief policies. This change was partly due to the appearance of federal relief programs in 1933.

Unfortunately, during the initial stages of the controversy between the mayor and the superintendent, many residents shared the former's anti-alien, antitransient sentiments, forcing many Mexicans to leave the Twin Cities. Removal from relief rolls, discrimination in hiring practices, and forced repatriations reduced their numbers from about 1,500 in 1929 to less than 500 in 1932.[30] In 1934, 328 more Mexicans were repatriated or deported at the request of relief authorities. Among them were children who had been born in the United States.[31]

By January 1931 the number of unemployed in Illinois had reached 700,000. One of the hardest hit areas was Cook County, which contained the largest concentration of Mexicans in the Midwest. Two years later unemployment in the state peaked at 1.5 million.[32] Children went to school without lunch, and hundreds of homeless women slept in Chicago's parks. Efforts to provide relief had been completely routed by 1933.[33]

The Mexican population in Chicago numbered about 21,000 in 1930; by 1938 it was less than 16,000. Mexicans were hard hit because most of them were unskilled laborers. By 1935 unemployment among Mexicans had reached more than 30 percent.[34] As elsewhere, many departed during the early years of the depression to seek work in other parts of the country. Between 1929 and 1933 most Mexicans who left the city did so voluntarily. During these years repatriation was funded by local private and public agencies, which considered it an economical, one-time alternative to long-term assistance. The Mexican consul openly supported these programs, calling them "a laudable undertaking."[35]

Chicagoans, however, did not exert a great deal of pressure on Mexicans to leave. This attitude reflected their treatment of Mexicans during the 1920s, when the immigrants had been subjected to a kind of benign neglect. Although interethnic conflict and tensions had plagued Chicago, they had not been as widespread or prolonged as in East Chicago and Gary. No campaign arose to force Mexicans to leave the Chicago area during the hard times after 1929.[36]

Despite this relatively benign attitude, Mexicans did encounter discrimination and harsh treatment during the depression. *El Nacional* complained that Mexicans were harassed and threatened by the police. "Every day the attitude of local police is more intolerable. Sometimes they imprison honest Mexicans who are not guilty of violating any law." The reporter described a raid on El Gato Negro, a local pool hall. The police had drawn their weapons and abused the patrons. "The policemen after using profane language and without explanation, took the . . . Mexicans away. It is funny that the policemen do not prosecute the real criminals, but cowardly beat and insult our defenseless compatriots."[37]

In another incident, two agents from the Immigration Department entered the home of a Mexican without a warrant. In searching the house they overturned furniture, after which they took the man into custody. Later it was discovered that Mr. Romero was a naturalized citizen who lived with his family "in a luxurious North Side apartment." An editorial in *La Defensa* lamented the plight of Mexicans in Chicago. "The prolonged industrial depression has made of us who compose the foreign element, the principle victims. The Mexican population is perhaps the most affected. The percentage of unemployed Mexicans is higher if we compare it with the other groups in Chicago. . . . More than twenty-five percent of the Mexicans in Chicago are unemployed, some have been for months, and many of them for years."[38]

Mexicans were the first to be laid off or fired. Some men deserted their families once they found they could not get employment or receive aid. This practice sometimes led to tragic consequences for the family. In 1932 *El Nacional* reported that a Mexican had been drawn to an old building by the plaintive cries of a six-week old infant. "When Manuel Castillo entered the building, he stood horrified at the sight of the baby making futile efforts to reach its mother's bosom. Her body was motionless. . . . Five small unclothed and hungry children were standing around the bed where the lifeless mother was stretched out. The windows of the house were boarded up, leaving the place in complete darkness."[39]

Mexicans in the Calumet Region

Mexicans in Gary, South Chicago, and Indiana Harbor were treated more harshly than they were in Chicago. This abuse was partly due to the long-standing ethnic tensions, which had marred relations between Mexicans and eastern Europeans in those communities. The depression exacerbated hostilities and hatched repatriation schemes designed to force Mexicans out of the region.

The drive was spearheaded by veterans of World War I, whose dislike of Mexicans dated back to the armistice and the disastrous steel strike of 1919. After being discharged, many servicemen had returned to find their jobs taken by "foreigners," southern Blacks, and women. This led to widespread demonstrations against employers who hired Mexicans and to the subsequent firing of Mexican nationals. The failure of the steel strike was mistakenly blamed on Mexican scab labor. Inter-ethnic violence during the 1920s and the belief that Mexicans lowered wage scales and deprived American citizens of jobs further solidified anti-Mexican attitudes in the Calumet region. In many respects, the repatriation drives that occurred in the region after 1932 were part of a continuum that extended back to 1918.

Before 1932 most Mexicans who left the Calumet region did so of their own volition. Assistance was provided by groups such as the Mt. Carmel Mission, the Emergency Relief Association, and the trustee's office. The International Institute, which had close ties to Mexicans in the area, demonstrated concern for their welfare. During the voluntary phase of repatriation, the institute attempted to secure free transportation for Mexicans from Gary's Council of Social Agencies. When this failed, the institute approached the Mexican consul in Chicago and arranged for free passes on Mexican railroads for those who reached the border on their own. Those who chose to remain pooled family resources or combined households, hoping the hard times would quickly subside.

Things went from bad to worse, however, and with them came a greater intolerance toward Mexicans. Anti-alien editorials, stories, and cartoons began appearing with regularity in the local press. In September 1931 the American Legion announced a program to combat the economic problems plaguing the community. A major part of the plan was to repatriate indigent aliens. Such a move, argued one member of this group, would end unemployment in Lake County and help in recovery. Secretary of Labor William Doak sanctioned the idea but cautioned organizers that the federal government could do little to help them because Mexicans had not violated any immigration laws.[40]

The lack of government assistance did not deter the proponents of repatriation. In seeking local support for their program, they argued that "the most effective plan of relief for this community would be the removal of the nationalists, especially the Mexicans."[41] The Mexicans became the scapegoats for the frustration, fear, and nativism the depression had unleashed. Their dark skin, Catholicism, and refusal to naturalize and assimilate, plus the popular stereotypes that enveloped them, "contributed to the ease with which Americans embraced the panacea of repatriation."[42]

By 1932 Mexicans were being forced to leave the Calumet region. The International Institute, which had supported voluntary departures, withdrew its support at the behest of its national office, the YWCA Department of Immigration and Foreign Communities. The DIFC urged that "no assistance in repatriation be given unless first investigated and ascertained that aliens will be better off in [their] homeland." Representatives of the Gary International Institute agreed: "The report is a confirmation of our contention that families who have been in this country many years should not be forced to leave." It also reported that "among 111 Mexicans who left a few days ago were several who went unwillingly."[43] Despite the objections of the institute, the movement continued, drawing support from local businessmen, nativists, township trustee officials, the local press, and the American Legion.

Businessmen and employers saw repatriation as a way of lowering taxes. Horace S. Norton of the U.S. Steel Corporation and president of the Gary Commercial Club and the Gary Chamber of Commerce, said that sending Mexicans back was an act of kindness. They had failed to assimilate and were unhappy in Gary. In an incredible statement, Norton disavowed his company's responsibility for having brought Mexican workers to Gary. "I personally know," he said, "that no Lake County concern made any effort to get them to come here."[44]

Township trustee officials believed that returning nationals to Mexico would significantly reduce relief costs. The local press agreed. The *Gary Post-Tribune* reported that each family on relief cost the township $336.00 per year, but the price for sending one family back to Mexico only amounted to $37.50.

Contributions for the drive were solicited from settlement houses and individuals. Money was also raised by sponsoring a stag party at a local Knights of Columbus Hall. To assuage those who might object to the gambling and other attractions at the event, the fundraiser was tagged as a "civic and patriotic duty" because "the proceeds will go to a worthy cause—that of unofficially deporting Mexicans from Gary to reduce the amount of poor relief."[45]

The money raised through these means, however, proved insufficient. To subsidize the campaign, the Lake County commissioners adopted the Wells Plan in March 1932, which authorized the removal of every Mexican family on public assistance. To defray expenses for implementing the plan, local businesses contributed money. In turn, they received scrip for use in paying local taxes. The scrip approved by the commissioners bore 6-percent interest. The funds collected from this venture paid for the repatriation of 3,600 Mexicans from Gary, East Chicago, and the rest of Lake County in 1933.[46]

Mexicans who were forcibly expelled during this phase expressed outrage and disappointment over their treatment. Most of them had no desire to return to Mexico, and many of them were either U.S. citizens or had children born in the United States. News from Mexico about the failure of the colonization projects, high unemployment, and shortages of all kinds further dissuaded them from leaving. A young girl who was deported said, "This is my country but after the way we have been treated I hope never to see it again. . . . [W]e can't get justice here."[47] Another East Chicago resident stated, "We weren't asked voluntarily if we wanted to go. . . . So they told you . . . 'We are going to take you off welfare.' 'Oh, God what are you going to do, take us off welfare? We'll starve.' 'No, no you have an alternative . . . go to Mexico. We have a train that is available. A train full of Mexican people.' So actually they weren't forcing you to leave, they gave you a choice, starve or go back to Mexico."[48]

The depression and the repatriation and deportation drives it inspired had a profound effect on Mexicans in the Midwest. The population significantly declined between 1929 and 1936 in many of the colonias. The Mexican population in Chicago fell from 21,000 in 1930 to 14,000 in 1933; by 1934 only 12,500 remained in the city. The colonia in the Calumet region, which had grown to about 15,000 inhabitants in 1926, was reduced to 5,354 in 1930. Detroit's Mexican population dropped from 15,000 in 1928 to 5,615 in 1930.[49]

Nationally the voluntary and involuntary repatriation of Mexicans caused about 500,000 (one-third of those in the United States) to leave the country. According to Paul Taylor, a disproportionate number of them came from the Midwest. Whereas Michigan, Indiana, and Illinois contained only 3.6 percent of all the Mexicans who were in the United States legally, they provided over 10 percent of the repatriates. His estimates, however, do not include U.S. citizens of Mexican descent who were also expelled. Between 1930 and 1932 more than 32,000 Mexicans left Illinois, Indiana, Michigan, and Ohio. In 1928 George Edson estimated that 63,780 Mexicans lived in the north-central states, which included the four listed above. That same year the Mexican consul in Chicago estimated that approximately 50,000 were in his jurisdiction. According to Edson's estimates, the repatriations resulted in more than half of the Mexican population leaving the region. According to the consul's figures, the repatriations forced more than 64 percent of the Mexican population to return to Mexico.[50]

Mexicans who avoided repatriation did not fare much better. They continued to suffer from privation, discrimination, and harassment from local authorities. Employers, under community pressure, hired only U.S. citizens. By 1932 the steel industry required employees to provide proof of citizenship or their "first papers" as a requisite for continued employment. This policy, which was in widespread use throughout the country after 1932, adversely affected people of Mexican descent. Municipalities and states enacted statutes requiring anyone employed on public works or receiving relief to be a citizen. In Detroit hundreds of Mexicans lost their street railway jobs as a result of this policy. Mexicans encountered the same problem under New Deal programs.

The repatriation and deportation drives that began in 1929 came as no big surprise to many Mexicans in the Midwest. Such programs had occurred throughout the 1920s after any major economic downturn or when nativistic attitudes reached a fever pitch. The events that followed closely on the heels of the depression simply confirmed what many of them already knew—they were welcome only as long as their labor was needed.

These realities, however, did not completely assuage the bitterness, frustration, and anger that the drives created among Mexicans. Some rued that their hard work and sacrifices had significantly contributed to the region's economic growth and development but that the wealth they helped generate had bypassed them and gone to others. For those who had become naturalized citizens or had been born in the United States, the uprooting was even harsher. Teachers, employers, the press, and social workers had couched the idea of "Americanization" in terms of greater opportunity and acceptance. Now the illusory nature of such promises was evident as citizens and noncitizens alike were herded onto trains for the return trip to Mexico.

Mexicans accepted their fate philosophically, if not cynically. "Things had always been difficult, so why should they be any different now?" remarked a deportee from East Chicago. Carey McWilliams observed, "They have been shunted back and forth across the border for so many years by war, revolution and the law of supply and demand, that it would seem that neither expatriation [nor] repatriation held any more terror for them."[51] If hard times lay ahead, others reasoned, then it was best to face them with friends or family back home. "If you were broke and without a job, would you rather be home, or in a foreign country?" queried one Mexican who had opted to repatriate. Another said that "in Mexico there are always beans and tortillas. You can eat whether you have money or not. In the United States if you have no money, you starve."[52] A Mexican repatriate was more than happy to leave. He found the winters "too cold" and the "gringos unfriendly."[53]

The major repatriation campaigns ended in 1935. Despite promises that "getting rid of the Mexican" would alleviate the burden on relief rolls, create jobs for American citizens, and place the country on the road to recovery, all failed to materialize. This failure was apparent in 1936, when President Franklin D. Roosevelt declared in his second inaugural address that he saw "one-third of a nation ill-housed, ill-clad, ill-nourished."[54] In retrospect, the number of Mexicans on relief between 1929 and 1935 had been small. The condition that afflicted American society was not due to the large numbers of Mexicans who had crossed the border in search of employment and opportunity. Their removal, therefore, did little to alleviate the suffering the depression created.

Epilogue

At the height of Michigan's repatriation campaign in 1933, S.L.A. Marshall, a *Detroit News* reporter, had written that the drive was "the closing of an epoch."[1] In some ways he was correct. By 1937 much of the so-called Immigrant Generation of Mexicans had been displaced and returned to the Southwest or Mexico. Most Mexican-based and Mexican-led organizations had also disappeared, and with them, the sponsorship of events and programs that underscored loyalty to Mexico and its culture. Decreased immigration further weakened the influence of Mexico in midwestern communities. Businesses catering to and operated by Mexicans folded. So did many of the Spanish-language newspapers that had served as the voice of a highly nationalistic elite. Families supplanted the large, transient, solo population that had predominated throughout the predepression era in the Midwest.

During the 1930s the gap in the ratio of men to women closed noticeably. In East Chicago there were seventy-six men to every twenty-four women. By 1940 the ratio of men to women was fifty-eight to forty-two. In 1930 less than 30 percent of Mexican-descent men in East Chicago had wives. Ten years later more than half of the men in the colonia were married. As a result the number of U.S.-born children also increased. By the mid-1930s many Mexican families in the region had become more deeply rooted in their communities. The average length of residence in the Midwest now stood at ten and one-half years.[2]

As the 1930s progressed, the number of Mexicans who were born in the United States or became naturalized citizens increased. For the first time since the great migration of Mexicans began around 1900, Mexican Americans made up more than half of the Mexican-descent population in the United States.[3] The rate of naturalization among Mexicans also rose. Many established residency and became citizens to qualify for jobs on public works. There was also a noticeable shift in the Immigrant

Generation's attitude toward the federal government. This change was partially due to the New Deal, whose programs brought direct and indirect benefits to Mexicans and Mexican Americans. To people of Mexican descent and to Americans in general, the federal government became a benefactor who assumed responsibility for their welfare, creating loyalty to that government and, by extension, to the Democratic party.

The repatriation drives and the intolerance spawned by the depression convinced many Mexicans of the importance of becoming U.S. citizens. A major rationale behind the repatriation and deportation schemes was that Mexicans were not assimilable and had refused naturalization. Most of the Mexicans who had been forced to leave were from the ranks of the most recent and least rooted members of the community—traits that added credence to this rationale. There were, of course, more compelling motives behind the drives, as evidenced by the large number of citizens who were returned to Mexico. Nonetheless, those who remained in the region appear to have taken the message to heart. By the mid-1930s Mexican enrollment in citizenship, Americanization, and English classes increased substantially.

The growing acculturation became evident in many midwestern Mexican communities. The number of Mexican-descent children enrolled in the public schools increased, as did their graduation rates. More children of Mexican descent were born in the United States. Intermarriages became more common. The forces of acculturation had already manifested themselves within many Mexican colonias during the highly nationalistic 1920s. The strength of these forces is reflected in the grave concern over Americanization and de-Mexicanization expressed by government officials, the Spanish-language press, and community leaders. The acculturation process accelerated, however, as the influence of the Immigrant Generation declined. With its demise as a guiding force in colonias, activities that reinforced traditional Mexican culture and values declined. Although elements of Mexican culture continued during the 1930s, they were increasingly merged with societal elements. For example, Mexicans had danced to their own music performed by their own bands and orchestras during the 1920s. In the 1930s those same bands, many of whom kept their Mexican names, played music from the big band era.

Social workers in Chicago and the Calumet region reported that Mexicans in the 1930s interacted more with other ethnic groups and patronized social events at the settlements that attracted culturally and ethnically diverse populations. Many of the events were planned around celebrations of American holidays such as Halloween, Thanksgiving, Christmas, New Year's Eve, and the Fourth of July. This intermingling represented a significant shift from the 1920s, when settlements had sponsored separate activities for each group in the neighborhood to avoid conflict.[4]

Mexicans also began to participate more openly in local politics and labor unions. In 1938 the First American Political Club was founded by a group of native-born and recently naturalized Mexicans. Many of its members came from the ranks of the professionals or union leaders. The club's goals were to unite the colonia, actively participate in political campaigns, and help those who wanted to become naturalized.[5] Although its members did not achieve those goals, the club's existence attests to the important change that had taken place within Mexican organizations. Whereas those of the Immigrant Generation saw themselves as temporary sojourners in the United States, those of the so-called Mexican American Generation, which emerged during the 1930s, thought of themselves as permanent residents and U.S. citizens. The new generation espoused the pursuit of the "American Dream" rather than the "Mexican Dream" and the achievement of integration and equality within American society.[6]

The ethnic tensions that had marred relations between Mexicans and European ethnic groups were ameliorated later in the depression. This improvement was partly due to the significant decline in the transient, solo and soltero population and the decrease in the number of Mexicans throughout the Midwest.

The depression itself exercised a leveling influence among Americans. Regardless of their ethnic origins or class, many Americans now shared a common experience and frame of reference. The emphasis was now on bread-and-butter issues, survival, and the need to close ranks. In many respects the depression created a greater sense of community and empathy among Americans. Although Mexicans were initially made scapegoats and their removal was heralded as a panacea for the nation's economic ills, sober reality set in after the massive repatriations failed to bring an end to the depression. Increasingly, Americans adopted a more religious explanation for their troubles. Rather than seeking ethnic scapegoats, they turned to their own acts of commission and omission as reasons for their suffering. Many came to believe that the depression represented God's retribution for their sins during the previous decade. At least for the time being, the desperate state in which so many Americans lived drew more attention to their similarities than their differences.

For most Mexicans and Mexican Americans, there was little comfort in this change of heart. The realization by Americans that Mexicans were not to blame for the depression came too late to spare many Mexicans from the agony, frustration, and despair of repatriation. Although acculturation became more prevalent among people of Mexican-descent, its adoption was often based on necessity and was not always embraced completely or enthusiastically. Mexicans continued to retain their basic institutions and values. Their sense of peoplehood and ethnicity, forged in the crucible of the immigrant process, did not dissipate in the face of economic hardship or external pressure. Even if they had thoroughly embraced the tenets of acculturation, they had not been integrated into the fabric of American society. Mexicans and Mexican Americans were continually reminded that they had not yet achieved equal status and that the problems associated with discrimination, exploitation, and prejudice still remained to be redressed.

In late 1937 and early 1938, the emigration process triggered by the events of 1929 began to reverse itself. This time, however, many of those who traveled to the Midwest were Mexican Americans from Texas and other southwestern states. Also on the increase were Hispanics from other regions such as Puerto Rico, Cuba, and Central and South America. Unlike their Mexican predecessors to the region, many of these Hispanics came with their families and with the intent of settling permanently. The onset of World War II accelerated the movement northward, as people of Latin descent returned in even greater numbers to revitalize a region and a country that had yielded little more than broken promises to their Mexican predecessors.

Notes

For complete citations for notes, see the bibliography.

Acronyms Used in Notes

AGN   Archivo General de la Nación, Mexico City

ARE   Archivo Histórico de la Secretaría de Relaciónes Exteriores, Mexico City

CRA   Calumet Regional Archives, Indiana University Northwest, Gary

FLPS   Foreign Language Press Survey, Chicago Public Library, Chicago

IPL   Immigrants' Protective League reports, University of Illinois Archives, Chicago

INS, RG 85   Immigration and Naturalization Service, Record Group 85, National Archives, Washington, D.C.

UCS   University of Chicago Settlement reports, Chicago Historical Society, Chicago

Chapter 1, Mexican Immigration to the United States, 1900–1917

1. Glaab and Brown, *History of Urban America*; Green, *American Cities*; Kramer and Holborn, *City in American Life*; McKelvey, *Urbanization of America*; Schlesinger, *Rise of the City*.

2. Garraty, *New Commonwealth*, chap. 3.

3. Adna Weber, *Growth of Cities*, pp. 22, 28; U.S. Bureau of the Census, *Fifteenth Census*, vol. 3, pt. 1, *Population*, p. 18.

4. For examples of the voluminous literature that presented the negative aspects of urban life, see *Spider and the Fly*; Buel, *Metropolitan Life*.

5. Cardoso, *Mexican Emigration*, p. 7. An estimated one million Mexicans fled to the United States during the Revolution—about 10 percent of Mexico's population.

6. Garraty, *New Commonwealth*, p. 87; George Taylor and Irene Neu, *American Railroad*, pp. 3–14, 16, 37, 47.

7. Cardoso, *Mexican Emigration*, pp. 13–14.

8. Martínez, *Mexican Emigration*, p. 4.

9. Cardoso, *Mexican Emigration*, pp. 26–27.

10. Laird, "Argentine, Kansas," p. 117.

11. Oppenheimer, "Acculturation," p. 435.

12. Oppenheimer, "Acculturation," p. 433.

13. Latino Oral History Project.

14. T. G. Pellicer, Consul, Philadelphia, to Cándido Aguilar, Consul General, Secretaría de Relaciónes Exteriores, 16 November 1916, "Visita que hizo nuestro Cónsul ... a los obreros mexicanos que trabajan en . . . Ferrocaril," File IV/524, 12-7-95, ARE.

15. Ibid.

16. Ibid.

17. Secretaría de Relaciónes Exteriores, Consulado de Mexico, St. Louis, Mo., "Remite informe de los trabajos ejucatidos por su Oficina Consular, durante los últimos seis meses del año próximo pasado" (1919), File IV/033(04)/1. 17-14-150, ARE, p. 5.

18. Valdés, *Al Norte*, pp. 12, 27. According to a study conducted in 1926, only about one-third of the Mexican beet workers in the upper Midwest returned south after the season ended. Paul Taylor, *Mexican Labor: Dimmit County*, pp. 308, 419, 420, 430; Edson, "North Central States," Taylor Collection, p. 156.

19. Valdés, "Betabeleros," pp. 2–3.

20. Ibid., p. 2.

21. Valdés, *Al Norte*, p. 4.

22. Valdés, *El Pueblo*, p. 8.

23. Valdés, "Betabeleros," p. 3.

24. U.S. Children's Bureau, *Child Labor*, p. 79.

25. Valdés, *Al Norte*, p. 3.

26. Oppenheimer, "Acculturation," p. 433.

27. Baba and Abonyi, *Mexicans of Detroit*, p. 43.

28. Ibid.

29. Ibid., p. 44.

30. Latino Oral History Project.

31. Ibid.

32. Murillo, "Detroit Mexican Colonia," pp. 13–14; S.L.A. Marshall, "Mexican Labor Leaving Michigan for Homeland," *Detroit News*, 9 November 1932, p. 6.

33. Vargas, *Proletarians*, p. 24.

34. Edson, "Detroit," Taylor Collection, p. 19; Edson, "Lorain," Taylor Collection, p. 10.

35. Amentrout, Brown, and Gibbons, *Child Labor*, pp. 6–7; House Committee, *National Defense Migration*, p. 7873.

36. Governor's Interracial Commission, *Race Relations in Minnesota*, p. 8; St. Paul Neighborhood House, "Mexicans in St. Paul," p. 5.

37. Information provided by J. L. Cook of Continental Sugar Co., "Reports," Taylor Collection.

38. Gamio, *Mexican Immigration*, p. 86.

39. Valdés, *El Pueblo*, p. 10; "Reports," Taylor Collection, p. 10; Cane, *Social Life*, p. 1. Not all housing was as dismal as this. Some sugar beet companies, such as the Minnesota Sugar Co., provided clean and adequate housing for their workers. Governor's Interracial Commission, *Race Relations in Minnesota*, p. 9.

40. Gamio, *Mexican Immigration*, p. 86.

41. Valdés, "Betabeleros", pp. 2–3.

42. In 1914, 1,218,480 persons entered the United States from abroad. By 1918, however, World War I and the *Immigration Act of 1917* had reduced immigration to less than 10 percent of what it had been in 1914. Cardoso, *Mexican Emigration*, p. 46.

43. Corwin, "Causes of Mexican Emigration," pp. 620–621.

44. John L. Burnett to William B. Wilson, 27 May 1917, File 54, 261/202, INS, RG 85. Burnett felt so strongly about the matter that he introduced legislation (H.R. 4852) to repeal the section of the *Immigration Act of 1917* that permitted the Secretary of Labor to suspend provisions within the act. H.R. 4852 was not acted upon. *Congressional Record*, 65th Cong., 1st sess., 1917, 55, pt. 3, p. 3253; Reisler, *Sweat of Their Brow*, pp. 28–29.

45. Senate Committee, *Emergency Immigration Legislation*, pp. 698–699.

46. Ibid., pp. 700, 703–707.

47. Ibid., p. 704.

48. Ibid., p. 708.

49. Ibid., p. 709; Anthony Caminetti, Commissioner-General of Immigration, to Commissioner of Immigration and Inspectors in Charge of Districts, memorandum, 3 January 1919, File 811.504/150, State Department, RG 59.

50. Reisler, *Sweat of Their Brow*, p. 34, 50.

51. The Border Patrol was not officially established until 1924. Before then, the border was patrolled mostly by Treasury agents looking for smugglers. Even after the Border Patrol was established, its main concern was controlling smugglers.

52. U.S. Department of Commerce and Labor, *Annual Report, 1911*, p. 21.

53. U.S. Department of Commerce and Labor, *Annual Report, 1906*, pp. 67–68.

54. J. R. Silver, employment agent, El Paso, Tex., interview by Paul Taylor, n.d. Field notes for Paul Taylor's book, *Mexican Labor: Dimmitt County,* folder, "Labor Contractors and Agencies," Box 74/187 C, Taylor Collection, p. 3.

55. Ibid.

56. Cardoso, *Mexican Emigration,* p. 22.

57. Folder, "Biographies and Case Histories," Gamio Collection, p. 1.

58. Secretaría de Relaciónes Exteriores, Consulado de Mexico, St. Louis, Mo., "Remite informe de los trabajos ejucatidos," p. 5.

Chapter 2, Mexicans in the Midwest, 1914–1922

1. Romo, "Urbanization," pp. 183–207; Castillo, "Chicanos and the City," p. 2.

2. Romo, "Urbanization," pp. 184–185.

3. U.S. Bureau of the Census, *Fifteenth Census,* vol. 3, pt. 1, *Population,* p. 65; Romo, "Urbanization," p. 193.

4. Vargas, *Proletarians,* p. 128.

5. Broadbent, "Distribution," table 3, p. 72.

6. Bernard, *American Immigration Policy,* p. 40; Reisler, "Always the Laborer," p. 35.

7. Manuel Contreras, interview by Victor Barrela and Grant Newsburger, Minneapolis, 16 July 1975, Minnesota Oral Histories.

8. Reisler, "Always the Laborer," p. 38.

9. U.S. Bureau of the Census, *Fourteenth Census,* vol. 3, *Population by State,* table 12, pp. 492–495.

10. Oppenheimer, "Acculturation," p. 434.

11. U.S. Bureau of the Census, *Abstracts of the Twelfth Census,* pp. 60–61.

12. Cardoso, *Mexican Emigration,* p. 46. In 1914, 1,218,480 persons entered the United States from abroad.

13. American Vice Consul, Piedras Negras, Coahuila, Mexico, to Secretary of State, 26 May 1917, State Department, RG 159, pp. 2–5.

14. *San Antonio Express,* 24 May 1917, p. 1.

15. American Vice Consul, Piedras Negras, Coahuila, Mexico, to Secretary of State, 18 May 1917, Dispatch 1146, State Department, RG 159, p. 4.

16. M. García, "Maltrato a los mexicanos por empleados de inmigración y sanidad," Laredo, Tex., 6 March 1916, correspondence 146, File IV/524, ARE; E. Garza Perez, Official Mayor, to Lic. Jesus Acuña, Secretario de Urbanición, 7 March 1916, File IV/524, ARE; Inspector James E. Trout, U.S. Department of Labor, Immigration Service, to M. García, 5 March 1916, File IV/524, ARE.

17. Alberto Franco, El Encargado de Negocios As-Interim, Habana, Cuba, to El Subsecretario del Despacho de Relaciónes Exteriores, 7 January 1917, File IV/524, ARE, p. 1–2.

18. Cardoso, *Mexican Emigration*, p. 50; Reisler, *Sweat of Their Brow*, p. 26.

19. *San Antonio Express*, 25 May 1917, p. 1.

20. *El Imparcial*, 21 May 1917, p. 1.

21. Reisler, *Sweat of Their Brow*, p. 27; Poster in Box 7574, State Department, RG 159. According to Reisler, the poster was incorrect in stating that immigrants had to demonstrate writing proficiency as a requirement for entering the United States.

22. *El Cosmopolita*, 19 January 1918, p. 1.

23. Duncan and Alanzo, *Guadalupe Center*, p. 15.

24. Valdés, *Al Norte*, p. 11.

25. Paul Taylor, *Mexican Labor: Chicago*, p. 67.

26. Valdés, *Al Norte*, pp. 13–15, 17, 26.

27. Ibid., pp. 13–14, 25.

28. Rosales, "Mexican Immigration," p. 141.

29. Folder, "Biographies and Case Histories," Gamio Collection, pp. 1–3.

30. Monita Esiguia, interview by Victor Barrela and Grant Newsburger, St. Paul, 7 July 1975, Minnesota Oral Histories.

31. Louis Medina, interview by Victor Barrela and Grant Newsburger, Minneapolis, 25 July 1975, Minnesota Oral Histories.

32. Paul Taylor, *Mexican Labor: Chicago*, p. 57.

33. Valdés, *Al Norte*, p. 26.

34. West, "Mexican Aztec Society," p. 99.

35. Ibid., p. 100.

36. See Gibson, *Black Legend*.

37. See Rosenbaum, *Mexican Resistance*.

38. See Powell, *Tree of Hate*; Wilson, *Cuban Crisis*; Beisner, *Twelve Against Empire*.

39. Rosales and Simon, "Chicago Steel Workers," pp. 267–275.

40. Sepulveda, "La Colonia del Harbor," pp. 51–52.

41. Ibid., p. 54.

42. Valdés, *El Pueblo*, p. 29.

43. José L. Sepulveda to Secretaría de Relaciónes Exteriores, report, 30 June 1919, File IV/664-1 (72-73)/1, 17-14-146, ARE, p. 1.

44. Sepulveda, "La Colonia del Harbor," p. 54; Paul Taylor, *Mexican Labor: Chicago,* p. 36.

45. Cardoso, *Mexican Emigration,* p. 86; Senate Committee, *Restriction of Western Hemisphere Immigration,* pp. 89–91, 111.

46. Rosales, "Mexican Immigration," p. 141, citing Inland Steel, personnel data cards.

47. Vargas, "New Ford Men," p. 4.

48. Paul Taylor, *Mexican Labor: Chicago,* pp. 71–72.

49. Ibid., p. 89.

50. "Reports," Taylor Collection, p. 4.

51. Gorton, Carruth and Associates, *Encyclopedia,* p. 459.

52. Cardoso, *Mexican Emigration,* p. 97.

53. Ibid.

54. Rosales, "Mexican Immigration," p. 148; Sepulveda, "La Colonia del Harbor," p. 62; Martínez, *Mexican Emigration,* pp. 52–53.

55. Oppenheimer, "Acculturation," p. 443.

56. Consul, Kansas City, Kans., report, 5 April 1921, Secretaría de Industria, AGN, p. 1–2.

57. Sepulveda, "La Colonia del Harbor," p. 61; Paul Taylor, *Mexican Labor: Chicago,* p. 36.

58. Vargas, *Proletarians,* pp. 81–82.

59. Many of these letters and telegrams are in Box 364, File 822-M-1, Calles-Obregón Papers, AGN.

60. Jesus S. Rodríguez, President, Sociedad Benito Juárez, Chicago, to Secretaría de Relaciónes Exteriores, 25 March 1921, File 241-R-R1-14, Calles-Obregón Papers, AGN.

61. Secretaría de Relaciónes Exteriores to Jesus S. Rodríguez, 14 May 1925, File 241-R-R1-14, Calles-Obregón Papers, AGN.

62. Ramon P. Denegri, Consul General, New York, to President Alvaro Obregón, 27 December 1920, File 822-M-1, Calles-Obregón Papers, AGN, p. 2.

63. Ibid.

64. Alvaro Obregón to Ramon P. Denegri, 29 December 1921, File 822-M-1, Calles-Obregón Papers, AGN.

65. Rosales, "Mexican Immigration," p. 181. This organization ceased to exist in 1923.

66. Cardoso, *Mexican Emigration,* p. 101.

67. Consul, Detroit, to Subsecretaría de Relaciónes Exteriores, 20 March 1922, File 822-D-3, Calles-Obregón Papers, AGN.

68. Cardoso, *Mexican Emigration*, p. 98.

69. *Detroit Free Press*, 20 March 1922, p. 7.

70. Martínez, *Mexican Emigration*, pp. 52–53; Sepulveda, "La Colonia del Harbor," p. 62.

71. *Detroit News*, 11 December 1920; *Detroit News*, 15 February 1921; Valdés, *El Pueblo*, p. 16.

72. Paul Taylor, *Mexican Labor: Chicago*, p. 35; Kerr, "Chicano Experience," p. 23.

73. Rosales, "Mexican Immigration," p. 181.

74. Vargas, *Proletarians*, p. 86.

75. Robert Jones and Louis Wilson, *Mexicans in Chicago*, p. 19.

Chapter 3, Housing and Labor

1. Sepulveda, "La Colonia del Harbor," p. 57; Murillo, "Detroit Mexican Colonia," p. 13.

2. Cardoso, *Mexican Emigration*, p. 96.

3. Ibid., p. 72.

4. Ibid., p. 73.

5. Secretaría de Industria, *La industria, el comerzio y el trabajo en Mexico*, vol. 3 (Mexico City: Tip. Galas, 1928), pp. 64–65; Gruening, *Mexico and Its Heritage*, pp. 136–137.

6. Gamio, *Mexican Immigration*, pp. 35–38.

7. Baba and Abonyi, *Mexicans of Detroit*, p. 28.

8. Secretaría de Industria, *Monografía sobre el estado actual de la industria en Mexico* (Mexico City: Talleres Gráficos de la Nación, 1929), pp. 63–66; Meyer, *Estado y sociedad*, pp. 154–174.

9. Gonzalo González to Alvaro Obregón, 7 March 1921, File 817-5-37, Calles-Obregón Papers, AGN.

10. Bailey, *Viva Cristo Rey*, passim; Mabry, "Mexican Anticlerics," pp. 81–92.

11. Paul Taylor, *Mexican Labor: Chicago*, p. 76.

12. See Higham, *Strangers;* Murphy, "Normalcy" and "Nature of Intolerance."

13. See Chalmers, *Hooded Americanism;* Degler, "Century of Klans"; Miller, "Ku Klux Klan"; Jackson, *Ku Klux Klan;* Moore, *Citizen Klansmen;* Blee, *Women of the Klan.*

14. Lipschultz, *American Attitudes*, pp. 1–10, 37–49; Reisler, *Sweat of Their Brow*, chaps. 6, 7, 8; Cardoso, *Mexican Emigration*, pp. 21–27.

15. "Reports," Taylor Collection, p. 10.

16. Hughes, *Living Conditions*, p. 13.

17. Rosales, "Mexican Immigration," p. 156.

18. Rosales and Simon, "Mexican Immigrant Experience," p. 337.

19. Nick Hernández, interview, East Chicago, 28 July 1928, "Reports," Taylor Collection.

20. Abbott, *Tenements of Chicago*, p. 136.

21. Paul Taylor, *Mexican Labor: Chicago*, p. 224.

22. Albig, "Opinions," p. 66.

23. Valdés, *El Pueblo*, p. 21.

24. Baba and Abonyi, *Mexicans of Detroit*, p. 56; Latino Oral History Project.

25. Paul Taylor, *Mexican Labor: Chicago*, p. 223.

26. Albig, "Opinions," p. 64.

27. Paul Taylor, *Mexican Labor: Chicago*, p. 227.

28. Walker, "East Chicago," pp. 24–32, 121–122.

29. Duncan and Alanzo, *Guadalupe Center*, p. 11.

30. Robert Jones and Louis Wilson, *Mexicans in Chicago*, p. 9.

31. Redfield, "Mexicans in Chicago," p. 50.

32. Abbott, *Tenements of Chicago*, p. 291.

33. Paul Taylor, *Mexican Labor: Chicago*, p. 226.

34. Duncan and Alanzo, *Guadalupe Center*, p. 11.

35. Vargas, *Proletarians*, pp. 66, 127.

36. Rosales and Simon, "Mexican Immigrant Experience," p. 341.

37. Abbott, *Tenements of Chicago*, p. 136.

38. Paul Taylor, *Mexican Labor: Chicago*, pp. 185–186.

39. *Calumet News*, 6 February 1926, p. 1.

40. Rosales and Simon, "Mexican Immigrant Experience," p. 341.

41. Reisler, "Mexican Immigrant," p. 151.

42. Hubert Herring, "Relations Between Americans and Mexicans in the United States," *Religious Education* (February 1931), quoted in Robert Jones and Louis Wilson, *Mexicans in Chicago*, p. 28.

43. Sepulveda, "Una Colonia de Obreros," p. 334.

44. McLean, *Northern Mexican*, pp. 10–12.

45. Vargas, *Proletarians*, pp. 110, 179.

46. Paul Taylor, *Mexican Labor: Chicago*, p. 79.

47. Ibid., p. 87.

48. Ibid., p. 88.

49. Ibid., p. 89.

50. Ibid.

51. Ibid., p. 97.

52. Ibid., p. 100.

53. Ibid., p. 101.

54. Ibid.

55. Vargas, "New Ford Men," pp. 9–10.

56. Ibid., p. 10.

57. Vargas, *Proletarians,* p. 94.

58. Paul Taylor, *Mexican Labor: Chicago,* p. 97.

59. Vargas, "Mexican Auto Workers," p. 107.

60. Ibid.

61. Ibid., p. 120; Vargas, *Proletarians,* p. 95.

62. Vargas, *Proletarians,* p. 114.

63. Peterson, "Automobile Workers," pp. 83, 90. Vargas states that most jobs at Ford could be learned in one week. Vargas, *Proletarians,* p. 114.

64. Paul Taylor, *Mexican Labor: Chicago,* p. 102.

65. Vargas, "New Ford Men," p. 12; Vargas, *Proletarians,* p. 119.

66. Paul Taylor, *Mexican Labor: Chicago,* p. 102.

67. Rosales, "Regional Origins," pp. 193–196.

68. Laird, "Argentine, Kansas," p. 84.

69. Gamio, *Mexican Immigration,* pp. 9–10.

70. Fine, *Automobile,* pp. 4–6; Nevins and Hill, *Ford,* pp. 526–527.

71. Nonetheless, when compared to other industries, the average yearly earnings of Detroit auto workers between 1914 and 1939 remained 40 percent higher than the national figure for all manufacturing wage earners. From 1919 to 1939, the real earnings of Detroit auto workers remained 15 to 35 percent higher than those of manufacturing workers in other major urban areas. Ticknor, "Motor City," pp. 151–152.

72. Paul Taylor, *Mexican Labor: Chicago,* p. 183; Paul Taylor, *Mexican Labor: Bethlehem,* p. 12.

73. Vargas, "Mexican Auto Workers," p. 183; Vargas, *Proletarians,* p. 67.

74. Senate Committee, *Restriction of Western Hemisphere Immigration,* p. 91.

75. Ibid., pp. 89–91, 111.

76. Paul Taylor, "Employment," p. 206.

77. Paul Taylor, *Mexican Labor: Chicago,* pp. 36–37, 117, 182; Rosales, "Mexican Immigration," p. 209.

78. Paul Taylor, *Mexican Labor: Chicago,* p. 207.

79. George T. Edson, "Mexicans in Our North Central States," in *Perspectives in Mexican American Studies,* vol. 2, *Mexicans in the Midwest,* edited by Juan R. García and Thomas Gelsinon (Tucson: Mexican American Studies and Research Center, 1989), p. 106; Valdés, *Al Norte,* p. 12.

80. Paul Taylor, *Mexican Labor: Chicago,* pp. 100–101.

81. Ibid., p. 77.

82. Vargas, "Mexican Auto Workers," p. 89.

83. Ibid., p. 85.

84. "Reports," Taylor Collection, p. 8.

85. Paul Taylor, *Mexican Labor: Chicago,* pp. 2, 3, 19.

86. Valdés, "Perspiring Capitalists," pp. 8, 11–12.

87. "Reports," Taylor Collection, p. 3.

88. Ibid., p. 6.

89. Ibid., p. 2.

90. Ibid., pp. 167–168; Kerr, "Chicano Experience," p. 22.

91. Murillo, "Detroit Mexican Colonia," p. 40. Mexican businesses also catered to other nationalities.

92. Goldner, *Northern Urban Area,* p. 6.

93. *Social Service Review* 2, no. 4 (1928), Reel 62, FLPS.

94. "Reports," Taylor Collection, p. 7.

95. Immigrants' Protective League, *Annual Report, 1930,* IPL, p. 19.

96. Redfield, "Mexicans in Chicago," pp. 42–46.

97. J. Xavier Mondragón, "El progreso del comercio mexicano de Chicago," *La Noticia Mundial,* 16 September 1927, p. 4.

98. Levenstein, "AFL," pp. 206–219.

99. Davidson, "Industrial Detroit," p. 34; Peterson, "Automobile Workers," p. 101; Ticknor, "Motor City," pp. 151–152.

100. Rosales and Simon, "Mexican Immigrant Experience," p. 351.

101. Vargas, *Proletarians,* p. 157.

102. Rosales and Simon, "Chicago Steel Workers," pp. 267–275.

103. Ibid.

104. Alvarado, "Mexican Immigration," p. 479.

105. Sepulveda, "La Colonia del Harbor," p. 147.

Chapter 4, Women and Work

1. Ms. Trini, interview, Detroit, Interview 4, folder, "Observations, Notes and an Itinerary of Trip to Mexico," Gamio Collection, p. 2.

2. U.S. Children's Bureau, *Child Labor,* pp. 2, 113.

3. Ibid., p. 113.

4. Ibid., p. 80.

5. House Committee, *Interstate Migration,* p. 7882. (Cited in text as the Tolan Committee.)

6. Ibid.

7. Valdés, *Al Norte,* pp. 6, 27.

8. U.S. Children's Bureau, *Child Labor,* p. 119.

9. Rosalinda González, "Chicanas," p. 68.

10. Deutsch, *No Separate Refuge,* p. 116, quoting D. L. Joehneck, "Next Year's Labor Contract" (paper presented at the 1st annual meeting of the Rocky Mountain Chapter, American Association of Sugar Beet Agriculturalists, Denver, Colo., January 1921), Great Western Sugar Co. Papers, Box 4, Western Historical Collections, University of Colorado, Boulder, pp. 1–2.

11. U.S. Children's Bureau, *Child Labor,* p. iii.

12. Ibid., p. 108.

13. Ibid.

14. Ibid.

15. Ibid., p. iii.

16. Ibid., p. 9.

17. Romo, "Urbanization," pp. 195–196.

18. Oppenheimer, "Acculturation," pp. 436–437.

19. Ibid.

20. Ibid.

21. Paul Taylor, *Mexican Labor: Chicago,* p. 199.

22. Anthony, *Mothers Who Must Earn,* p. 16; Tentler, *Wage-Earning Women,* p. 139.

23. Tentler, *Wage-Earning Women,* p. 15.

24. Houghteling, *Income,* pp. 23–25.

25. Tentler, *Wage-Earning Women,* p. 85; Monroe, *Chicago Families,* pp. 173–174.

26. Rosalinda González, "Chicanas," pp. 72–73.

27. Tentler, *Wage-Earning Women*, pp. 20, 25, 35.

28. Montgomery, *American Girl*, p. 27.

29. Rosalinda González, "Chicanas," p. 72.

30. Tentler, *Wage-Earning Women*, p. 89.

31. Paul Taylor, *Mexican Labor: Chicago*, p. 20.

32. Ibid., p. 200.

33. Ibid., pp. 199–200.

34. Ibid., p. 199.

35. Ibid., pp. 199–200.

36. Ibid., p. 199.

37. Ibid., p. 197.

38. Ibid.

39. Tentler, *Wage-Earning Women*, p. 80.

40. *La Noticia Mundial*, 18 December 1927, p. 7.

41. Paul Taylor, *Mexican Labor: Chicago*, p. 198.

42. *Mexico*, 9 October 1927.

43. Gamio, *Mexican Immigrant*, pp. 46–47.

44. Paul Taylor, *Mexican Labor: Chicago*, p. 79.

45. Ibid.

46. *La Noticia Mundial*, 2 October 1927, p. 6.

47. Paul Taylor, *Mexican Labor: Chicago*, p. 199.

48. U.S. Bureau of the Census, *Fifteenth Census, Population: Special Report*, pp. 211, 213, 217; Rosales and Simon, "Mexican Immigrant Experience," p. 341.

49. Hughes, *Living Conditions*, p. 13.

50. "Reports," Taylor Collection, pp. 13, 17.

51. Paul Taylor, *Mexican Labor: Chicago*, p. 190.

52. Ibid., p. 194.

53. Ibid., p. 195.

54. Ibid.

55. Ibid., p. 194.

56. Ibid., p. 195.

57. *Mexico*, 9 May 1928.

58. Paul Taylor, *Mexican Labor: Chicago*, p. 196.

59. Ibid.

60. *Mexico,* 2 October 1926, pp. 3, 5.

61. Rosalinda González, "Chicanas," p. 74.

Chapter 5, Mexican Consuls

1. Cardoso, *Mexican Emigration,* p. 32.

2. Rosales, "Mexican Immigration," p. 56.

3. Cardoso, *Mexican Emigration,* p. 57.

4. Consul, Galveston, Tex., to Secretaría de Fomento, 3 October 1913, File IV/241, ARE.

5. T. G. Pellicer to Cándido Aguilar, 16 November 1916, p. 2, ARE.

6. Cornelius Ferris, Consul, Mexico City, to Robert Lansing, Secretary of State, 11 March 1920, State Department, RG 59.

7. "Report to the President," 10 June 1922, Box 206, File 711-M-30, Calles-Obregón Papers, AGN; Ramon P. Denegri to Alvaro Obregón, 27 December 1920, p. 2.

8. "Report to the President," p. 1.

9. Cardoso, *Mexican Emigration,* pp. 109–110.

10. Secretaría de Relaciónes Exteriores, *Guía Diplomática y Consular* (Mexico City: Imprenta de Francisco Ciaz de Leon, 1902), p. 79.

11. Ibid., p. 78.

12. Oppenheimer, "Acculturation," p. 434.

13. Secretaría de Relaciónes Exteriores, "Informes sobre protección, 1929, Kansas City, Missouri," File IV/241 (04) (73-75)/1. IV-70-5, ARE.

14. Samuel J. McWilliams, Kansas City, Mo., to Jack Danciger, Consul, Kansas City, Mo., 6 July 1916, File 1241 (73-72). 12-7-74, ARE.

15. J. B. Vega to Juan T. Burns, Consul General, New York, 28 July 1916, File 1241 (73-72). 12-7-74, ARE.

16. *El Cosmopolita,* 2 March 1918, p. 3; Secretaría de Relaciónes Exteriores, Protección, "Informe de Cónsul de Mexico en Detroit, Michigan, sobre el tratamiento dado a mexicanos en prisiónes en los Estados Unidos de America" (1927), File VI/241 (73-14) /533. 20-19-126, ARE.

17. *El Cosmopolita,* 2 March 1918, p. 3.

18. Enrique Colunga-Rubrica, El Jefe del Departamento Consultivo, memorandum, 18 March 1921, File IV/241, ARE.

19. I. Magaña, Cónsul Comisionado, to Secretaría de Relaciónes Exteriores, "Asunto: Debilisma protección a nuestros nacionales en Estados Unidos. Sus principales

causas y como podría mejorarse" (1922), File IV/241 (73) "22" /1, 11-6-232, ARE, p. 1.

20. Ibid.

21. Ibid., p. 3.

22. Secretaría de Relaciónes Exteriores, "Detención y atentados contra mexicanos en el extranjero" (1920), File IV/241, 11/242 (72:73) /14. 12-7-72, ARE.

23. Esteban Morales to Ramon P. Denegri, 12 August 1921, File IV/241, ARE.

24. Gilberto Crespo y Martínez to Philander C. Knox, 9 October 1911, File 1910–1929, Box 3574, File 311.122 R 14, State Department, RG 59.

25. W. R. Stubbs to Philander C. Knox, 16 November 1922, File 1910–1929, Box 3574, File 311.122 R 14, State Department, RG 59, pp. 1–2.

26. Ibid., p. 2.

27. *El Cosmopolita,* 27 February 1915, p. 3.

28. Paul Taylor, *Mexican Labor: Chicago,* p. 151.

29. *Mexico,* 11 April 1925, p. 1.

30. Paul Taylor, *Mexican Labor: Chicago,* p. 150.

31. Ibid., p. 151.

32. *Mexico,* 27 November 1926; 11 December 1926.

33. *La Prensa,* 8 July 1931.

34. Secretaría de Relaciónes Exteriores, "Informes sobre protección."

35. Alvaro Obregón to Alberto J. Pani, Secretary of Foreign Relations, 19 May 1921, File 814-R-5, Calles-Obregón Papers, AGN; Circular 31, 21 October 1921, File 2214-1, ARE; Alberto J. Pani to all consuls, 1 November 1922, ARE.

36. Cardoso, *Mexican Emigration,* p. 113.

37. Edmundo E. Martínez, Consul, St. Louis, Mo., to Ernesto Garza Perez, Sub-secretario del Despacho de Relaciónes Exteriores, Mexico City, report, 15 January 1919, File IV/033 (04)/1. 17-14-150, ARE, p. 1–2.

38. Copy of a letter from F. C. D., El Paso, Tex., to Gen. L. T., 5 October 1919, attached to a note from Y. Bonnillai, Mexican Ambassador, Washington, D.C., to Lic. Hilario Medina, Subsecretario de Relaciónes Exteriores, 17 October 1919, forwarded from the Consul General, New York, to Lic. Manuel Aguirre Berlanga, Secretario de Gobernación, Confidential, 20 December 1919, ARE.

39. Ibid.

40. *El Cosmopolita,* 11 December 1916, p. 1; *El Cosmopolita,* 1 January 1917, p. 1.

41. File on discrimination against Mexican school children by Kansas City, Kans., authorities, 12 January, 4 February, 21 September, and 25 October 1925, State

Decimal File 1910–1929, Box 3573, File 311. 1215/Kansas City, State Department, RG 59.

42. Rafael Aveleyra, Consul, "Informe de protección del Consulado de Mexico en Chicago," 30 March 1930, File IV/524, ARE, p. 4.

43. Rafael Aveleyra, "Informe de protección del Consulado de Mexico en Chicago," 18 February 1930, File IV/524, ARE, p. 3.

44. I. Magaña to Secretaría de Reláciones Exteriores, "Mexicanos en Estados Unidos—Protección" (1922), File IV/241 (73) "22"/1, 11-6-232, ARE, p. 1–6.

45. Memorandum, 10 June 1922, File 711-M-30, Calles-Obregón Papers, AGN.

46. Cardoso, *Mexican Emigration*, p. 109.

47. Enrique A. González, Consul General, Mexico, Visitada de Consulados, "Informes sobre las Comisiónes Honoríficas, Brigadas de Cruz Azul y situación general de los mexicanos en Estados Unidos" (1930), File IV/524 (73) "30"/1. 18-22-7, ARE, pp. 3–4.

48. Ibid.

49. Ibid., pp. 4–5.

50. Ibid., p. 6.

51. Ibid.

52. Cardoso, *Mexican Emigration*, p. 109. Mexico's failure to adequately finance consular programs was due to its depressed economy and its need to use available monies for high-priority endeavors, such as stopping rebellions.

53. *La Prensa*, 1 June 1916.

54. Cardoso, "Mexican Community Leadership," pp. 15–16.

55. Gomez-Quiñones, "Piedras Contra la Luna," passim.

Chapter 6, Issues Affecting Mexican Organizational Efforts

1. Laird, "Argentine, Kansas," pp. 80, 84, 87–89.

2. Oppenheimer, "Acculturation," p. 435.

3. Rosales, "Regional Origins," p. 196.

4. Vargas, *Proletarians*, p. 94.

5. Paul Taylor, *Mexican Labor: Chicago*, pp. 48–50.

6. Board of Public Welfare, *Social Prospectus*, p. 6.

7. Edson, "Gary," Taylor Collection, p. 3.

8. Edson, "Indiana Harbor," Taylor Collection, p. 1.

9. West, "Mexican Aztec Society," pp. 103–104.

10. *Correo Mexicano*, 8 September 1926, p. 2.

11. "Nuestra campaña en contra de la marijuana," *El Eco de la Patria*, n.d., Gamio Collection.

12. Vaughn, "Women," p. 136.

13. Hart, *Revolutionary Mexico*, pp. 277–278.

14. Secretaría de Instrucción Pública y Bellas Artes, *Boletín de Educación* (Mexico City) 1, no. 1 (1914), p. 126.

15. Vaughn, "Women," p. 146.

16. Griswold del Castillo, *La Familia*, p. 28.

17. Arrom, "Women and the Family," p. 162.

18. Ibid., p. 138.

19. Sierra, *Obras completas*, p. 329.

20. Vaughn, "Women," p. 142.

21. Secretaría de Instrucción Pública y Bellas Artes, *Boletín de Educación* 1, no. 1 (1914), p. 126.

22. Palavicimi, *Problemas de la educación*, pp. 12–15.

23. Many elitist organizations dropped their overt anticlerical stance because of its divisive and controversial nature.

24. Gamio, *Mexican Immigration*, p. 94.

25. *Mexico*, 8 December 1926, p. 3.

26. Augusto Franco, "Los hijos del desterrado," *La Noticia Mundial*, 16 September 1927, p. 12.

27. *La Noticia Mundial*, 18 December 1927, p. 3.

28. Ibid.

29. Alfredo Vasquez, Consul, Kansas City, Mo., report, "Su visita a la colonia mexicana en Scottsbluff, Nebraska," 30 March 1930, File IV/523 (73-25)/6, IV-100-2, ARE, p. 6.

30. Paul Taylor, *Mexican Labor: Chicago*, p. 218.

31. *El Cosmopolita*, 8 January 1916, p. 3; *La Noticia Mundial*, 23 October 1927, p. 8. *Adelitas* was another name for the *soldaderas*, Mexican women who fought alongside their husbands and mates during the 1910 revolution.

32. *El Cosmopolita*, 5 December 1914, p. 2.

33. *El Cosmopolita*, 22 October 1914, p. 3.

34. *La Noticia Mundial*, 23 October 1927, p. 8. Interestingly, very few articles were written about the evils of drinking and alcoholism. More concern was voiced about smoking among women because the consequences of drinking were largely economic, whereas smoking supposedly led to greater vices and more degenerate

behavior. Mexican leaders also held the mistaken notion that women did not drink and that it was more difficult to acquire alcoholic beverages because of Prohibition.

35. The burning of Judas effigies on the day before Easter dates back to colonial Spain. These Judas burnings served important social functions and were considered a form of social parody in Mexican culture. Although their origins are unknown, their inspiration was biblical: according to the Bible, Judas Iscariot hanged himself after betraying Jesus; his body then exploded. After Mexican independence in 1821, the practice became more secular: effigies resembled people or images that represented fashion, authority, or manners. Burning them provided Mexicans with a "harmless, humorous safety valve [that] released hostility without disrupting society." Beezley, *Judas*, pp. 3–4.

36. Beezley, *Judas*, pp. 14–16.

37. Luís González, *San José de García*, p. 112.

38. Schmidt, *Roots of Lo Mexicano*, chaps. 3, 4.

39. *Mexico*, 3 November 1928, p. 3.

40. *La Noticia Mundial*, 21 August 1927, p. 3.

41. "Los Primeros Papeles," *La Noticia Mundial*, 25 September 1927, p. 8.

42. U.S. Bureau of the Census, *Fifteenth Census*, vol. 3, pt. 1, *Population*, pp. 2, 446; James J. Davis to Senator William Harris, 28 December 1928, *Congressional Record*, 70th Cong., 2d sess., 1928, 70, pt. 2, p. 117.

43. Reisler, "Always the Laborer," p. 240.

44. Lin, "Voluntary Kinship," p. 58.

45. *Mexican Review* 2, no. 8 (1918), p. 8; Lipschultz, *American Attitudes*, pp. 44–49.

46. *New York Times*, 16 May 1930, p. 2.

47. Paul Taylor, *Mexican Labor: Chicago*, p. 217.

48. "Reports," Taylor Collection, p. 14.

49. Hoffman, *Unwanted Mexican Americans*, p. 20.

50. "Reports," Taylor Collection, p. 13.

51. Ibid., p. 14.

52. Immigrants' Protective League, *Annual Report, 1930*, IPL.

53. Edson, "Indiana Harbor," Taylor Collection, p. 13.

54. *La Noticia Mundial*, 11 December 1927, p. 3.

55. *El Cosmopolita*, 10 April 1915, p. 2.

56. The Chicago community rallied behind Mrs. Juanita de Guevara and raised money for her defense. During the trial, it was proven that Mrs. Guevara had

been beaten by the deceased before the shooting and had acted in self-defense. It was also noted that the man she shot was an ex-sheriff. She was acquitted of all charges. *La Noticia Mundial,* 28 August 1927, p. 1; 4 December 1927, p. 1; 18 December 1927, p. 1.

57. *La Noticia Mundial,* 4 September 1927, p. 3.

58. Paul Taylor, *Mexican Labor: Chicago,* p. 149.

59. "Reports," Taylor Collection, p. 13.

60. *Lake County Times,* 9 January 1930, p. 1.

61. Paul Taylor, *Mexican Labor: Chicago,* p. 150.

62. *Mexico,* 17 August 1929, p. 1.

63. "Reports," Taylor Collection, p. 8.

64. Paul Taylor, *Mexican Labor: Chicago,* p. 141.

65. See Rosales, "Interethnic Violence," for a more thorough discussion about some of the incidents and causes that attracted widespread support from the Mexican community in the Chicago area.

66. Baur, *Delinquency,* p. 14.

67. Seller, *America,* p. 49.

68. *Correo Mexicano,* 6 September 1926, p. 2.

69. Kerr, "Mexican Chicago," p. 294.

Chapter 7, Mexican Mutual Aid Societies

1. Gamio, *Mexican Immigration,* p. 132.

2. Juan García, "Midwest Mexicanos," p. 93.

3. West, "Mexican Aztec Society," p. 204.

4. Sepulveda, "La Colonia del Harbor," p. 70; *El Amigo del Hogar,* 25 November 1925.

5. Angel Cal, *"El Amigo del Hogar,"* unpublished paper in author's files (n.d.), pp. 2–3.

6. A term used by Francisco Rosales to describe an exalted form of nationalism among Mexican immigrants before the Great Depression. Rosales, "Interethnic Violence," p. 63.

7. West, "Mexican Aztec Society," p. 155.

8. *El Cosmopolita,* 6 September 1919, p. 1; Lin, "Voluntary Kinship," p. 93; Laird, "Argentine, Kansas," pp. 52–54.

9. Laird, "Argentine, Kansas," p. 53.

10. *El Cosmopolita,* 22 October 1914, pp. 1, 4; Duncan and Alanzo, *Guadalupe Center,* pp. 28–30.

11. Duncan and Alanzo, *Guadalupe Center,* p. 30.

12. Ibid., pp. 32, 38, 41.

13. *Kansas City (Mo.) Journal-Post,* 28 March 1926.

14. Rosales and Simon, "Mexican Immigrant Experience," pp. 338–339.

15. Leitman, "Exile and Union," p. 50.

16. Rosales, "Mexican Immigration," p. 189.

17. Ibid., p. 165.

18. Muñoz had visited Indiana Harbor in late 1924 to give sermons and do missionary work.

19. Rosales, "Mexican Immigration," p. 189.

20. *El Amigo del Hogar,* 22 November 1925, 24 January 1926, 28 March 1926; Sepulveda, "La Colonia del Harbor," p. 81.

21. Sepulveda, "La Colonia del Harbor," pp. 83–84.

22. Rosales and Simon, "Mexican Immigrant Experience," p. 339.

23. Figueroa, interview, "Reports," Taylor Collection.

24. J. Jesus Cortés, President, Círculo de Obreros Católicos "San José," to George Edson, Special Agent of the Department of Labor, November 1926, Edson, "Indiana Harbor," Taylor Collection.

25. *El Amigo del Hogar,* 22 November 1925; Rogers, "Our Lady of Guadalupe," pp. 14–17.

26. For a more thorough discussion of *El Amigo del Hogar*'s contents and focus, see Leitman, "Exile and Union"; Juan García and Angel Cal, "El Círculo," pp. 95–114.

27. Paul Taylor, *Mexican Labor: Chicago,* p. 241.

28. National Conference of Catholic Charities, *Proceedings,* 11th annual meeting (Kansas City, Mo., 1925), p. 214.

29. *El Amigo del Hogar,* 16 October 1927; 13 November 1927.

30. Paul Taylor, *Mexican Labor: Chicago,* p. 176.

31. Sepulveda, "La Colonia del Harbor," p. 102.

32. Rosales and Simon, "Mexican Immigrant Experience," p. 340.

33. Kanellos, "Mexican Community Theatre," p. 45.

34. *El Amigo del Hogar,* 12 and 16 May 1926; 15 May, 10 July, and 24 July 1927; 7 October 1928; Rogers, "Our Lady of Guadalupe," pp. 14–34.

35. Sepulveda, "La Colonia del Harbor," p. 107.

36. Cortés to Edson, November 1926.

37. Calumet region Mexicans, interview, 1929, call no. 74/187c, "Calumet Region: Mexicans," in "Reports," Taylor Collection, pp. 1–2.

38. Ibid., p. 2.

39. Paul Taylor, *Mexican Labor: Chicago*, p. 134.

40. Agustín Angel, interview, East Chicago, Ind., "Calumet Region: Mexicans," in "Reports," Taylor Collection, p. 1.

41. *El Amigo del Hogar*, 11 April 1928, p. 3.

42. Interview, Document 88-260, "Reports," Taylor Collection.

43. Rosales, "Mexican Immigration," pp. 200–201.

44. Sepulveda, "La Colonia del Harbor," p. 75. The membership in the Cuauhtémoc society was between 100 and 150. Rosales, "Mexican Immigration," p. 206.

45. Sepulveda, "La Colonia del Harbor," p. 69; Edson, "Indiana Harbor," Taylor Collection, p. 6; Rosales and Simon, "Mexican Immigrant Experience," p. 339.

46. U.S. Bureau of the Census, *Fourteenth Census*, vol. 3, *Population by State*, table 12, pp. 492–495.

47. *Detroit Free Press*, 20 March 1922, p. 7.

48. Valdés, *El Pueblo*, p. 4.

49. Skendzel, *Detroit's Pioneer Mexicans*, p. 10.

50. *Detroit News*, 26 January 1931, p. 6. The Detroit International Institute, which served a large portion of Detroit's Mexican community, estimated the number in 1928 at 10,000. Detroit International Institute, *Annual Report* (Detroit: Detroit International Institute, 1926).

51. Valdés, "Perspiring Capitalists," p. 5.

52. Ibid.

53. Ibid.

54. Ibid., p. 7.

55. Valdés, *El Pueblo*, p. 18.

56. Baba and Abonyi, *Mexicans of Detroit*, p. 52.

57. Ibid., p. 53.

58. *El Eco de la Patria* 1, no. 12 (20 June 1926), Gamio Collection.

59. Skendzel, *Detroit's Pioneer Mexicans*, p. 58.

60. Ibid., p. 60. Adding to the group's exuberance over aviation was the recently completed flight of Charles Lindbergh.

61. Skendzel, *Detroit's Pioneer Mexicans*, p. 15.

62. Baba and Abonyi, *Mexicans of Detroit*, p. 54.

63. Vargas, *Proletarians*, p. 74, quoted from the *Detroit News*, 27 March 1920.

64. Vargas, *Proletarians*, p. 75.

65. *Detroit News*, 3 October 1920.

66. Ibid.; "Our Spaniards and Aztecs," *Detroit Saturday Night*, 16 October 1926.

67. Humphrey, "Integration," p. 160; Murillo, "Detroit Mexican Colonia," p. 36.

68. "Our Spaniards."

69. Edson, "Detroit," Taylor Collection, p. 1.

70. Gamio, *Mexican Immigrant*, pp. 226–229.

71. Humphrey, "Integration," p. 164.

72. Ibid., p. 163.

73. Ibid.

74. Ibid., p. 160.

75. Ibid., p. 165.

76. Ibid., p. 161.

77. Rosales, "Mexican Immigration," p. 207.

78. *El Amigo del Hogar*, 17 September 1926; Sepulveda, "La Colonia del Harbor," p. 83.

79. Juan García, "Midwest Mexicanos," p. 94; Cardoso, "Mexican Community Leadership," p. 5.

80. *El Cosmopolita*, 2 January 1915, pp. 1, 4.

81. Paul Taylor, *Mexican Labor: Chicago*, p. 135.

82. Humphrey, "Integration," p. 159.

83. Hernández, "Mutual Aid Societies," p. 174.

84. *La Noticia Mundial*, 29 January 1928, p. 2.

85. *El Trabajo*, 19 June 1925, p. 4.

86. Paul Taylor, *Mexican Labor: Chicago*, pp. 138–139.

87. Edson, "Chicago," Taylor Collection, pp. 1–2.

88. Paul Taylor, *Mexican Labor: Chicago*, pp. 134–141; *Mexico*, 26 August 1926.

89. Hernández, "Mutual Aid Societies," p. 144.

90. Cardoso, "Mexican Community Leadership," p. 9.

91. Edson, "East Chicago," Taylor Collection, p. 6; Edson, "North Central States," Taylor Collection.

92. "Reports," Taylor Collection, p. 13.

93. Sepulveda, "La Colonia del Harbor," pp. 71–72; *El Amigo del Hogar*, 22 November 1925; Rogers, "Our Lady of Guadalupe," pp. 14–17.

94. Cardoso, "Mexican Community Leadership," p. 10.

95. Ibid.

96. Paul Taylor, *Mexican Labor: Chicago*, p. 128.

97. Hernández, "Mutual Aid Societies," p. 9.

98. Rosales, "Mexicanos in Indiana Harbor," p. 97.

99. Ricardo Parra, "Mid-West Chicano Organizations: Past, Present, and Possibilities" (n.d.), Midwest Council of *La Raza*, p. 24.

100. Cardoso, "Mexican Community Leadership," p. 9.

Chapter 8, Social and Cultural Life of Mexicans in Some Midwestern Cities

1. West, "Mexican Aztec Society," pp. 130–131.

2. Edson, "Minnesota," Taylor Collection, p. 11.

3. Paul Taylor, *Mexican Labor: Chicago*, pp. 270–271.

4. Ibid.

5. Paul Taylor, *Mexican Labor: Chicago*, pp. 168–169; Robert Jones and Louis Wilson, *Mexicans in Chicago*, p. 9.

6. Rosales, "Mexican Immigration," p. 207.

7. Laird, "Argentine, Kansas," pp. 52–53; *El Cosmopolita*, 22 August 1914, p. 1; 29 April 1916, p. 1.

8. Robert Jones and Louis Wilson, *Mexicans in Chicago*, p. 9.

9. Ibid.

10. Valdés, *El Pueblo*, pp. 17–18; Foreign Student Records, Accession 774, Henry Ford Service School; Sepulveda, "La Colonia del Harbor," p. 61.

11. Sepulveda, "La Colonia del Harbor," p. 101.

12. Paul Taylor, *Mexican Labor: Chicago*, p. 232.

13. Augustin Angel, interview by Paul Taylor, East Chicago, Ind., July 1928, "Calumet Region: Mexicans," in "Reports," Taylor Collection, p. 4.

14. Edson, "Chicago," Taylor Collection, p. 7.

15. Cesario Hernández, interview by Paul Taylor, East Chicago, Ind., July 1928, "Calumet Region: Mexicans," in "Reports," Taylor Collection, p. 6.

16. Edson, "Chicago," Taylor Collection, pp. 7–8.

17. Paul Taylor, *Mexican Labor: Chicago*, pp. 227–228.

18. Alvarado, "Mexican Immigration," p. 480.

19. *Mexican Review* 2, no. 8 (1918), p. 8.

20. Woll, *Latin Image*, p. 17.

21. Newspaper clipping, no author, n.d., Gamio Collection.

22. *La Noticia Mundial*, 9 October 1927, p. 7.

23. Rosales, "Mexican Immigration," p. 220.

24. J. Xavier Mondragón, "A pesar de todo somos mexicanos," *La Noticia Mundial,* 23 October 1927, p. 7.

25. Robert Jones and Louis Wilson, *Mexicans in Chicago,* pp. 1–2.

26. Edson, "Indiana Harbor," Taylor Collection, p. 17.

27. Beezley, *Judas,* pp. 23–26.

28. Sepulveda, "La Colonia del Harbor," p. 111; *El Amigo del Hogar,* 10 June 1927, p. 3.

29. Rosales, "Mexican Immigration," p. 220.

30. Duncan and Alanzo, *Guadalupe Center,* p. 10.

31. Vargas, *Proletarians,* p. 162.

32. Mr. Herrera, interview by Paul Taylor, Chicago, July 1928, "Calumet Region: Mexicans," in "Reports," Taylor Collection, p. 1.

33. Leila Gutierrez, interview by Juan R. García, Indiana Harbor, 2 September 1979.

34. Kanellos, "Two Centuries," p. 19.

35. Ibid., pp. 27–28.

36. Ibid., p. 30.

37. Kanellos, "Fifty Years of Theatre," pp. 255–256.

38. Edson, "Indiana Harbor," Taylor Collection, pp. 17–18.

39. Kanellos, "Two Centuries," p. 19.

40. *La Noticia Mundial,* 18 September 1927, p. 13.

41. David Weber, "Anglo Views," p. 162.

42. University of Chicago Settlement, *Annual Report, 1923–1924,* Box 19, UCS, p. 3. Anita Jones was the resident who was working on her Master's degree. She did some of the earliest research on Mexicans in Chicago. See Anita Jones, "Conditions."

43. M. R. Ibañez, "Report of the Mexican Work at the University of Chicago Settlement for the Year 1930–1931," in University of Chicago Settlement, *Annual Report, 1930–1931,* Box 21, UCS, p. 2.

44. Ibid., pp. 1–2.

45. Ibid., pp. 2, 10.

46. Robert C. Jones, interview by Paul Taylor, Chicago, July 1928, "Calumet Region: Observations," in "Reports," Taylor Collection, p. 3.

47. University of Chicago Settlement, "Mexican Work Report," Summer 1930, Box 21, UCS, p. 1.

48. Paul Taylor, *Mexican Labor: Chicago,* p. 131.

49. University of Chicago Settlement, "Report of Mexican Work, 1930–1932," Box 21, UCS, p. 11.

50. Hull House Studies, 20 June 1928, "Reports," Taylor Collection, p. 9.

51. Ibid., p. 8.

52. *Mexico,* 5 June 1926, p. 2.

53. *El Trabajo,* 4 April 1925, p. 4.

54. "La instrucción de la mujer," *Mexico,* 14 May 1927, p. 3.

55. Immigrants' Protective League, *Annual Report, 1930,* IPL, p. 19.

56. Edson, "Chicago," Taylor Collection, p. 9.

57. University of Chicago Settlement, *Annual Report, 1929–1930,* Box 21, UCS, p. 2.

58. Skendzel, *Detroit's Pioneer Mexicans,* pp. 78–79; Vargas, "New Ford Men," pp. 9, 14.

59. Edson, "North Central States," Taylor Collection, p. 23. The 2 percent who spoke English fluently also included "American-born" Mexicans.

60. Oppenheimer, "Acculturation," pp. 440–441.

61. McLean, *Northern Mexican,* p. 17; David Weber, "Anglo Views,"p. 175.

62. University of Chicago Settlement, *Annual Report, 1928–1929,* Box 21, UCS, p. 4; University of Chicago Settlement, *Annual Report, 1929–1930,* Box 21, UCS, p. 2.

63. Kerr, "Chicano Experience," p. 52.

64. University of Chicago Settlement, *Annual Report, 1928–1929,* Box 21, UCS, p. 6.

65. Lane, "Extranjeros," p. 28.

66. International Institute, memorandums, "Mexican Colony," and "History of the Mexican Colony," International Institute Papers, CRA; Paul Taylor, *Mexican Labor: Chicago,* pp. 135–136.

67. Vargas, "New Ford Men," pp. 7, 9, 14; Skendzel, *Detroit's Pioneer Mexicans,* pp. 78–79. This is not to say that Mexicans were not subjected to discriminatory treatment in these communities; ample evidence shows the contrary. The ethnic tensions and conflicts, however, never approached those in the Calumet region during the 1920s.

68. Nick Hernández, interview by Paul Taylor, Chicago, 22 July 1928, "Calumet Region: Mexicans," in "Reports," Taylor Collection, p. 2.

69. J. M. Guajardo, interview by Paul Taylor, Gary, August 1928, "Calumet Region: Mexicans," in "Reports," Taylor Collection, p. 2.

70. Edson, "Gary," Taylor Collection, p. 5.

71. Ellis, *Americanization,* p. 31.

72. Sanchez, "Go After the Women," p. 1.

73. Mr. Armandaez, interview by Paul Taylor, Chicago, 26 July 1928, "Calumet Region: Mexicans," in "Reports," Taylor Collection, p. 2.

74. Bogardus, *Mexican in the United States,* p. 79.

75. Gary Neighborhood House, "Minutes," 17 November 1925, CRA, p. 156.

76. Crocker, "Gary Mexicans," p. 121, citing International Institute, "Survey of the Foreign Born" (1929), Interview 11, International Institute Papers, CRA.

77. Crocker, "Gary Mexicans," p. 122.

78. Ibid., quoting Bishop Herman J. Alerding to Reverend J. E. Burke, Chairman of the Catholic Welfare Council, 14 March 1920, Alerding correspondence, Chancery of the Diocese of Fort Wayne, Ind.

79. Crocker, "Gary Mexicans," p. 125, citing Bishop Alerding to Elbert Gary, 14 March 1920, Alerding correspondence.

80. Crocker, "Gary Mexicans," p. 123–134.

81. Ibid., p. 127.

82. Edson, "Gary," Taylor Collection, p. 11.

83. *Gary Post-Tribune,* 23 January 1927, p. 1.

84. *Gary Post-Tribune,* 3 March 1927, pp. 1–2.

85. *Gary Post-Tribune,* 23 January 1927, p. 5; *Gary Daily Tribune,* 13 December 1926, p. 13.

86. David Weber, "Anglo Views," p. 162.

87. The percentage is based upon estimates of Mexicans enrolled in English classes provided by Paul Taylor, George Edson, Manuel Gamio, and the "Monthly Reports of Activities" for 1924 to 1930, found in the records of Hull House and the University of Chicago Settlement.

88. J. M. Guajardo, interview by Paul Taylor, Gary, 26 August 1928, "Reports," Taylor Collection, p. 3.

89. Edson, "Gary," Taylor Collection, p. 14.

90. Agustín Angel, interview by Paul Taylor, East Chicago, Ind., July 1928, "Reports," Taylor Collection, p. 4.

Chapter 9, Mexicans and the Early Years of the Depression, 1929–1932

1. *Inaugural Addresses,* p. 233.

2. M. R. Ibañez, "Mexican Work, 1929–1930," in University of Chicago Settlement, *Annual Report, 1929–1930,* Box 21, UCS, pp. 10–11.

3. Baba and Abonyi, *Mexicans of Detroit,* p. 32.

4. Vargas, "Great Depression."

5. Rosales and Simon, "Mexican Immigrant Experience," p. 344.

6. In 1927 the number of Mexicans employed in steel mills and foundries was estimated at about 17,000. Ignacio Batiza, Consul, Detroit, to Manuel Tellez, Minister of the Exterior, 7 March 1930, File 73-14/17, IV-76-3, ARE; Hoffman, *Unwanted Mexican Americans,* pp. 120–122; Cardoso, *Mexican Emigration,* p. 145.

7. Oppenheimer, "Acculturation," pp. 444–445.

8. West, "Mexican Aztec Society," p. 145.

9. Reisler, *Sweat of Their Brow,* p. 228.

10. Governor's Interracial Commission, *Race Relations in Minnesota,* p. 9.

11. Oppenheimer, "Acculturation," p. 446.

12. Carlota F. Arellano, interview by Victor Barrela and Grant Newsburger, Minneapolis, 30 July 1975, Minnesota Oral Histories.

13. Feldman, *Racial Factors,* p. 107.

14. Governor's Interracial Commission, *Race Relations in Minnesota,* p. 10.

15. Humphrey, "Mexican Repatriation," p. 511.

16. Secretaría de Relaciónes Exteriores, Departmento Consular, Repatriaciónes, "Chicago, Consulado. Repatriación de colonos mexicanos en Rockdale," 30 December 1930, File IV/524.5 (73-10)14, IV-354-4, ARE.

17. Grupo de Mexicanos to Consul Aveleyra, 31 December 1930, and Secretaría de Relaciónes Exteriores to Consulado, Chicago, 19 January 1931, File IV/524.5 (73-10)14, IV-354-4, ARE.

18. Cardoso, *Mexican Emigration,* p. 148; Enrique González, "Brigadas de Cruz Azul."

19. *Excelsior,* 2 January 1930, pp. 1, 4.

20. *Mexico,* 27 October 1928, p. 2.

21. E. D. Ruiz, Consul General, New York, to Subsecretario de Relaciónes Exteriores, Mexico City, 29 October 1929, "Declaraciónes del Cónsul a *La Raza,* sobre movimiento en Chicago para repatriación de algunos elementos mexicanos," File IV/524.5 (73-32)/7. IV-110-47, ARE.

22. Feldman, *Racial Factors,* p. 67.

23. Valdés, *El Pueblo,* p. 32. Rivera had come to Detroit to paint his mural, *Man and Machine,* at the Detroit Institute of Arts.

24. *Detroit News,* 16 November 1932, p. 1.

25. Hoffman, *Unwanted Mexican Americans,* pp. 128–129.

26. Ibid., pp. 136–137, 140.

27. John L. Zurbrick to Commissioner General of Immigration, memorandum, 20 October 1932, File 55784/585, INS, RG 85.

28. Valdés, *El Pueblo,* p. 31; *Detroit Free Press,* 15 November 1932, p. 1.

29. Humphrey, "Mexican Repatriation," pp. 508–509.

30. Koch, "Politics and Relief," pp. 153–159.

31. Governor's Interracial Commission, *Race Relations in Minnesota,* p. 42.

32. *First Annual Report of the Illinois Emergency Relief Commission, for the Year Ending February 5, 1937* (n.p., n.d.), Chicago Historical Society, pp. 3, 33.

33. Maurer, "Unemployment in Illinois," p. 124.

34. Hughes, *Illinois Persons on Relief,* p. xvi.

35. *La Raza,* 19 October 1929, p. 1.

36. David Weber, "Anglo Views," p. 66.

37. *El Nacional,* 7 January 1931, Reel 62, FLPS.

38. *El Nacional,* 13 August 1932, Reel 62, FLPS; *La Defensa* 2, no. 9 (29 February 1936), Reel 63, FLPS.

39. *El Nacional,* 14 May 1932, Reel 62, FLPS.

40. Rosales and Simon, "Mexican Immigrant Experience," pp. 345, 347–348.

41. Paul E. Kelly, "Mexicans in East Chicago Deportations, 1932," November 1932, Emergency Relief Association, Repatriation File, East Chicago Public Library, East Chicago, Ind., p. 3.

42. Mohl and Betten, "Discrimination," p. 171.

43. Ibid., p. 177, quoting Elizabeth N. Wilson, "Notes on the Early History of the International Institute of Gary" (n.d., typescript), International Institute Papers, CRA.

44. *Gary Post-Tribune,* 14 January and 12 May 1932.

45. *Gary Post-Tribune,* 5 and 27 February 1932; 16 March 1932.

46. Mohl and Betten, "Discrimination," p. 176.

47. Ibid., p. 178.

48. Vernon Fernandez, interview by Ciro Sepulveda, Indiana Harbor, 14 and 17 February 1974, cited in Sepulveda, "La Colonia del Harbor," pp. 144–145.

49. Kerr, "Chicano Experience," p. 75; Rosales and Simon, "Mexican Immigrant Experience," p. 348; Skendzel, *Detroit's Pioneer Mexicans,* p. 10, citing U.S. Bureau of the Census, *Population Bulletin,* vol. 31, *Michigan* (Washington, D.C.: GPO, 1931), p. 42.

50. Hoffman, *Unwanted Mexican Americans,* p. 120; Edson, "North Central States," Taylor Collection, p. 6; "Informe sobre los ciudadanos mexicanos residentes en la jurisdicción del Consulado de Mexico en Chicago, Illinois" (1926), "Reports," Taylor Collection, p. 1–2.

51. McWilliams, "Getting Rid of the Mexican."

52. McLean, "Goodbye, Vicente," pp. 195–196.

53. Ipulito Sandoval, interview by Juan R. García, Chicago Heights, Ill., 25 June 1975.

54. *Inaugural Addresses*, p. 243.

Epilogue

1. *Detroit News*, 11 November 1933.

2. Rosales and Simon, "Mexican Immigrant Experience," p. 349; Hines, *Study of Minority Groups*, p. xi.

3. A total of 56.6 percent of the 1,422,533 Mexicans counted in the 1930 census were Americans of Mexican descent. U.S. Bureau of the Census, *Abstract of the Fifteenth Census*, p. 81.

4. University of Chicago Settlement, "Report: Mexican Work," 30 April 1929, Box 21, UCS.

5. Rosales and Simon, "Mexican Immigrant Experience," p. 351.

6. Mario García, *Mexican Americans*, pp. 14–16.

Bibliography

Primary Sources

Archive Inventories

Archivo General de la Nación. Papeles Presidenciales de Plutarco E. Calles y de Alvaro Obregón. Mexico City. (Cited in notes as Calles-Obregón Papers, AGN.)

Archivo Histórico de la Secretaría de Relaciónes Exteriores. Mexico City. (Cited in notes as ARE.)

Edson, George T. "Mexicans in Aurora, Illinois." Paul S. Taylor Collection, Bancroft Library, University of California, Berkeley, 1926. (Cited in notes as Edson, "Aurora," Taylor Collection.)

———. "Mexicans in Chicago, Illinois." Paul S. Taylor Collection, Bancroft Library, University of California, Berkeley, 1927. (Cited in notes as Edson, "Chicago," Taylor Collection.)

———. "Mexicans in Detroit, Michigan." Paul S. Taylor Collection, Bancroft Library, University of California, Berkeley, 1926. (Cited in notes as Edson, "Detroit," Taylor Collection.)

———. "Mexicans in East Chicago." Paul S. Taylor Collection, Bancroft Library, University of California, Berkeley, 1926. (Cited in notes as Edson, "East Chicago," Taylor Collection.)

———. "Mexicans in Gary, Indiana." Paul S. Taylor Collection, Bancroft Library, University of California, Berkeley, 1926. (Cited in notes as Edson, "Gary," Taylor Collection.)

———. "Mexicans in Indiana Harbor, Indiana." Paul S. Taylor Collection, Bancroft Library, University of California, Berkeley, 1926. (Cited in notes as Edson, "Indiana Harbor," Taylor Collection.)

———. "Mexicans in Lorain, Ohio." Paul S. Taylor Collection, Bancroft Library, University of California, Berkeley, 1926. (Cited in notes as Edson, "Lorain," Taylor Collection.)

———. "Mexicans in Minnesota." Paul S. Taylor Collection, Bancroft Library, University of California, Berkeley, 1926. (Cited in notes as Edson, "Minnesota," Taylor Collection.)

———. "Mexicans in Our North Central States." Paul S. Taylor Collection, Bancroft Library, University of California, Berkeley, 1927. (Cited in notes as Edson, "North Central States," Taylor Collection.)

——. "Northern Sugar Beet Mexicans." Paul S. Taylor Collection, Bancroft Library, University of California, Berkeley, 1927. (Cited in notes as Edson, "Northern Sugar Beet," Taylor Collection.)

Foreign Language Press Survey. Chicago Public Library, Chicago. (Cited in notes as FLPS.)

Gary Neighborhood House. "Minutes." 17 November 1925. Calumet Regional Archives, Indiana University Northwest, Gary. (Cited in notes as CRA.)

Henry Ford Service School. Foreign Student Research. Accession ARG-15. Edison Industrial Archives, Edison Institute, Ford Motor Co., Dearborn, Mich.

Immigrants' Protective League. *Annual Report, 1930.* Annual Report 2, Supp. 2. Folder 60. University of Illinois Archives, Chicago. (Cited in notes as IPL.)

Immigration and Naturalization Service. Record Group 85. National Archives, Washington, D.C. (Cited in notes as INS, RG 85.)

International Institute. Memorandums. "The Mexican Colony, 1921–1926," November 1926, and "History of the Mexican Colony, 1927–1928," 22 November 1928. Calumet Regional Archives, Indiana University Northwest, Gary. (Cited in notes as International Institute Papers, CRA.)

Latino Senior Citizens Oral History Project. Wayne State University, Detroit, October 1973. (Cited in notes as Latino Oral History Project.)

Manuel Gamio Papers. Packet, "Prensa Mexicana Editada en Michigan." Bancroft Library, University of California, Berkeley. (Cited in notes as Gamio Collection.)

Minnesota Historical Society, Archives and Manuscripts Division. Oral Histories Collection, St. Paul. (Cited in notes as Minnesota Oral Histories.)

Paul S. Taylor Collection. Folder, "Reports and Correspondence regarding Mexican Labor in the Midwest." Bancroft Library, University of California, Berkeley. (Cited in notes as "Reports," Taylor Collection.)

Redfield, Robert. "Mexicans in Chicago, 1924–1925." Robert Redfield Collection, Regenstein Library, University of Chicago, Chicago.

Secretaría de Industria, Comercio y Trabajo, Departamento de Trabajo, Box 333, No. 25 F:4, Archivo General de la Nación, Mexico City. (Cited in notes as Secretaría de Industria, AGN.)

St. Paul Neighborhood House. "The Mexicans in St. Paul." In *Annual Reports.* St. Paul: 1960.

University of Chicago Settlement. Annual Reports, 1923–1932. Boxes 19 and 21. Chicago Historical Society, Chicago. (Cited in notes as UCS.)

U.S. Department of State. Record Group 59. National Archives, Washington, D.C. (Cited in notes as State Department, RG 59.)

U.S. Department of State. Record Group 159, Decimal File, 1910–1929, 811.504/86. National Archives, Washington, D.C. (Cited in notes as State Department, RG 159.)

Censuses and Government Reports

Board of Public Welfare. *Social Prospectus of Kansas City, Missouri*. Kansas City, Mo.: Research Bureau of Public Welfare, 1913.

Governor's Interracial Commission. *Race Relations in Minnesota*. St. Paul: 1948.

U.S. Bureau of the Census. *Abstract of the Fifteenth Census of the United States*. Washington, D.C.: GPO, 1933.

——. *Abstracts of the Twelfth Census of the United States, 1900*. Washington, D.C.: GPO, 1904.

——. *Fifteenth Census of the United States, 1930*. Vol. 3, pt. 1, *Population*. Washington, D.C.: GPO, 1932.

——. *Fifteenth Census of the United States, 1930. Population: Special Report on Foreign-Born White Families*. Washington, D.C.: GPO, 1933.

——. *Fourteenth Census of the United States, 1920*. Vol. 3, *Composition and Characteristics of Population by State*. Washington, D.C.: GPO, 1921.

U.S. Children's Bureau. *Child Labor and the Work of Mothers in the Beet Fields of Colorado and Michigan*. Publication No. 115. Washington, D.C.: GPO, 1923.

U.S. Department of Commerce and Labor. *Annual Report of the Commissioner-General of Immigration*. Washington, D.C.: GPO, 1906.

——. *Annual Report of the Commissioner-General of Immigration*. Washington, D.C.: GPO, 1911.

U.S. House. Committee on Immigration. *National Defense Migration Hearings*. 77th Cong., 1st sess., pt. 19, 1941.

——. Select Committee to Investigate the Interstate Migration of Destitite Citizens. *Hearings on Interstate Migration*. 77th Cong., 3d sess., 1941.

U.S. Senate. Committee on Immigration. *Hearings on Emergency Immigration Legislation*. 66th Cong., 3d sess., 1921.

——. *Hearings on Restriction of Western Hemisphere Immigration*. 70th Cong., 1st sess., 1928.

Walker, James. "Planning for the Future of East Chicago: A General Survey of Its Social and Economic Problems, Prepared for the East Chicago Chamber of Commerce, 1926." East Chicago Public Library, East Chicago, Ind.

Newspapers

Calumet News (East Chicago, Ind.)

Chicago Sunday Times

Correo Mexicano (Chicago)

Detroit Free Press

Detroit News

Detroit Saturday Night

El Amigo del Hogar (Indiana Harbor, Ind.)

El Cosmopolita (Kansas City, Mo.)

El Eco de la Patria (Detroit)

El Imparcial (San Antonio)

El Nacional (Mexico City)

El Trabajo (Davenport, Iowa)

Excelsior (Mexico City)

Gary Daily Tribune

Gary Post-Tribune

Kansas City (Mo.) Journal Post

La Defensa (Chicago)

Lake County Times (Hammond, Ind.)

La Noticia Mundial (Chicago)

La Prensa (San Antonio)

La Raza (Chicago)

Mexico (Chicago)

Michigan Catholic (Detroit)

New York Times

San Antonio Express

Secondary Sources

Books, Theses, and Dissertations

Abbott, Edith. *The Tenements of Chicago, 1908–1925.* Chicago: University of Chicago Press, 1936.

Amentrout, Walter M., Sarah A. Brown, and Charles E. Gibbons. *Child Labor in the Sugar Beet Fields of Michigan.* New York: National Child Labor Committee, 1923.

Anthony, Katherine. *Mothers Who Must Earn.* New York: Russell Sage Foundation, 1914.

Arrom, Sylvia M. "Women and the Family in Mexico City, 1800–1867." Ph.D. diss., Stanford University, 1976.

Baba, Marietta Lynn, and Malvina Hauk Abonyi. *Mexicans of Detroit.* Detroit: Wayne State University, Center for Urban Studies, 1979.

Bailey, David C. *Viva Cristo Rey: The Cristero Rebellion and the Church-State Conflict in Mexico.* Austin: University of Texas Press, 1974.

Baur, Jackson. *Delinquency Among Mexican Boys in South Chicago.* WPA Report 165-54-6999. Chicago: Works Progress Administration, 1938.

Beezley, William H. *Judas at the Jockey Club and Other Episodes of Porfirian Mexico.* Lincoln: University of Nebraska Press, 1987.

Beisner, Robert L. *Twelve Against Empire: The Anti-Imperialists, 1898–1900.* New York: McGraw-Hill, 1968.

Bernard, William S. *American Immigration Policy.* New York: Harper, 1950.

Blee, Kathleen M. *Women of the Klan: Racism and Gender in the 1920s.* Berkeley: University of California Press, 1991.

Bogardus, Emory S. *The Mexican in the United States.* New York: Arno Press, 1970.

Broadbent, Elizabeth. "The Distribution of the Mexican Population in the United States." Ph.D. diss., University of Chicago, 1941.

Buel, James W. *Metropolitan Life Unveiled; or the Mysteries and Miseries of America's Great Cities.* St. Louis: Historical Publishing Co., 1882.

Cane, Allen T. *Social Life in a Mexican American Community.* San Francisco: R and E Research Associates, 1974.

Cardoso, Lawrence. *Mexican Emigration to the United States, 1897 to 1931.* Tucson: University of Arizona Press, 1980.

Chalmers, John H. *Hooded Americanism: The First Century of the Ku Klux Klan, 1865–1965.* New York: Doubleday, 1965.

Davidson, George W. "Industrial Detroit after World War I, 1919–1921." Master's thesis, Wayne State University–Detroit, 1953.

Deutsch, Sarah. *No Separate Refuge: Culture, Class, and Gender on an Anglo-Hispanic Frontier in the American Southwest, 1880–1940.* New York: Oxford University Press, 1987.

Duncan, John T., and Severiano Alanzo. *Guadalupe Center, Fifty Years of Service.* Kansas City, Mo.: Guadalupe Center, 1972.

Ellis, Pearl I. *Americanization Through Homemaking.* Los Angeles: Wetzel Publishing Co., 1929.

Feldman, Herman. *Racial Factors in American Industry.* New York: Harper and Brothers, 1931.

Fine, Sidney. *The Automobile Under the Blue Eagle.* Ann Arbor: University of Michigan Press, 1963.

Gamio, Manuel. *The Mexican Immigrant: His Life Story.* Chicago: University of Chicago Press, 1931.

——. *Mexican Immigration to the United States: A Study of Human Migration and Adjustment.* Chicago: University of Chicago Press, 1930.

García, Mario T. *Mexican Americans: Leadership, Ideology and Identity, 1930–1960.* New Haven: Yale University Press, 1989.

Garraty, John. *The New Commonwealth, 1877–1890.* New York: Harper Torchbooks, 1968.

Gibson, Charles, ed. *The Black Legend: Anti-Spanish Attitudes in the Old World and the New.* New York: Alfred A. Knopf, 1971.

Glaab, Charles N., and A. Theodore Brown. *A History of Urban America.* New York: Macmillan, 1971.

Goldner, Norman. *The Mexican in the Northern Urban Area: A Comparison of Two Generations.* San Francisco: R and E Research Associates, 1972.

González, Luís. *San José de García: Mexican Town in Transition.* Austin: University of Texas Press, 1972.

Gorton, Carruth and Associates, eds. *The Encyclopedia of American Facts and Dates.* New York: Thomas Y. Crowell Publishers, 1979.

Green, Constance M. *American Cities in the Growth of the Nation.* London: Athlom Press, 1957.

Griswold del Castillo, Richard. *La Familia: Chicano Families in the Urban Southwest, 1848 to the Present.* Notre Dame: Notre Dame Press, 1984.

Gruening, Ernest. *Mexico and Its Heritage.* New York: Appleton-Century-Crofts, 1929.

Hart, John M. *Revolutionary Mexico.* Berkeley: University of California Press, 1987.

Hernández, José A. "The Political Development of Mutual Aid Societies in the Mexican American Community: Ideals and Principles." Ph.D. diss., University of California–Riverside, 1979.

Higham, John. *Strangers in the Land: Patterns of American Nativism, 1860–1925.* New York: Atheneum, 1963.

Hines, Edna. *A Study of Minority Groups and Race Relations.* Public Works Administration, Study Project 665-54-3-79, n.d. National Archives, Washington, D.C.

Hoffman, Abraham. *Unwanted Mexican Americans in the Great Depression: Repatriation Pressures, 1929–1939.* Tucson: University of Arizona Press, 1974.

Houghteling, Leila. *The Income and Standard of Living of Unskilled Workers in Chicago.* Chicago: University of Chicago Press, 1927.

Hughes, Elizabeth A. *Illinois Persons on Relief in 1935.* WPA Report 165-54-6018. Chicago: Works Progress Administration, 1937.

——. *Living Conditions for Small-Wage Earners in Chicago.* Chicago: Department of Public Welfare, 1925.

Inaugural Addresses of the Presidents of the United States from George Washington, 1789, to John F. Kennedy, 1961. Washington, D.C.: GPO, 1961.

Jackson, Kenneth. *The Ku Klux Klan in the City, 1915–1930.* New York: Oxford University Press, 1967.

Jones, Anita Edgar. "Conditions Surrounding Mexicans in Chicago." Master's thesis, University of Chicago, 1928. Reprint, San Francisco: R and E Research Associates, 1971.

Jones, Robert C., and Louis R. Wilson. *The Mexicans in Chicago.* Chicago: Comity Commission of the Chicago Church Federation, 1931.

Kerr, Louise Año Nuevo. "The Chicano Experience in Chicago, 1920–1970." Ph.D. diss., University of Illinois, 1976.

Kramer, Paul, and Frederick L. Holborn, eds. *The City in American Life from Colonial Times to the Present.* New York: Capricorn Books, 1971.

Laird, Judith A. "Argentine, Kansas: The Evolution of a Mexican-American Community, 1905–1940." Ph.D. diss., University of Kansas, 1975.

Lin, Paul. "Voluntary Kinship and Voluntary Associations in a Mexican American Community." Master's thesis, University of Kansas, 1963.

Lipschultz, Robert J. *American Attitudes Toward Mexican Immigration.* San Francisco: R and E Research Associates, 1971.

Martínez, John. *Mexican Emigration to the U.S.* San Francisco: R and E Research Associates, 1971.

McKelvey, Blake. *The Urbanization of America, 1820–1915.* New Brunswick, N.J.: Rutgers University Press, 1963.

McLean, Robert N. *The Northern Mexican.* New York: Home Missions Council, n.d.

Meyer, Jean. *Estado y sociedad con Calles.* Mexico City: Colegio de Mexico, 1977.

Monroe, Day. *Chicago Families: A Study of Unpublished Census Data.* Chicago: University of Chicago Press, 1932.

Montgomery, Louise. *The American Girl in the Stockyards District.* Vol. 2. Chicago: University of Chicago Press, 1913.

Moore, Leonard J. *Citizen Klansmen: The Ku Klux Klan in Indiana, 1921–1928.* Chapel Hill: University of North Carolina Press, 1991.

Murillo, Louis C. "The Detroit Mexican Colonia from 1920 to 1930: Implications for Social and Educational Policy." Ph.D. diss., Michigan State University, 1981.

Nevins, Allan, and Ernest Hill. *Ford: Expansion and Challenge, 1915–1933.* New York: Charles Scribners, 1957.

Palavicimi, Felix F. *Problemas de la educación.* Valencia, Spain: F. Sempere y Compañía, Editores, 1910.

Peterson, Joyce Shaw. "A Social History of Automobile Workers Before Unionization, 1918–1933." Ph.D. diss., University of Wisconsin–Madison, 1976.

Powell, Philip Wayne. *The Tree of Hate: Propaganda and Prejudices Affecting United States Relations with the Hispanic World*. New York: Basic Books, 1971.

Reisler, Mark. *By the Sweat of Their Brow: Mexican Immigrant Labor in the United States, 1900 to 1940*. Westport, Conn.: Greenwood Press, 1976.

Rogers, Mary Helen. "The Role of Our Lady of Guadalupe Parish in the Adjustment of the Mexican Community to Life in the Indiana Harbor Area." Master's thesis, Loyola University–Chicago, 1952.

Rosales, Francisco A. "Mexican Immigration to the Urban Midwest During the 1920s." Ph.D. diss., Indiana University–Bloomington, 1978.

Rosenbaum, Robert. *Mexican Resistance in the Southwest*. Austin: University of Texas Press, 1981.

Schlesinger, Arthur M. *The Rise of the City*. Chicago: Quadrangle Books, 1971.

Schmidt, Henry C. *The Roots of Lo Mexicano: Self and Society in Mexican Thought, 1900–1934*. College Station: Texas A & M University Press, 1978.

Seller, Maxine. *America: A History of Ethnic Life in the United States*. New York: Jerome S. Ozer, 1977.

Sepulveda, Ciro. "La Colonia del Harbor: A History of Mexicanos in East Chicago, Indiana, 1919–1932." Ph.D. diss., University of Notre Dame, 1976.

Sierra, Justo. *Obras completas*. Vol. 8, *La educación nacional*. Mexico City: Universidad Nacional Autonoma de Mexico, 1948.

Skendzel, Eduard Adam. *Detroit's Pioneer Mexicans: A Historical Study of the Mexican Colony in Detroit*. Grand Rapids, Mich.: Littleshield Press, 1980.

The Spider and the Fly; or Tricks, Traps, and Pitfalls of City Life by One Who Knows. New York, 1873.

Taylor, George R., and Irene D. Neu. *The American Railroad Network, 1861–1890*. Cambridge, Mass.: Harvard University Press, 1956.

Taylor, Paul S. *Mexican Labor in the United States: Bethlehem, Pennsylvania*. University of California Publications in Economics, vol. 2, no. 6. Berkeley: University of California Press, 1931.

———. *Mexican Labor in the United States: Chicago and the Calumet Region*. University of California Publications in Economics, vol. 7, no. 2. Berkeley: University of California Press, 1932.

———. *Mexican Labor in the United States: Dimmit County, Winter Garden District, South Texas*. University of California Publications in Economics, vol. 6, no. 5. Berkeley: University of California Press, 1930.

Tentler, Leslie W. *Wage-Earning Women: Industrial Work and Family Life, 1900 to 1930*. New York: Oxford University Press, 1982.

Ticknor, Thomas J. "Motor City: The Impact of the Automobile Industry upon Detroit, 1900–1975." Ph.D. diss., University of Michigan, 1978.

Valdés, Dennis. *Al Norte. Agricultural Workers in the Great Lakes Region, 1917–1970*. Austin: University of Texas Press, 1991.

——. *El Pueblo Mexicano en Detroit y Michigan: A Social History*. Detroit: Wayne State University, College of Education, 1982.

Vargas, Zaragosa. "Mexican Auto Workers at Ford Motor Company, 1918–1933." Ph.D. diss., University of Michigan, 1984.

——. *Proletarians of the North: A History of Mexican Industrial Workers in Detroit and the Midwest, 1917–1933*. Berkeley: University of California Press, 1993.

Weber, Adna F. *The Growth of Cities in the Nineteenth Century: A Study in Statistics*. Ithaca: Cornell University Press, 1963.

Weber, David S. "Anglo Views of Mexican Immigrants: Popular Perceptions and Neighborhood Realities in Chicago, 1900–1940." Ph.D. diss., Ohio State University, 1982.

West, Stanley A. "The Mexican Aztec Society: A Mexican-American Voluntary Association in Diachronic Perspective." Ph.D. diss., Syracuse University, 1973.

Wilson, Joseph E. *The Cuban Crisis as Reflected in the New York Press, 1895–1898*. New York: Columbia University Press, 1934.

Woll, Allen L. *The Latin Image in American Film*. Los Angeles: UCLA Latin American Center Publications, 1977.

Articles and Papers

Albig, William. "Opinions Concerning Unskilled Mexican Immigrants." *Sociology and Social Research* 15, no. 1 (1931): 62–72.

Alvarado, Ernestine M. "Mexican Immigration to the United States." In *Proceedings of the National Conference of Social Work, 47th Annual Session*, 479–480. Chicago: University of Chicago Press, 1920.

Cardoso, Lawrence. "Mexican Community Leadership in the 1920s: The Struggle for Civil, Cultural, and Economic Rights." Paper presented at the annual meeting of the American Historical Association, Washington, D.C., 28 December 1980.

Castillo, Pedro. "Chicanos and the City." Paper presented at the International Conference on Current Trends in the Study of America, Sevilla, Spain, 17 December 1976.

Corwin, Arthur. "Causes of Mexican Emigration to the United States: A Summary View." In *Perspectives in American History*, edited by Donald Fleming and Bernard Bailyn, 557–635. Cambridge, Mass.: Harvard University Press, 1973.

Crocker, Ruth H. "Gary Mexicans and 'Christian Americanization': A Study in Cultural Conflict." In *Forging a Community: The Latino Experience in Northwest Indiana,*

1919–1975, edited by James B. Lane and Edward J. Escobar, 115–134. Chicago: Cattails Press, 1987.

Degler, Carl. "A Century of Klans: A Review Article." *Journal of Southern History* 31, no. 4 (1965): 435–443.

García, Juan R. "Midwest Mexicanos in the 1920s: Issues, Questions, and Directions." *Social Science Journal* 19, no. 2 (1982): 88–99.

García, Juan R., and Angel Cal. "El Círculo de Obreros Católicos 'San José.' " In *Forging a Community: The Latino Experience in Northwest Indiana, 1919–1975*, edited by James B. Lane and Edward J. Escobar, 95–114. Chicago: Cattails Press, 1987.

Gomez-Quiñones, Juan. "Piedras Contra la Luna, Mexico en Aztlán y Aztlán en Mexico: Chicano-Mexicano Relations and the Mexican Consulates, 1900–1920." In *Contemporary Mexico*, edited by James W. Wilkie, Michael C. Meyer, and Edna M. de Wilkie, 494–523. Berkeley: University of California Press, 1976.

González, Rosalinda M. "Chicanas and Mexican Immigrant Families 1920–1940: Women's Subordination and Family Exploitation." In *Decades of Discontent: The Women's Movement, 1920–1940*, edited by Lois Scharf and Joan M. Jensen, 59–84. Westport, Conn.: Greenwood Press, 1983.

Humphrey, Norman D. "The Integration of the Detroit Mexican Colony." *American Journal of Economics and Sociology* 3, no. 2 (1944): 155–166.

———. "Mexican Repatriation from Michigan: Public Assistance in Historical Perspective." *Social Science Review* 15, no. 3 (1941): 497–513.

Kanellos, Nicolas. "Fifty Years of Theatre in the Latino Communities of Northwest Indiana." *Aztlán* 7, no. 2 (1976): 255–265.

———. "Mexican Community Theatre in a Midwestern City." *Latin American Theatre Review* 7, no. 1 (1973): 43–48.

———. "Two Centuries of Hispanic Theatre in the Southwest." In *Mexican American Theatre, Then and Now*, edited by Nicolas Kanellos, 17–40. Houston: Arte Público Press, 1983.

Kerr, Louise Año Nuevo. "Mexican Chicago: Chicano Assimilation Aborted, 1939–1954." In *The Ethnic Frontier: Essays in the History of Group Survival in Chicago and the Midwest*, edited by Melvin G. Holli and Peter d'Alroy Jones, 293–328. Grand Rapids, Mich.: William Eerdmans Publishing Co., 1977.

Koch, Raymond L. "Politics and Relief in Minneapolis During the 1930s." *Minnesota History* 41, no. 4 (1968): 153–159.

Lane, James B. "Extranjeros en La Patria: Mexican Immigrants." In *Forging a Community: The Latino Experience in Northwest Indiana, 1919–1975*, edited by James B. Lane and Edward J. Escobar, 25–30. Chicago: Cattails Press, 1987.

Leitman, Spencer. "Exile and Union in Indiana Harbor: Los Obreros Católicos 'San

José' and *El Amigo del Hogar,* 1925–1930." *Revista Chicano Riqueña* 2, no. 1 (1974): 50–57.

Levenstein, Harvey A. "The AFL and Mexican Immigration in the 1920s: An Experiment in Labor Diplomacy." *Hispanic American Historical Review* 48, no. 2 (1968): 206–219.

Mabry, Donald J. "Mexican Anticlerics, Bishops, Cristeros and the Devout During the 1920s: A Scholarly Debate." *Journal of Church and State* 20, no. 1 (1978): 81–92.

Maurer, David J. "Unemployment in Illinois During the Great Depression." In *Essays in Illinois History in Honor of Glenn Huron Seymour,* edited by Donald F. Tingley, 120–132. Carbondale: Southern Illinois University Press, 1968.

McLean, Robert N. "Goodbye, Vicente." *Survey* 56, no. 1 (1931): 195–197.

McWilliams, Carey. "Getting Rid of the Mexican." *American Mercury* 28, no. 111 (1933): 322–324.

Miller, Robert. "The Ku Klux Klan." In *Change and Continuity in the Twentieth Century: The 1920s,* edited by John Braeman, et al., 215–255. Columbus: Ohio State University Press, 1968.

Mohl, Raymond A., and Neil Betten. "Discrimination and Repatriation: Mexican Life in Gary." In *Forging a Community: The Latino Experience in Northwest Indiana, 1919–1975,* edited by James Lane and Edward Escobar, 161–186. Chicago: Cattails Press, 1987.

Murphy, Paul L. "Normalcy, Intolerance, and the American Character." *Virginia Quarterly Review* 40, no. 3 (1964): 445–459.

——. "Sources and Nature of Intolerance in the 1920s." *Journal of Southern History* 31, no. 4 (1964): 60–76.

Oppenheimer, Robert. "Acculturation or Assimilation: Mexican Immigrants in Kansas, 1900 to World War II." *Western Historical Quarterly* 16, no. 4 (1985): 429–448.

Reisler, Mark. "Always the Laborer, Never the Citizen: Anglo Perceptions of the Mexican Immigrant During the 1920s." *Pacific Historical Review* 45, no. 2 (1976): 231–254.

——. "The Mexican Immigrant in the Chicago Area During the 1920s." *Illinois State Historical Society Journal* 66, no. 2 (1976): 144–158.

Romo, Ricardo. "The Urbanization of Southwestern Chicanos in the Early Twentieth Century." *New Scholar* 6 (Fall 1977): 183–207.

Rosales, Francisco A. "Mexicanos in Indiana Harbor During the 1920s: Prosperity and Depression." *Revista Chicano Riqueña* 4, no. 4 (1976): 88–98.

——. "Mexicans, Interethnic Violence, and Crime in the Chicago Area During the 1920s and 1930s: The Struggle to Achieve Ethnic Consciousness." In *Perspectives in Mexican American Studies,* vol. 2, *Mexicans in the Midwest,* edited by Juan R. García and Ignacio García, 59–97. Tucson: Mexican American Studies and Research Center, 1990.

———. "The Regional Origins of Mexican Immigrants to Chicago During the 1920s." *Aztlán* 7, no. 2 (1976): 187–201.

Rosales, Francisco A., and Daniel T. Simon. "Chicano Steel Workers and Unionism in the Midwest, 1919–1945." *Aztlán* 6, no. 2 (1976): 267–275.

———. "Mexican Immigrant Experience in the Urban Midwest: East Chicago, Indiana, 1919–1945." *Indiana Magazine of History* 77, no. 4 (1981): 333–357.

Sanchez, George J. " 'Go After the Women': Americanization and the Mexican Immigrant Woman, 1915–1929." Working Paper Series No. 6. Stanford: Stanford Center for Chicano Research, 1984.

Sepulveda, Ciro. "Una Colonia de Obreros: East Chicago, Indiana." *Aztlán* 7, no. 2 (1976): 327–336.

Taylor, Paul S. "Employment of Mexicans in Chicago and the Calumet Region." *Journal of the American Statistical Association* 25, no. 107 (1930): 206–207.

Valdés, Dennis. "Betabeleros in the Midwest: The Formation of a Class Segment, 1900 to 1930." Paper presented at the 12th annual meeting of the National Association for Chicano Studies, Austin, Tex., 4 March 1984.

———. "Perspiring Capitalists: Latinos and the Henry Ford Service School, 1918–1928." Paper presented at the 74th annual meeting of the Organization of American Historians, Detroit, 3 April 1981.

Vargas, Zaragosa. "The Great Depression and Mexicans." Paper presented at the annual meeting of the National Association for Chicano Studies, Salt Lake City, Utah, 11 April 1987.

———. "The New Ford Men: Mexican Auto Workers at the Ford Motor Company, 1919–1933." Paper presented at the North American Labor History Conference, Detroit, Mich., 15 October 1983.

Vaughn, Mary K. "Women, Class, and Education in Mexico, 1880–1928." *Latin American Perspectives* 4, no. 1–2, issue 12–13 (1977): 135–152.

Index

About the Author

Juan R. García received his Ph.D. degree from the University of Notre Dame in 1977. His major fields were U.S. history and Mexican American studies. He also holds two M.A. degrees, one from De Paul University in Latin American history, and the other from the University of Notre Dame in U.S. history.

García served as director of the Chicano Studies Center at the University of Michigan in Flint. He is currently an associate professor of history and the associate dean of instruction in the College of Social and Behavioral Sciences at the University of Arizona. His current research is about Mexicans during the Great Depression.

García's first book was a community study of Chicago Heights, Illinois. He has also published *Operation Wetback*, a study of the Bracero Program and the mass repatriation of Mexicans during the 1950s. He served as a consultant on the fifth-grade textbook, *The Latino Experience in U.S. History*, and is writing another fifth-grade textbook on general U.S. history. García is the editor of *Perspectives in Mexican American Studies*.